ISBN 978-1-331-72062-1
PIBN 10225946

1 MONTH OF
FREE
READING

at
www.ForgottenBooks.com

By purchasing this book you are eligible for one month membership to ForgottenBooks.com, giving you unlimited access to our entire collection of over 700,000 titles via our web site and mobile apps.

To claim your free month visit:
www.forgottenbooks.com/free225946

Similar Books Are Available from
www.forgottenbooks.com

B. Danks
York
April 10.th 1883

THE CRUCIFIXION AND RESURRECTION.   LAURENTIAN M.S., A.D. 586.

THE ART TEACHIN

OF THE

PRIMITIVE CHURCH;

WITH AN

Index of Subjects, Historical and Emblema

BY THE

REV. R. ST. JOHN TYRWHITT, M.A.,

FORMERLY STUDENT AND TUTOR OF CHRIST CHURCH, OXFORD.

Published under the Direction of the Committee of General Literature
and Education appointed by the Society for Promoting
Christian Knowledge.

LONDON:

SOCIETY FOR PROMOTING CHRISTIAN KNOWLEDG

SOLD AT THE DEPOSITORIES ·

77, Great Queen Street, Lincoln's Inn Fields;

4, Royal Exchange; 48, Piccadilly;

AND RY ALL BOOKSELLERS.

LONDON
R. CLAY, SONS, AND TAYLOR, PRINTERS,
BREAD STREET HILL.

PREFACE.

THIS volume contains some notes of the traditionary subjects of Early Christian art as far as the first Italian Renaissance. That period, it seems, may be best marked by the name of Niccola Pisano. Whatever the unknown artists of the earliest Lombard churches may have done, the careful study of Ancient or Attic-Greek models, as distinguished from those of the Byzantine school, is held to begin with that great master; whose life marks the commencement of Modern art. By his time, the Gothic or Mediæval choice of subject and treatment was fully established. It is an object of this work to point out some of the differences in these respects, between mediæval and primitive Church-art, and to give some notes of the progressive intrusion of legend and polytheism into the ancient cycle of Scriptural art-teaching.

The various references have of course cost some labour. For the Catacombs, the works of Bosio,

Aringhi, and Bottari are all due to the labours of the first, and his plates were used to illustrate them all: Aringhi's Symbolic Index is a mine of learned comment and reference. One book or the other will generally be found accessible. Though these plates give no idea of the present appearance, or rather the gradual disappearance, of the buried frescoes, they may probably be accurate records of the subjects once represented. Cardinal Bosio's integrity was equal to his enthusiasm, and he had no polemical motive in his work of re-discovery. It is therefore generally assumed in this book, that his authority is sufficient to prove that such and such subjects (of often un-certain date within the first eight centuries) have been found in Christian sepulchres, whether the latter were of greater antiquity than their decorations or not.

For modern text-books on this subject, Alt's " Heiligenbilder," and Martigny's " Dictionnaire des Antiquités Chrétiennes," will supply the reader with ample information, and open to him a vast range of reference for more extended study, which is sure to increase in interest, as the connection between early art, archæology, and history is better understood.

For the present state of monuments and examples, Mr. J. H. Parker's collection of Roman and other photographs stands by itself as a unique and invaluable addition to modern means of accurate knowledge.

I have expressed my obligations to Professor Westwood more than once in the text; but I have to thank him particularly for access to his large collection of ivories; and for a sight of a valuable monograph on Christian sculpture, by Dr. Appell, of the South Kensington Museum.

R. St. J. T.

CONTENTS.

CONTENTS.

CHAPTER VII.

LIST OF ILLUSTRATIONS.

PRIMITIVE CHURCH ART.

INTRODUCTORY.

THE ancient relics and monuments of Christian
art are a portion of the history of the Primitive
Church. All historians acknowledge their importance as documents; and several attempts are made
in these pages to illustrate their connection with
doctrine. But the chief practical object of this work
is to indicate and appeal to that tradition of sacred
art, for the plain purposes of Gospel education, which
the writer believes to have been continued in use in
the Church from her earliest paintings,—the " Ciclo
Biblico" of the Catacombs.

The religious paintings and carvings of any race
of men are, in fact, evidence of the belief of the
people, and let us know the actual thoughts and hopes
of ordinary persons about the faith they hold. The
Catacomb pictures are a standard of religious intelligence, which show us how people received and
understood the word preached and written. To a practical man, interested in, yet distressed by, the ways
of common life in any age, thoughts of the Christian

faith are inseparable from thoughts of death: and
in the earliest paintings we have the ideas which
martyrs and hearers of Apostles themselves dwelt
on and commended to others in the hour of death.
They attempted no description of Paradise or of
Heaven; they did not, for centuries, dwell on the Glory
of Christ the Lord, as seen in Apocalyptic vision:
they scarcely appealed to the judgment to come,
they denounced no vengeance from Heaven on those
who sought their lives.   These were not the great
and leading thoughts of the faith, which the early
Church desired plain men to dwell on in the most
solemn hours of life, and at its end.   She continued
the teaching of St. Peter and St. Paul, and appealed
to the ancient Law and the Prophets, asserting the
connection of the Mosaic and the Christian dispen
sations.   If the multitude of the first Pentecost
believed the witness of the patriarch David about
the Holy One Who should not be suffered to see
corruption, they must repent and be baptized every
one in the name of Jesus Christ.   If the Sanhedrim
would hearken, Stephen would tell them the history
of their fathers from Abraham, and its real meaning
for them.   If King Agrippa believed the Prophets,
his place, in logic and right reason, was in the Church
with St. Paul.   There had been, from the time of the
Fall, a promise of deliverance from corruption, evil,
and pain; some great good had been determined by
God's fore-knowledge for man.   Since Abraham, the
" lively oracles " concerning it had been in Abraham's
race, not dumb, but speaking.   Accordingly the first
lesson of Apostolic preaching was sustained appeal to
the Old Testament, as typical and confirmatory of the

New. This was enforced by the earliest paintings; and St. Paulinus of Nola, about A.D. 400, wrote in the spirit of the earliest Gospel when he said, "The Ancient Law confirms the New, the New fulfils the Old."

It seems to have been the special work of this remarkable person to call the attention of the Italian Church, in its hours of intense suffering and terror, to those powerful means of instructive appeal to the barbarian mind, which the relics of Græco-Roman art yet afforded.[1] Accordingly we have evidence of the

[1] His reasons for church painting are very simple—the poor people understand the pictures, and can think about them, and so learn better behaviour in church.

> " Forte requiratur, quanam ratione gerendi
>   Sederit hæc nobis sententia, pingere sanctas
>   Raro more domos animantibus adsimulatis.
>   *   *   *   turba frequentior hic est
>   Rusticitas non casta fide, neque docta legendi
>   Hæc adsueta diu sacris servire profanis,
>   Ventre Deo, tandem convertitur advena Christo,
>   Dum sanctorum opera in Christo miratur aperta.
>   Propterea visum nobis opus utile, totis
>   Felices domibus picturâ illudere sanctâ ;
>   Si forte attonitas hæc per spectacula mentes
>   Agrestum caperet fucata coloribus umbra
>   Quæ super exprimitur literis, ut litera monstret
>   Quod manus explicuit ; dumque omnes picta vicissim
>   Ostendunt releguntque sibi, vel tardius escæ
>   Sunt memores, dum grata oculis jejunia pascunt ;
>   Atque ita se melior stupefactis inserit usus,
>   Dum fallit pictura famem, sanctasque legenti
>   Historias castorum operum subrepit honestas
>   Exemplis inducta piis; potatur hianti
>   Sobrietas, nimii subeunt oblivia vini :
>   Dumque diem ducunt spatio majore tuentes,
>   Pocula rarescunt, quia per mirantia tracto
>   Tempore, jam paucæ superant epulantibus horæ."
>   *In Natal. Felic.* poem ix.

On the Ark, &c. :

> " Quo duce Jordanus suspenso gurgite fixis
>   Fluctibus, a facie divinæ restitit arcæ,
>   Vis nova divisit flumen ; pars amne recluso   [Constitit

B 2

energies of the Church, indomitable at the time when
all else was crushed by Alaric's capture of Rome, in
the great historical mosaics of St. Sabina, commenced
in 424, and those of St. Maria Maggiore in 432 ; the
latter setting forth the history of the Hebrew Law from
Abraham downwards.   There can be no doubt that
the lost paintings by Paulinus in the Church of St.
Felix at Nola must be connected, as history, with
the mosaics of St. M. Maggiore.   Among them were
scenes from the Old Testament; the Passage of the
Red Sea ; Joshua and the Ark of God; Ruth and
Orpah, as typical of the faithful and the backsliders
from faith.   "These," says Milman, "must have
involved decided attempts at landscape, composition,
and expression."[1]   There can be no doubt to anyone
who has seen the Old Testament mosaics of St. M.
Maggiore, that if the spirit and vigour of those
works had continued in a succession of students, a
powerful school might have risen from them; as the
great school of Florence, in after days, struck its roots
in the Lombard work along the southern spurs of
the Alps from the 8th to the 11th century.   And,
indeed, it is hard to say that these mosaics may not

> Constitit, et fluvii pars in mare lapsa cucurrit,
> Destituitque vadum : et validus qui forte fuehat
> Impetus, adstrictas altè cumulaverat undas,
> Et tremulâ compage minax pendebat aquæ mons
> Despectans transire pedes arente profundo,
> Et medio pedibus siccis in flumine ferri
> Pulverulenta hominum duro vestigia limo."

Orpah and Ruth:

> " Qnum geminæ scindunt sese in diversa sorores ;
> Ruth sequitur sanctam, quam deserit Orpa, parentem ;
> Perfidiam nurus una, fidem nurus altera monstrat,
> Præfert una Deum patriæ, patriam altera vitæ."— Nat. F. ix.

[1] See Parker's Photographs, and Ciampini's plates there repeated.

have influenced the monk Jacobus, or Torrita, or the various and undistinguishable authors of the Pisan and Florentine inlayings. But the careful appeal of the earliest art to Hebrew history and prophecy is our main point; together with the fact that it repeats the arguments of St. Peter and St. Paul from the Old Testament to the New. Their preaching was argumentative and not emotional, as far as we know; and the same remark applies to the early paintings. Similar principles of teaching are greatly to be desired in our own days. There is an unity of purpose and of theology, which runs from the first century to our own, and expresses itself in marble, mosaic, and painting. For centuries it was altogether good or harmless, while it expressed the faith of the people, that God had come on earth as Man to deliver them from evil, and had lately submitted to human life and death with them and for them: that the New Testament was the history of that endurance and action, and the Old the record of the world's preparation for it.

A parallel degeneracy in pictorial expression marks the failure of the popular standard of faith. Personal trust in Our Lord dies away; saints, martyrs, angels, and the Virgin Mother are invoked to mediate with Him. His Form, first symbolized, then painted with artless imaginations of human beauty, recedes by degrees; and constantly the images of saints take His place, or He appears, after the tenth century, as the unpitying Judge: while the Christian ideal of Him becomes that of sad severity, as if mourning over the inefficacy of His own Act of Redemption. But yet again, with the early Renais sance of Pisa and Florence, the strength of young Italy resumes much of the ancient hope and joy in Him ; and by the side of His sufferings and His judgment it is asserted, vividly and gloriously, that He rose and ascended, and that His mercy endureth for ever.

When Primitive Art is not historical, for narrative teaching of the facts of the Old and New Dispensations and their mutual relation, it is symbolical, for enforcement of Doctrine ;—that is to say, of the facts or truths in possession of the Christian soul, and *teachable* by man to man. The Corruption or Fall of man, and the Cross as the sign of the Redeemer ; [1] sin, and deliverance by sacrifice—these were the key-notes of Christian art for the people, because they were the broad and fundamental truths which upheld the personal hope of every individual of the people. So it was in the earliest days, when Our Lord's Person and Life were most dwelt on ; so in after time, from the 6th century, when the manner of His Death filled men's hearts ; and so it is, down to the Sacramental instructions of Bishop Wilson, the " Christús Consolator" of Ary Scheffer, and that important relic of mediæval Christianity, the Passion-play of Ammergau. The Christian use of art, graphic or scenic, is not for emotion or sensation ; it is to enforce the reality of History, and the permanence of Doctrine.

[1] Not, in the first instance, of the manner of His death. See Chapter on Crosses and Crucifixes.

CRUCIFIX.—THE GRAFFITO BLASFEMO.

CHAPTER I.

RELIGIOUS ART-HISTORY.

IT is a remark of the late Dean of St. Paul's in a note to his "History of Christianity,"[1] that the Iconoclasts had, probably, more influence in barbarising the East, than the Barbarians themselves had in the West. The observation has all the in-

[1] Book iv. chap. iv. Compare "Christian Remembrancer," vol. lv. pp. 333-4, where the connection between Manicheism and Iconoclasm is pointed out. The author calls attention also to the sweeping nature of the destruction of Christian documents in the eighth century, including great numbers of precious MSS. ; and to the Iconodulist influence, in Italy and the Western world, of the great number of monastic artists who sought refuge from Eastern persecution.

terest which an apparent paradox by a great writer always possesses; and it is, after all, highly probable as a conjecture. The chief inference to which it leads is the principle which justifies the writing, or compilation, of this book. It is that no means of popular education, religious or secular, is to be neglected; that to refuse means of right development and instruction to one's neighbour, when it is fairly in our power to give them, can come to no good; and, that instruction of the most varied and valuable character is to be conveyed (and with especial force and clearness in the case of rude and simple minds), by means of symbols in form, or colour, or both. They appeal to the imagination; and through it they set the mind in action, and supply it with matter to work on. It is appointed for man, by his Maker, that he should learn and teach through the eye, through the sense of likeness and the sense of beauty; for likeness or resemblance is the lowest form of pictorial beauty, and the pleasure of observ ing a resemblance is really that of studying two forms by comparing them. If this means of teaching be neglected or forbidden, a means of instruction is closed, which all Theists must consider Divinely appointed. The world suffers accordingly; men are deprived of light, of sweetness, of fresh and right thought. Iconoclasm, certainly, had this result in the East, urged as it was to its results by Christians, Jews, and Mohammedans; and with the more sustained violence, as the latter conquering race insisted on it with the most crushing vigour; forbidding, even to this day, all the wholesome secular uses of naturalist art in representing the works of God on earth. I am unable to find this definite prohibition in the Koran; but it certainly has been stringently carried out in the Mohammedan world. The common derivation of the word *arabesque* turns on it. The Lions of the Alhambra are an exception to it, and are believed to be a dubious indulgence in representative art; neither they nor the building of which they form a part require notice here. Much conventional ornament, founded on nature, and executed by Greek mosaicists or carvers, will be found in Saracenic work at Cairo, Damascus, and Jerusalem. It is probable that the rule of prohibition was originally adopted from Hebrew law, and given in the Hebrew sense, which admitted certain exceptions in practice, and, indeed, in the text of Holy Scripture.[1] "It was contrary to the religion of the Arab to introduce any animal form into his ornament, but though all the radiance of colour, and all proportion and design were open to him, he could not produce any noble work without an abstraction of the forms of leafage, in his capitals, and as the ground-plan of his chased ornament." Eastern art perished or grew monstrous by neglect of nature, for want of faithful study of present beauty, through the merciless prohibition, insisted on with all the vehemence of ignorance, to record, at all or for any purpose, the form of any living thing which God has made.

Though they seem to have given but little trouble, the questions of religious art must have been before the Church of Christ from the very earliest times. Pictorial decoration of every kind, from the

[1] See *infra*, and "Stones of Venice," vol. i., end of chap. xx,

statues of gods and heroes to mosaics of ducks and doves, and from thence again to the "inscripta lintea" of wine-shops and gladiators' schools, was the rule of Greek and Roman life. In the very earliest days of the Church, Christian congregations must have met in decorated rooms, without noticing or caring for their decoration. To the Pauline or Gentile school of converts, filled, through long spaces of life, with one all-sufficient idea, that their God had come to them and was theirs, the graven image was what it was to him of Tarsus—nothing at all. The easy way in which Christians adopted heathen ornament is noticed by writers of all views. "I have constantly observed," says the Commendatore de Rossi, "in the subterranean cemeteries, that the early Christians possessed sculptured sarcophagi which bear no sign of Christian faith, and seem to have issued from Gentile workshops; adorned with images of the firmament, scenes of shepherd-life, agricul ture, the chase, games, &c. The Christian interpre tation given to agricultural or pastoral scenes, to personifications of the seasons, to dolphins and other marine creatures, is obvious and universally ac- knowledged. When the faithful could not obtain sarcophagi adorned with sacred sculpture, it . is evident that they took great trouble in selecting those which contained nothing directly offensive to the faith, and did not represent idolatrous rites, images of false gods, or subjects too evidently belonging to Pagan theogony." There was, how- ever, another great class of Christians—perhaps, as Milman suggests, it existed in every city—which would feel differently. To the Hebrew Christian, still zealous of the law, the representation of any uncommanded and unprescribed form in any place of worship would be matter for alarm and earnest protest, at the least. And later on in time, the austerer and harsher minds among Gentile Christians would object to picture-ornament as an indulgence, as lust of the flesh and of the eye. Tertullian's condemnation of all images and forms whatever[1] seems connected with the natural severity of his temper. There can be no doubt, however, that the strictness of Hebrew rule and feeling against idolatry would and did postpone the use of art by the Church, even for instruction in historical pictures of events. The well-known decree of the Council of Illiberis forbids them generally (Can. 36), as it, seems by way of caution:—" It is ordered, that there be no pictures in Church, lest that which we worship and adore (come to) be painted on the walls."

Still Hebrew usage itself had its well-remembered exceptions, of which the brazen serpent is perhaps the most striking. The cherubs, the oxen, the pomegranates and flower-work of the ancient Temple were doubtless repeated in that of Herod—they certainly never could be forgotten by the Jewish people: and thus the difference between symbolic ornament (however significant) and idolatrous creature-worship, was virtually understood by the Hebrew. Even Tertullian[2] is checked in his sweeping condemnation of all representation whatever, by his recollection of the serpent in the wilderness, which he excuses as virtually a Christian symbol. But all the casuistry of the subject, all the distinctions

[1] " De Idolatria," c. iii.   [2] Ibid. c. iv.

between the use of emblems for instruction, their misuse to excite feeling, and their final abuse as *objects* of worship, must have been only too familiar to a race in whose history the calf-worship (or probably cherub-worship) of Jeroboam formed a part.[1] It seems likely that in his day the cherubs on the veil and doors of the Temple, seen there daily without harm by priests and people, were set up as objects of worship in Dan and Bethel. It is probable, however, that in the first and second age of the Primitive Church both Hebrew and Gentile Christians may have been accustomed to use variously decorated rooms without scruple. They may have met, even for prayer and the Eucharistic celebration, without giving a thought to the fact that vines, or boys, or pictures of the seasons, or of shepherds, may have been painted on their walls, roughly or elaborately. This is virtually proved, for the western world, by the quotation given above from De Rossi, founded on the earliest known works in the catacombs; as in that of St. Prætextatus, A.D. 150.[2] It is admitted on all hands that Pagan decorations were accepted, and invested with meaning by the Christian imagination. There is little or no doubt that vines and shepherds adorned Roman chambers of all kinds before the Christian era · there is no doubt at all that, after the Lord's words "I am the Vine," "I am the Good Shepherd," those images were repeated continually in all places where Christians met to worship Him. But when decorations began to be widely adopted by the

[1] See Chapter on Symbolism.
[2] Parker, 615, 1822, and Chapter on Catacombs.

Church, we must believe that the Hebrew dread of idolatry in all representations, at least in all portraits or images of mankind, arose in the earlier Christian world, as it has existed ever since; not as an apprehension confined to the Hebrew or Semitic mind, but as the reasoning scruple of all who, like ourselves, are or should be zealous of the moral law. The second commandment does undoubtedly stand on primal revelation of God's will to man; and it was repeated and ratified to Moses on the Mount. In the Christian Church, as among all worshippers of One God, questions have arisen, and will for ever arise, on this great point of conscience. It cannot, in logic, right reason, charity, or common sense, be absolutely ruled either way. There is no doubt that from the second or third century the Christian imagination began to employ itself in picture—first for instruction and declaration of the faith, then for splendour and for dedicative sacrifice; that excesses created alarm from time to time, though rarely at first; that sometimes an ornament may have been held to express a wrong or false idea, as did the Gnostic symbols; that sometimes human or animal figures may have appeared in themselves idolatrous. On the other hand, few sects or parties have ever been able to dispense long with pictorial means of teaching and self-expression. Doctrinal formulæ, definitions, and developments, as well as error and heresy, began to be set forth in decorative art, almost as soon as they were expressed in forms of words. Had the printing-press been in use in that age to express and propagate opinion, Christianity, heresy, and Paganism would have used it alike: and picture-symbols and letter-symbols are really different forms of the same thing; connected with each other by the derivation of letters from drawings.[1]   And exactly as the undefinable pleasure called beauty (to use the term in its widest and vaguest sense) was sought for in picture-teaching for the sake of impressiveness, as soon as the artist was able to produce it ; so in all ages and to all times beauty, so-called, of spoken or written words will be used for the sake of power.   At all times, perhaps, scrupulous-minded and excellent men, entitled to great attention, have expressed natural suspicion or objection to pictorial beauty as an abuse, while they adorned their philippics against it with all the flowers of rhetoric ; and perhaps tampered more with truth and the simplicity of the faith in speech or writing, than those who wrote the Lord's parables on the wall in colour, or carved His miracles of mercy on their sarcophagi.

The existence, at a very early date, of many Gnostic emblems need not surprise anyone who will take into consideration the necessary secrecy so long practised in the Christian Church.   Orthodox Christianity had its mysteries, too great and precious to the believer to be freely named to the Gentiles.   These were embodied in Christian symbols as the Fish, the Bread, and the Monogram—the Vine, the Lamb, and countless others, being at the same time adopted from Gentile fancy.   But meanwhile all manner of intricacies of Cerinthian and Gnostic opinion flourished either just within or just without the assembly of the Church ; and new brotherhoods were formed, which in some degree imitated or

[1] See Chapter on Symbolism.

emulated the original brotherhood in Christ. These would either submit to the faith in the end, or die away without it, or take new forms of error: but meanwhile there seems to have been a great variety of Gnostic symbols and passwords, which are enumerated and described with great learning by Mr. King; to whom Christianity seems to appear rather in the light of a variety of Gnosticism, than Gnosticism as a reflection of Christianity.[1] There can be no doubt, however, that necessary secrecy was a principal cause, alike of the Church's use of symbolism, and its occasional adoption of heathen emblems.

There was another reason for the use of art which had special application in Rome. Christians of all nations and languages met in the central city of the world; and pictures of the Gospel history and the Lord's preaching told their tale with equal force to all. Art was an universal form of expression, and the artist not only spoke in all men's tongues, but spoke in them with a force of his own. The difference between having a story told and having a scene before one is very great to simple-minded people, to all, in fact, whose minds are not vivid enough to realize and represent the facts of history on the retina of imagination. And this brings us to our first and broadest division of Christian art, into historical and symbolic representations. Of symbolisms we must speak hereafter—for the present, there are a few observations to be made on the general use of pictorial art for historical teaching, and educational purposes in general. We can then give some account, either in the body of this work or

[1] "The Gnostics and their Remains." C. W. King, M.A.

in its descriptive Index, of the historical pictures and bas-reliefs of the early Church; especially of that large and important class of them which has reference to prophecy, and those typical events in Hebrew history which are specially connected with the Christian faith in which they find fulfilment

It has often seemed to us, that what clergy and teachers of religious history are apt to complain of as diluted scepticism, and haziness of belief in facts, extends, in the British mind, to all history alike. It is as if nobody thought there ever had been any past at all. History, the bygone reality of great and noble things and men, seems altogether unlikely—in a country where all things grow daily newer, meaner, more crowded and common, less abiding or deserving of continuance. An age of journalism, or of contemporary history told in party interests, is sure to be fruitful in general scepticism and disgust about history altogether. When every daily sketch of daily events is coloured or distorted by the political connections and interests of the day, men cease, in fact, to believe each other. Contemporary history is universally written by political attorneys or advocates ; and nobody in his heart ever believes an advocate. Accomplished scholars and students of history say it is a Mississippi of falsehood. We are taunted with religious panic, because Christian men are startled, and alarmed at each other's alarm, about the literal truth of parts of the sacred narratives. Their panic is really a sign of faith : it proves the paramount importance which they attribute to those narratives, as bearing on their own lives. The Bible has a practical meaning for them, of which they do not intend to be deprived. For secular history, men let it slip altogether, and are content to be not only incredulous but ignorant of it. One can hardly be surprised, when one considers how it used to be taught : for though great improvement has been made by earnest and brilliant teachers, their efforts are still isolated, and they have a heavy balance of dulness against them. In our own day, at all events, we were taught to "get up" history by rote, rather than to make use of the feelings and the imagination to assist the memory. We had to try to remember men and facts by the dates, instead of the dates by the men and their great deeds. It is obvious that if knowledge is to· be acquired by the imagination, which, as metaphysicians say, deals with individual men and events, then pictures which represent either are the most forcible means of impressing the imagination into the· service of knowledge. When imagination is deficient, and the rote-memory powerful, what we say does not apply ; but there can be no doubt that in most schools the rote-memory is or was encouraged at the expense of the imagination, even in the study of history. A framework of dates was insisted on, and the facts were to be learnt by them : the dates were somehow got up, generally by some hateful *memoria technica* of horrid misspelt sounds, and we learnt to· sort kings and heroes out among them as well as· we could. It certainly seems to us now that it would have been better to remember the period by the men than the men by the period first to possess the imagination with the sense of good or heroic presences in history, doing and suffering great things ; then to group the events round the

men, and let the chronological arrangement come
last. What is a name in a school-book now was once
a man ; and what he did or said may have something
to do with us still. To be taught early to realize the
personality of men, to have some image of the
actuality of an event, must be of unlimited advantage
to the student : and it is here that art bears so
strongly on historical knowledge. Every pilgrimage
to the scene of great events, or to the habitat and
faint visible traces on earth of some great one, is a
testimony to the power of imagination over the
understanding, and virtually of art over the imagination. It is true that the first lessons in the use of
the latter are best given, not in school, but in the
preliminary teaching of mothers and nurses; but
they, too, appeal indefinitely to pictures and prints,
to rhymed verses, to everything which can call out
the imaginative power ; and the impressions they
thus convey are often indelible.

"Pictures are poor men's books," says John
Damascenus ; and the principle of illustration
or illumination of books to help instruction and
memory was recognized in the first ages, in the
very infancy of Record, as well as now. It appears
certain, in fact, that if letters be universally derived
from hieroglyphics, as in Egypt, the pictorial records
are the earliest. Those Eastern travellers who have
visited the ancient turquoise, iron, and copper mines
of Wady Maghárah, in the Desert of Mount Sinai,
will remember the great Egyptian tablets, beginning
with the earliest kings of the fourth or Memphite
dynasty, which are cut in the sandstone cliffs of that
strange and rough valley, neither eared nor sown. We

saw five in 1862, some near the mine and the traces of the Pharaonic entrenched camp, others at some distance up the valley. They are some of the most ancient historical documents in the world, and their authenticity is absolutely without dispute. They are picture-hieroglyphics of considerable beauty; partly relating to the conquest of the country by Egypt, partly to its zoology and metallic products. Cheops and Kephren hew down their prisoners in person, according to the prevailing tradition of Egyptian record, which makes every king his own butcher. Considerable graphic power and comprehension of character are shown in the bas-reliefs of animals, which are not for the most part intaglioed or engraven, but raised in clear, sharp, and shallow projection. They are done on tablets carefully prepared at considerable height, and in situations specially chosen to avoid those rapid eddies of the mountain winds, which, carrying the sharp sand before them, act in the course of years like a file on the plane surface of the weathered rock, and make clean round holes like an auger or centre-bit, wherever the polishing medium is whirled round by eddies of wind. The tablets were of course cut and smoothed in the selected places first, and had their surface removed according to drawings then made on it. The results are so near being imperishable as to remain quite intelligible to the present time; and are still so far distant from civilization and so difficult of discovery that their still further endurance may be hoped for.[1]

[1] There is a cursory and imperfect account of these turquoise mines in a paper by the author, in "Vacation Tourists" (1862, Macmillan); but it is entirely superseded by the complete and most valuable description (accompanied by admirable photographs

It will be seen that the main principle of transition from picture-writing to letter-writing is to make the picture of an object represent the initial sound of its name. The picture sign can thus be used for other words in which the same sound occurs. The Hebrew ⊐ is the rude picture of a house, black tent, or goat's-hair screen, such as is used in the desert to this day. The corresponding name is Beth in Hebrew, Beyt in Arabic. Let the picture stand for its initial sound B; it may then be used as a letter to write down the names Bara, Ben, &c., and any other words or names in which the B sound occurs. It is like the all-important change from printing-blocks to movable type.

History then was all pictures in the earliest times, and is now greatly assisted by such records in the present, if she is not dependent on them.

It is not in our way now to consider how our modern historical teaching seems to suffer from neglect of the imaginative power. Indeed, that power is now appealed to in education through poetry and romance, and archæology begins to be called to their aid; so it may be hoped that this book may fall in with and supplement others. But that great department of the world's records called Church History is, was, and for ever will be, specially associated with art; if for no other reason, because many works of art in churches or cemeteries are historical docu-

and drawings) lately issued by the authors of the Sinai Survey. The change or progress from earlier to later hieroglyphic, arrangement in columns, &c., is very interesting. A short and clear account (with illustrations) of the transition from hieroglyphics into characters, will be found in the Appendix to Rawlinson's "Herodotus," vol. ii. book ii.

ments of special value and indisputable genuineness. There can be no doubt that the catacombs themselves, as places of Christian burial, and sometimes of refuge and martyrdom, have had vast influence on Christianity [1] Their undiminished importance to Christian thought in our own days rests on the paintings they contain, which give us at least an approximative idea of the personal hopes and expectations in death of whole generations of believers. The credibility of history may depend on contemporaneous evidence of this kind, especially in our own days, when the increase of knowledge appears to be the increase of doubt, if not of sorrow. One may judge of the value which time gives to picture-record from the importance which the blasphemous scrawl of some unknown slave assumes, when treated as what it really is, a decisive proof of Christian worship of the Crucified Lord in the days of Severus or Caracalla.[2] That a Pagan caricature of the rudest

[1] "Dum essem Romæ puer, et a liberalibus studiis erudirer, solebam cum cæteris ejusdem ætatis et propositi, diebus Dominicis sepulcra Apostolorum et Martyrum circumire; crebroque cryptas ingredi, quæ in terrarum profundo defossæ, ex utraque parte ingredientium per parietes habent corpora sepultorum, et ita obscura sunt omnia, ut propemodum illud Propheticum compleatur, 'Descendunt in infernum viventes,' et raro desuper lumen admissum, horrorem temperat tenebrarum; ut non tam fenestram, quam foramen demissi luminis putes; rursumque pedetentim acceditur, et cæca nocte circumdatis, illud Virgilianum proponitur—

'Horror ubique animos, simul ipsa silentia terrent.'"

Continual pilgrimages, from St. Paulinus of Nola's time to the 11th century, testified to the interest of the Christian world in these monuments of the early Church.

The above often-quoted passage from St. Jerome (Com. in Ezech. xii. c. 40) applied to many besides himself, as he says. Migne, t. xxv. p. 375.

[2] See p. 7: for festivals held in the cemeteries see the note on Agapæ, Chapter on the Catacombs.

kind should become an interesting point of Christian
evidence, when its only intention was to express and
excite feelings of. dull ridicule and hatred of the
Christian faith, is at least a remarkable coinci-
deuce.[1]

This rude appeal to passion may lead us to another
part of our subject; which is that the principle of
early Christian art was instruction rather than
emotion ; and that commentless statement of the
facts of the faith, and pictorial repetition of the
Lord's words, furnish between them the whole
original stock of Christian subjects for artistic
representation.   Beauty is faintly attempted ; the
workman does as well as he can for the work's
sake : but his motive is plain narrative.   Such a
parable the Lord spoke about Himself, and it is
painted ; such a miracle of mercy He wrought, and
it is carved in bas-relief.   To pursue beauty and the
associations which are connected with it; to throw
out power and delight from one's own spirit and
appeal to others through delight—these are the gifts
and the aspirations of men who live in ages of
culture, of physical progress, of national energy.
But the Christian faith was made for all races,
periods, and conditions of the human mind and body ;
it was meant to avail man in his need, the weakest
of men and women in the most extreme need.   Such
persons seem to have made use of the language of
picture in the primitive ages, for the sake of its
vividness, because it assisted oral teaching.   What

[1] See Dr. Liddon's " Bampton Lectures," p. 396, ed. 1868, with
reference to the paper of Father Garrucci, Rome, 1862; and compare
woodcut in this volume, p. 7.

remnants of beauty in execution or design thev possessed, were really inherited from ancient Greece and Rome. By the end of the sixth century, an Eastern sense of colour and some faint relics of graphic power, were all the gifts which were left to Christian art from the heathen ages; and men made the best of these in preaching the faith they held, exactly as St. Chrysostom and St. Augustine may have obeyed the rules of the Rhetoric of Aristotle and the Institutions of Quintilian They had no scruples in using the traditions of heathen skill; they were easily able to draw the distinction between Gentile and Pagan art—between the witty inventions of human genius, itself the gift of God, and their misapplication to image-worship. They were willing to bury their dead witnesses, and celebrate the Communion of the Body and Blood of Christ, surrounded by rude paintings of shepherds and vintagers; which they understood with reference to Him, and which the heathen did not understand at all. But rather than do reverence or burn incense to the marble Jove or Apollo, they would face the lions and endure the violence of fire.

We are concerned in this chapter with the historical division of primitive art as distinguished from the symbolical: and it has seemed best to include in this volume a descriptive index of subjects of Christian art, particularly of such representations of persons and events in the Old Testament as are and have been held to be typical of others in the New. And the author must state a conviction here, which higher authorities have expressed before

him,[1] that the scope of primitive subject, so far
as the ancient cemeteries go, is almost entirely
Scriptural. The Monogram and the Anagram ; the
initials of the Lord's name, and the Fish, which
indicates the initials of His name and titles, are not
important as exceptions to this rule, though in themselves so deeply interesting. Nor, on the other hand,
is there any sign of trenchantly exclusive rule, forbidding non-Scriptural subjects. As has been observed,
Greek and Roman Christians were well used to
ornament of all kinds, and seem for the first four
centuries to have habitually drawn the motives of
their pictures from Holy Scripture, without rejecting
any detail or ornament which was not obviously connected with Polytheism. The progress from the symbolical representation of Our Lord as Shepherd of
Israel to portrait forms of Him (though we can hardly
suppose that any actual likeness to His bodily countenance was ever attempted)—the surrounding His
conventional portrait with choirs of angels and the
holy fellowship of the Apostles—the gradual introduction of His Virgin Mother as a proper object
of worship, and hearer and granter of prayer ;
and, finally, the increasing definiteness given to
her cultus and that of the saints, until the mediatorial office of Our Lord Himself was forgotten,—
this is all matter of ecclesiastical history. Some
account will be found of this transition in the
Chapter on Mosaics ; and the evidence given by those
monuments to a certain progress in the direction of
creature-worship is there in some degree made out.

[1] See De Rossi, Rom. Sott. part 1, with Mr. Wharton Marriott's
preface to " The Testimony of the Catacombs."

It is very difficult to say how far the introduction of figures of saints like those of St. Prassede and St. Pudentiana, was felt to be an innovation in churches of the sixth century. It is probable that the Anglican Church resembles the primitive, in permitting representations of saints engaged in ministry, as actors in historical pictures, or even as ornamental forms—in any position and gesture, in fact, save that of standing to accept the worship of the people, or, in the mediatorial office, to receive and present their prayers before God.

The Portrait, whether its features be traditional or ideal, is defended alike by Hindu and Italian ingenuity, as an assistance to devotional feeling. And had any record been left in Holy Scripture of the outward appearance of the Divine Man or of any of His followers, it would have been doubtless both right and advisable to repeat His, if not theirs, in every temple of the faith; such portraits would then have been matter of historical record. It is matter of history that He likened Himself to the Shepherd of Mankind; and we are right in setting forth the likeness of the symbolic Pastor. It is only repeating His Parable about Himself. But to look for sacred emotion from pictures is a vague expression, and we should like to know what it really means. In as far as the picture bears on the facts it narrates to the mind, it is instructive, and we defend it. But a conventional portrait figure asserts no historic fact, and it seems a doubtful proceeding either to stimulate or allow baseless, or at least unreasoning, emotion in the act of prayer, either to ourselves or others. The beauty of a picture has, primarily, nothing to do with the matter, unless we are to adore the picture. To allow oneself to feel, or persuade oneself that one feels, greater devotion to Christ our Lord before a Raffaelle than before a Byzantine mosaic, or before a mosaic than before nothing at all, is to make Raffaelle or the mosaicist our mediator with the Redeemer. Prayer is too serious a matter for this, to those who know need and pain, and are really calling for help to body and soul. In as far as a picture helps us to realize facts of the faith, its function is historical, and the mind may proceed from it as a theme of meditation, and so wax earnest and aspire. But to make use of a picture methodically and regularly to excite a dubious devotion by its beauty must be a questionable proceeding, for it involves the making the picture a means of grace in itself. To ourselves, the real principle of edification in pictures, considered as beautiful things, seems to be the devout or earnest spirit of the painter, if we can see it in his work. Some of Angelico's or Perugino's works seem to demonstrate that their author believed, with deep happiness, in what he painted, so that his life and being went into his hands and eyes, and every stroke of his brush was like a pulse of delight. Some of Botticelli's, in the Early Renaissance, show the happiness of a Christian lay-mind of great power, in joyfully repeating, by painted symbol, the main facts of its own faith. Some of Michael Angelo's, in the Late Renaissance, are the troubled and painful utterance of a suffering and misled genius to a suffering Lord, to Whom he holds, and by Whom he is held, against all trial. Of all modern men, perhaps, Holman Hunt has most in common with the last. But all these men's sacred works appeal to the emotions of the spectator, as it seems to us in a perfectly right way, as follows. They show him, beyond doubt that another man, of the highest powers, has here and hereby given his heart to God: they plead with the spectator, whatever be his humour for the time, that a man like him, or abler than he, did exert all the powers of his spirit, felt and was upborne beyond his normal state of mind, in realizing thoughts of sacred things, and writing them down for a record to all men, in the universal speech of colour and form. The picture is a monument of the soul's desire of its author : sometimes it is an evidence that his soul desired the Kingdom of God ; and so far it is his witness on earth to that Kingdom.

All these men, however, excepting perhaps Perugino, have principally left behind them historical groups in action, records of what God has done, rather than quasi-portraits of saints standing to receive adoration. The distinctions between *latria* (worship), veneration, &c., whether they were known to them or not by any name or formula, may have been real to their minds ; as indeed they may be to us in the English Church, or to other Protestant bodies. For those who believe in the existence of saints, and in the Communion of Saints, cannot surely repudiate feelings of reverence, at least, towards their elder brethren in Christ. But it can hardly be right now,— it certainly was wrong in the fifth and sixth centuries of the Church,—to expect whole crowds of zealous untaught people to hold by this distinction. *Latria, dulia, hyperdulia,* " worship, serving, devotion," are words invented for the exigencies of controversy. and

point to shades of difference which the popular eye can
hardly see. Moreover, if these classifications of the
council and the library were rightly made by the
people (as the teachers of the people assert them to
be, when pressed by controversy),.a change of things
would at once ensue which is simply incalculable.
Moreover, as has been hinted, parallel uses of the
Image-portrait are constant (and somewhat scandalous
and dreadful) in other than Christian countries ; the
setting up a signum or statue of the object of worship
being a simply human propensity.   Hindu idolaters,
for instance, defend themselves as ably, and to a
certain extent as justly, as John Damascene himself
on this matter. " Let us hear," says Professor Max
Müller,[1] " one of the mass of the people, a Hindu of
Benares, who, in a lecture delivered before an English
and native audience, defends his faith and the faith
of his forefathers against such sweeping accusations "
as that Indian popular religion is idol-worship and
nothing else.   " ' If by idolatry,' he says, ' is meant
a system of worship which confines our ideas of the
Deity to a mere image of clay and stone ; which pre-
vents our hearts from being expanded and elevated
with lofty notions of the attributes of God ; if this
is what is meant by idolatry, we abhor idolatry, and
deplore the ignorance or uncharitableness of those
who charge us with this grovelling system of worship.
But if, firmly believing, as we do, in the omnipresence
of God, we behold, by the aid of our imagination, in
the form of an image, any of His glorious manifestations, ought we to be charged with identifying
them with the matter of the image, when during

[1] "Chips frcm a German Workshop," vol. i. pref. p. 17.

those moments of devotion we do not even think of matter ? If at the sight of a portrait of a beloved and venerated friend *no longer existing in this world*, our heart is filled with sentiments of love and reverence—if we fancy him *present in the picture*, still looking upon us with his wonted tenderness and affection, and then indulge our feelings of love and gratitude, should we be charged with offering the grossest insult to him—that of fancying him to be no other than a piece of painted paper ?'"

This, it will be seen, is a valid protest against the accusation of fetichism, or attributing virtue and power locally to this or that particular image. It also appears to involve an excuse for the idolater, which his Master and ours will well know how to appreciate, and which we have no further business with than to remember that it exists. For ourselves, we can only say that in the south of Europe, from the fifth and sixth centuries, there has been frequent and general identification of the matter of the image with the saint,[1] and of the saint himself with God, as a hearer of prayer. But let us, if we can, suppose that the Hindu's heart is filled with sentiments of love and reverence at beholding a dragon-bodied and many-handed image; hideous and degrading as it seems, alike to us and to his Mohammedan kindred. Let this pass for a sincere though clumsy symbolism of omnipotence. Is it the same to all Hindus, educated and uneducated ? and might not a devout Hindu, possessed of the subtle power of mind which the Benares lecturer showed, go so far as to dispense with the image itself, and tell others like himself that they might

[1] See passage from Milman, *infra*.

do so as well ?   Was he not addressing himself *ad homines*, to the English part of his English and Hindu audience ?   While we ourselves acknowledge the difficulties and temptations which led to the error of Christians in past time, we cannot follow them in error, from motives of historical charity; and we cannot but see that the use of the portrait-image has led, and leads, masses of the people into a worship of the image as a present Deity. For its beauty, that seems to have little to do with the matter.   In modern times, appeals have been made to Beauty in religious art; sometimes, as it seems to us, in a luscious and abominably wicked manner.   There are impersonations of Saints and Magdalens which we are thankful to pass, and *not* look on.   But as to the more beautiful picture excit ing the more devotion, or, at least, drawing the greater crowds of worshippers, experience is practically against it, as Goethe observed.   Miraculous pictures are seldom well painted; nor are wonders of healing wrought before the Dresden Madonna or the Paradise of Tin toret.   The fact is that the idea of local and personal virtue, inherent in the image, belongs to times and states of society which are generally unable to understand artistic beauty, or to ally it with religion at all.

"Let the Pope and Cardinals reform the times," quoth Michael Angelo, "and the times will reform the pictures."   It is so; the spirit of pictures depends on the spirit of the men who produce them. The most elaborate and learned compositions may be done in a religious spirit, as many of Overbeck's and Ary Scheffer's works; and then they have their value as efforts of devout intellect, whatever grade of power that intellect may possess. And the simplest and rudest image only proves that those who made and who use it are rough and simple persons, not that they are good Christians ; on the contrary, the most elaborately insinuated blasphemy in modern polemics does not spring from a fiercer hatred than the scrawled graffito of the slave of Severus's household.[1]

For ourselves, there is one sufficient ground for the use of religious art, that it instructs in the facts and doctrines of religion. Further, where great human genius, labour, and sacrifice have evidently been applied to works in this department of intellect, we are or ought to be edified ; because the painter evidently desired to be, and *ipso facto* has made himself, a Christian preacher. If this were generally acknowledged and understood, as it is in part, how great would be the encouragement and support in heart and spirit, which such thoughts would convey to the painter. To find that his daily work does spiritual good ought, at all events, to make a man's heart to sing for joy over it ; it should teach him the greatness of life, in a way to make life happy; and that in the highest sense of the word happiness. But such work is not done, nor such happiness gained, by painting religious pictures for the market ; and the path of sacred art is straiter and narrower than it may seem. It is useless to dedicate impotence to God's service instead of power; and of all distressing things in the world, nothing can be more so than mistaken ambition in this matter. A school of church decoration possessed of some power and patronage,

[1] See p. 7.

and directed by critics alike able and just, well read and technically skilled, would go far to adjust all questions about the historic or instructive use of religious painting for generations to come.

vINE NO. 1.—CALLIXTINE CATACOMB

c 3

STATION CROSS OF MAYENCE

CHAPTER II.

THE word Symbol, σύμβολον (συμβάλλω, to put together, guess, conjecture), possesses a very wide range of meanings; through all which there seems to run a leading notion of the σύμβολον, or present and visible object, standing for something of greater importance not actually producible. Τὰ σύμβολα were strictly the two halves of a bone or coin, which two ξένοι, or any two contracting parties, broke between them and preserved. The tickets given the Athenian dikasts on entering a court, in exchange for which they received their fee at the end of the day, bore this name; and it was applied to many similar uses · thence it came to bear the meaning of a verbal signal or watchword, like *tessera* in Latin; and to be applied at last to the Creed or Confession of Faith of the Christian body, as their distinguishing mark (Lat. *symbolum*), and generally, to any outward sign of a conception or idea. In this sense symbolism, or the use of such signs, has been employed in the Church since the earliest times. Though verbal symbolism and figurative expressions are of course coeval with spoken language, and anterior to either writing or painting, there can be no doubt that the parable or metaphor corresponds to the carved or

painted symbol, and conveys ideas in the same
way, by analogy, or similar relation. It has been
observed that letters themselves are symbols based
on representative arts, and originally formed from
hieroglyphic pictures of objects. Again, as a matter
of fact, art has, from its very earliest periods, been
employed in symbolic teaching, almost entirely on
religious subjects. Further, the teaching of our Lord
by spoken parable involves His sanction to instruction by painted parable and allegory, which is virtually the same method. The connection between
hieroglyphics, or picture-writing, and phonetics, or
letter-writing, is perhaps not always clearly understood, and may be again briefly repeated here. First
comes the hieroglyphic representing an object; that,
in course of time, is taken to mean the initial sound
(*i. e.* the first letter) of the name of that object.
Beth or Beit is the name of a house; and B, its
initial sound, is represented by ב, a rude sketch of
an Arab screen or tent, the house of the desert, as it
is still called. The camel's neck and foreleg remain
in the letter Gimel. Sin or Shin, S, is the coiled
and hissing serpent; and so forth, till a limited
alphabet of written sounds has taken the place of
an endless quantity of rudely drawn signs. The
advantage is of course that the letters are inter-
changeable; and that the B sound, once represented
by a commonly-agreed sign, will do for Bara, for
Ben, and for "*omne quod incipit in B.*"[1] Yet though
letters are fittest for the intercourse of common life,

---

[1] Ingenious symbolical meanings were added or deduced from
primary hieroglyphs; as in Egypt the hawk stands for the Sun,
and the two lily-stems for Upper and Lower Egypt; but this must
have involved great complication and inconvenience.

pictures have still an expressive force of their own; and a few seem to have been used from a very early time of the Church. There is no saying on what principles, or by what steps of progress, painted or carved objects were allowed in Christian assemblies, or places of assembly for prayer and Sacraments. Christians in the first instance met where they could, and almost all halls and large rooms were more or less ornamented by painting or carving in the larger towns of Greece and Rome. It is possible that most congregations of the Church were early accustomed to pictures, with subjects of every-day character, on the walls within which they assembled. The question of decoration in the Primitive Church was probably never raised at all for two centuries; and it should be considered, that during that time the faithful had grown thoroughly accustomed to the graceful, and perhaps, in many places, somewhat unmeaning, grotesques and flower-ornaments of ordinary Greek or Roman life. It is fully understood, how in the earlier tombs and catacombs—as that of St. Domitilla, with the catacomb attached to it, and particularly in the catacomb of St. Prætextatus—we have instances of Gentile work invested with Christian meaning. The same thing occurs very frequently in the earlier work of other cemeteries, and it seems probable that the vine mosaics of St. Constantia at Rome are instances of the adoption of heathen imagery, to express Christian ideas. The transition from merely tolerating heathen ornament as unmeaning, to this way of utilizing it, was a natural one, and probably was made very early. And this would probably be, correctly speaking, the origin of Christian art-symbolism : that congregations long accustomed to animals, flowers, landscapes, and figures of all sorts on the walls of rooms of all kinds, at length chose special subjects of their own for decoration—such as the Dove, Fish, Vine, or Shepherd—all generally known and favourite representations, which awakened no particular attention on the part of the heathen, and in fact must often have appeared to all parties in the light of harmless concession. But as greater attention, more thought and intellectual power began to be applied to symbolic teaching, both verbal and pictorial, so must various questions, as to the danger of approximation to idolatry, have risen on the Christian mind. Some brief account of these must be given in this chapter. What is to be here noticed in this connection is that idolatry is a matter of *actual* and *direct* representation ; and that true symbolism represents an object of worship *indirectly*. This distinction was made in the Hebrew Church, and recognized from the first in the Christian symbolisms ; which appealed to the thoughts as the actual or direct picture does to the senses. The actual image is supposed to be *like* its subject, the symbol is not. This distinction, that the supposed portrait-image represents the outward form of its subject, and the symbol makes you think of the inner essence or being of its subject, is, we apprehend, real and vital. But it is unsatisfactorily subtle, and difficult of practical adjustment ; and it is continually infringed on, and finally destroyed, when the æsthetic spirit is abroad calling for visible images of objects of faith ; as from the fifth to the fifteenth century ;

and at the present time in the Roman Catholic
Church, and of late in the Anglican.

It is not to be wondered at, then, if in the first
and second centuries, the turn of the Churches'
practice in the Roman, or Græco-Roman world, was
to tolerate, or perhaps enjoy trivial ornament; and
latterly to attach special meanings to such details
of it as could be made into Christian tokens. And
here we enter on two distinctions, one of which will
have to be carried through the whole of this inquiry : between adopted and invented symbols, Scriptural and non-Scriptural emblems, or visible signs.
It should be noticed, that the earlier Christian emblems were for the most part taken from the Lord's
mouth, and that it is a leading feature of His parabolic teaching to adopt the employments, the sights
and thoughts of ordinary life, and invest them with
spiritual meaning. This is familiar to every school-
child ; and as our matured knowledge and experience
in spiritual matters does little more than enable us
to realize in part what we learnt as children, so it
is with the imagery of the Gospel. All remember
the awful contrast between the sheep and the goats,
and how it has impressed itself on the Christian
imagination : but few are aware of how vividly it
returns to the mind of the traveller, probably in his
very first day's journey through the land of Israel.
The terraces of the low hills are dotted with white
sheep and black goats ; so white and so black, that
their contrast of colour must attract even careless
eyes, and add force to our Lord's description of the
judgment. Again, on the way from Jaffa to Jerusalem, generally the first ride in the Holy Land, the

wayfarer will probably see the flocks watered from deep wells, like that of Sychar, where the hidden fountain springs up unto life, and the thin limestone strata are pierced through by living waters. The ancient vines which are still dressed on the slope of Olivet, recall the parable of the Vine, there delivered to all Christian eyes; the Shepherd and his stray flock are everywhere in the hill-country and throughout Palestine; the Fig-tree, the Sower and his Seed, the nets and fish of Tiberias, all point to Our Lord's custom of adopting daily things to the purposes of His teaching. Less frequently, He invented parables or symbolic relations of possible events; as those of the Steward, the Talents, and the Wise and Foolish Virgins, &c.—seldom or never descending to fable or apologue, like Jotham, in his story of the Trees. Both these classes of symbol were well known to the early Church. Many were adopted from the Lord's own words, a few were invented, as the Ship, the Anchor, and the Lyre. Some were adopted from heathen or secular use, as the Peacock, Olive and other trees, and much bird and flower decoration, and these of course appear in the most ancient examples we possess. The Monogram of the Lord's name; the anagrammatic Fish, IXΘΤΣ, of the initials of His name and titles; the palm-branch of death in Christ; and the adopted imagery of birds and flowers, are the oldest Christian symbols yet remaining. The Vine and the Good Shepherd accompany them in the earliest paintings of the catacombs, though the brief and easily-cut letter-symbol of the monogram is naturally more frequent in inscriptions. Setting this last aside, it may be repeated that the two former emblems were sanctioned by our Lord's use of them with reference to Himself.

Considered as the substitution of a producible or visible idea for another, verbal and pictorial symbolisms are the same thing. It can hardly be denied, that the symbolic picture of the Vine, or the Pastor bearing the lost lamb, are simply picture-writing of the words " I am the true Vine," or " I am the Good Shepherd." They attempt to impress a personality; they call to mind certain Divine Functions of the Divine Man; they make no appeal to the emotious through the eye; only indicating to the spectator the thought of the artist, and his desire that that thought might pass through other Christian souls also. The Lord's speech in parables, "because of the hardness of the hearts" of his hearers, is strictly an anticipation and a parallel of the use of pictured symbols for gradual instruction, because of the dul ness and the weakness of men's souls. He has not given to us to exchange ideas like pure intelligences; and the use of symbolism is a mere question of language, of the conveyance and transmission of ideas. Words are defined in logic as arbitrary signs of things, or of our ideas of things. They pass instead of things; they manifest and communicate ideas. Paper money is an arbitrary symbol of gold; leather might have been, and has been, used instead, and has answered the purpose of being exchanged for labour as well as gold. The words "five pounds" cannot *be substituted* in the market for the things they represent: nevertheless they *manifest* to the hearer, that the speaker has the idea of that sum before his mind. Words pass instead of things in the mind; they cannot be used instead of things in fact. And for this we have reason to be thankful, as otherwise the truth of the comfortable maxim, that hard words break no bones, might be seriously disputed; —and indeed it is so, by the lamenting bitterness of the Psalmist's symbolism, " His words were smoother than oil, and yet be they very swords."

Now, when the symbol stands instead of the thing symbolized as a word for a thing, or as a note for money, and is identified with it in the mind, it may come under the imputation of idolatry, or of approach to idolatry. When the symbol only manifests to the mind of the spectator that the painter intended him to think of the thing symbolized, that imputation cannot hold. No man (probably) ever fell down and worshipped a picture or image of a Vine or of a Fish: no man for six centuries ever worshipped the wood, stone, or metal of the Cross. But the portrait-representation of Our Lord (not that in symbolic form, of the Good Shepherd) became, though it ought not logically to have become, the first step in a course of image-worship. This will be hereafter traced through the Roman mosaics of the Greek school.

There can be no doubt, moreover, that the ancient Hebrew dread of the graven image, of every form of idolatry or approach to it, was present, through the first five centuries at least. As we shall hereafter observe, this scruple is one of the points of divergence between the Eastern and the Græco-Roman, or afterwards the Gothic, mind; the Mediæval Church being more impressed by the value of eye-art and picture-teaching, and also being led by her veneration for Rome to follow, as Rome followed, the *ancient* Greek tendency to Personification of the Deity or His manifestations. The Eastern mind, and that of the Byzantine, or later Greek Church, has, however, greater facility in understanding the difference between symbolism and personification in art, and in reducing it to practice. That difference or distinction has been already hinted at; the symbol indicates the thought of its object; the personification calls up a visible image of its object. Athene was thought of by the earlier Greek races, perhaps, as the queen of the air, or the breath of life and of thought, of the health, spirit and wisdom of man. And so she was thought of as a part of Zeus, the one supreme being; as something coming from him, springing unborn from him, to be the guide and helper of man. Some such thoughts and worship of the spirit of health and wisdom, with a name, but without an image, are conceivable, and probably were entertained for a time by the earlier Aryan races. But the Greek was impelled by the intensity of his perceptions and conceptions, or by the very perfection of his senses to desire, to see, and to touch. Like a child, he desired to have in his own hands that which he most desired; and he would be content no more with the majestic symbols of Egypt; he not only personified the powers of nature, but realized that personification in wood and stone, in his own image, according to the fashion of the beauty of man.[1] The final compromise of Iconoclasm,[2] as the late

---

[1] See Ruskin, "Queen of the Air," and Max Müller, "Chips from a German Workshop," vol. i.

[2] Milman's "Latin Christianity," chap ix. book xiv. (ed. i. p. 597, vol. vi.). It appears not how far sculpture had dared to embody

Dean of St. Paul's points out, may illustrate this distinction. The carved image seems to have been felt to be nearer to the idol; as more solidly and literally representative of its subjects, and in fact more like a living being; the picture appears more in the light of an emblem, a purely symbolic aid to thought and emotion. This distinction, however subtle, has been maintained thus in the Eastern Church ever since the ninth century; and it leads us to notice the necessary inaccuracy with which the words Greek and Eastern have to be used on this and kindred subjects. There is no doubt that the art of ancient Greece was

in brass or in marble the hallowed and awful objects of Christian worship. * * * Probably statues of this kind were extremely rare ; and when image-worship was restored, what may be called its song of victory is silent as to sculptures. See Poem in the Anthologia, Χριστιανικὰ Ἐπιγράμματα, Jacobs, i. 28.

Ἔλαμψεν ἀκτὶς τῆς ἀληθείας πάλιν * * *
ἰδοῦ γὰρ αὖθις Χριστὸς εἰκονισμένος
λάμπει πρὸς ὕψος τῆς καθέδρας τοῦ κράτους * * *
τῆς εἰσόδου δ᾽ ὕπερθεν, ὡς θεία πύλη
στηλογραφεῖται, καὶ φύλαξ, ἡ παρθένος, &c.

"The Lord, the Virgin, the angels, saints, martyrs, priesthood, take their place over the portal entrance ; but shining in colours to blind the eyes of the heretics. To the keener perception of the Greeks there may have risen a feeling that in its more rigid and solid form the image was more near to the idol. At the same time the art of sculpture and casting in bronze was probably degenerate and out of use ; at all events it was too slow and laborious to supply the demands of triumphant zeal in the restoration of the persecuted images. There was, therefore, a tacit compromise ; nothing appeared but painting, mosaics, engraving on cup and chalice, embroidery on vestments. The renunciation of sculpture grew into a rigid, passionate aversion. The Greek at length learned to contemplate that kind of full representation of the Deity or the Saints with the aversion of a Jew or a Mohammedan." See also Bingham, xii. ch. 8, and chapter on Christian sculpture.

On Perret's work, and the Catacomb paintings, see note in Milman, vol. vi. book xiv. chap. 9, p. 604.

linked with idolatry, from the natural tendency of the Greek to set forth to himself gods in his own image. The unconscious personifications of the elements and their working, which are the basis of Aryan mythology, were developed and realized by that wonderful race, with their acute senses, their great personal beauty, and their intense appreciation of all outer loveliness. The root of Western idolatry seems to be man's specially Greek tendency to set himself up as an anthropomorphic sign of Deity, rather than accept the signs already given—the rain and sunset and sunrise which Our Lord Himself pointed as the works of His Father. Greek art, then, till the absorption of Greece into Rome, was idolatrous, and the cause of idolatry. But after that event, Rome adopts and imitates Athens, and the centre and stronghold of the making and worship of the graven image is in the central city. From the day of the Empire, in fact, Greek or Græco-Roman art has represented the principle of idolatrous personification; and so far we speak of Greek work as that of ancient Athens, modified by time, degeneracy, and transference to Italy. But after Constantine, Greek means Byzantine, as Byzantium gradually becomes the centre of the Eastern part of the Church of Christ. It is there, accordingly, that we may expect to see the Eastern tendency to pure or non-representative symbolism, in the first place; and in the second, supposing symbolism to have degenerated into image worship, we may look to Byzantium for a revival of the Hebrew protest against idolatry; which is, in fact, found in the Iconoclasm of the eighth century. The use of the word " Greek " for the Eastern Church

is so immeasurably different from all its other uses
as to lead to confusion of ideas.   One may say that
on the question of images the Eastern element in the
Byzantine Church was protesting against the ancient
Hellenic, or idolatrous Greek, for great part of the
eighth century.

But a further question has exercised the Christian
Church from the third or fourth century at latest, as
to the degeneracy of symbolism—that is to say, the
natural tendency of mankind either to turn symbols
into images or fetiches, or to substitute beautiful
personifications or supposed portraits of divine or
sacred persons, for ancient symbols of Deity and the
Presence of the Invisible Lord.   Considering that
the distinction between symbolism and personification, or actual resemblance, is not likely to be
rightly understood by large masses of the people,
who cannot see the difference between that·which
indicates and that which represents, it is held best
by many to dispense with art and symbol altogether.[1]
This is arguing from abuse of a thing to its disuse, as
is so frequently done; but the Church has never
yet consented to lose illustrative art or emblematic
means of instruction.[2] This prohibition, in its strictest

---

[1] "Latin Christianity," book iv. vol. ii. p. 344, quoted in Chap.
iii. on Iconoclasm.

[2] Fairly argued thus by John Damascene. De Imag. Orat. ii.
p. 747, ὅτι βίβλοι τοῖς ἀγραμμάτοις εἰσὶν αἱ εἰκόνες ἐν ἀήχῳ φωνῇ τ.
ὁρῶντας διδάσκουσαι, &c.   Οὐκ εὐπορῶ βίβλων, οὐ σχόλην ἄγω πρὸ
τὴν ἀνάγνωσιν· εἴσειμι εἰς τὸ κοινὸν τῶν ψυχῶν ἰατρεῖον, τὴν ἐκκλη-
σίαν, ὥσπερ ἀκάνθαις τοῖς λογισμοῖς συναπνιγόμενος· ἕλκει με πρὸς
θεὸν τῆς γραφῆς τὸ ἄνθος, καὶ ὡς λειμὼν τέρπει τὴν ὅρασιν, &c. &c.

Pope Gregory II., in his letter to Leo Isaurian, enumerates a list
of subjects which instruct and edify him personally.   All are. historical and Scriptural: the Madonna and choirs of angels, The
Miracles of Mercy, Last Supper, Loaves in the Desert, Transfigu-

form, is more Mohammedan than Hebrew, and is by no means Scriptural; for the distinction between symbolic teaching and idolatrous representation is recognized from the first under the Mosaic dispensation. The cherubic forms used in the Ark, in the Tabernacle, and in the Temple, are the earliest instances of permitted or enjoined symbol; and on their use all Christian use of art in the same way may rest.[1]

First, the cherubic emblem or symbol was not only permitted, but enjoined and dictated to Moses on the Mount. No contradiction to the spirit of the Second Commandment seems to have been felt by the use of it, either during the period of the Tabernacle or that of the Temple of Solomon. We are led to suppose, also, from the vision of Ezekiel (chs. i. and x.), that the forms represented, as well as symbolized, real existences, glorious and awful created beings superior to man. Still, it is probable that the carved or embossed cherubs were understood as symbols only by the people : though Ezekiel, who was a priest, was able to recognize the hieratic Form, as it may be called, which he had seen upon the Ark of God. It will be remembered (see Numb. iv. 5, 19, 20) that this form was known only to the priests, as the Ark was always covered threefold, and by their hands, before it was moved. Its bearers might

---

ration, Sacrifice of Isaac, Pentecost, Crucifixion, and Resurrection. He appeals to the use of the Cherubic forms in the Hebrew Dispensation.

[1] For an exhaustive dissertation on this subject, reference should be made to the word "Cherub" in Smith's Dictionary of the Bible, by Dr. Hayman ; but some of its leading facts may be repeated here.

not enter till it was covered. Josephus says no one
can conjecture of what form (ὁποῖαί τινες), these
cherubim of Glory were. This expression must
relate to those on the Ark ; since the larger forms of
those made by Solomon must have been seen by
both Levites and people, as well as the cherubs
on the Temple doors, along with the forms of lions
and palm-trees, and those which supported the
great lavers (1 Kings vii.).

This crucial example of enjoined and commanded
symbolism has, of course, been cited throughout all
the long Iconoclastic divisions of Christendom. It
was referred to throughout the second Council of
Nice ; and Gregory II. makes especial reference to it.
In the passages quoted in Milman's "Latin Christianity," and repeated above, from that Pope, and from
Joannes Damascenus, the case in favour of *some*
use of painting for purposes of instruction is fairly
stated. The Dean seems, however, to have doubted the
possibility of maintaining the distinction between a
symbolic representation and an actual portrait-image
in an age of undiscriminating devotion. It had certainly ceased to be felt in the age he is describing,
when to all intents and purposes the image was the
saint. But it must be remarked that the Hebrews
were expected to understand and abide by it, even
immediately after their escape from the image-worship
of Egypt. Though graven images stood in their Holy
of Holies, they were forbidden to address them in
prayer, or to think of them as representing Him of
Whose state they were a part. And it would seem
that there were what may be called precautions which
secured the people from the danger of cherub-worship ;

at least till the time of Jeroboam, whose calves at
Dan and Bethel may be supposed to have partaken of
the cherubic form, most probably that known to the
people as represented on the doors of the Temple.
That form must have borne some relation or resemblance to the vast images of Assyria, and Egypt, and
Persia. There is no necessity for regarding it as a
mere Hebrew adoption of Egyptian ritual: it is
more like a special sanction of the use of a world-
wide symbol, which is represented in the imagination
of the Greek and Gothic races by the various forms
and stories of the Griffin or gryps. This word
is doubtless connected by its etymology with the
Hebrew כְּרוּב Cherub; and the universality of the
traditional idea of these composite creatures is a
highly significant fact. It would seem, in truth, that
all the chief races of men have been taught to set
forth to their own sight such mysterious forms, not
believing in them as existing beings, and therefore
without incurring the guilt of idolatry; not worshipping their vast images, but expressing to themselves by forms of bull, lion, and eagle, combined
with the human face of thought and command, some
of the attributes of the Divine Being. Some form
of this kind, of which the winged bulls or lions of
Nineveh, or the sphinxes of Egypt, may be taken as
types, must have been the popular form of the cherub
known to the children of Israel. They were guarded
from worshipping this form, though it was used as
a part of their ritual, partly by the fact that two
images, not one, were placed by command in the
Tabernacle: partly by these two being represented
as attending on and ministering to some actual and

special Presence of God; and again, probably, by their appearing to be without share in human sympathies. They stood forth as adoring, admiring, and contemplating beings; angels of knowledge, as Hebrew tradition calls them, not, as like the seraphim, angels of love and protection to mankind. Their number is suggested as two or four in the Old Testament, as the Apocalyptic creatures are four in the vision of St. John. It will be remembered that in the Temple of Solomon, the Ark, with its two cherubs of glory, was overshadowed by a second pair of colossal size. But when we come to the description by Ezekiel of his visions of the glory of God, we are led further:[1] "In ch. i. he speaks of them as living creatures, " animal forms. In ch. x., v. 14, the remarkable ex- " pression 'the face of a cherub' is introduced; and " the prophet refers to his former vision, and identi- " fies these creatures with the cherubim. 'I knew " '(v. 20) that they were cherubim.' On the whole, it " seems likely that the word cherub means not only " the composite creature form of which the man, lion, " bull, and eagle were the elements; but, further, " some peculiar and mystical form, which Ezekiel, " being a priest, would know and recognize as the " 'face of a cherub' κατ᾽ ἐξοχὴν, but which was kept " secret from all others—and such, probably, were " those on the Ark, which, when it was moved, was " always covered, &c. This mysterious form might " well be the symbol of Him Whom none could behold " and live. And as symbols of divine attributes, not " as representations of actual beings (Clem. Alex. " Strom. v. p. 241), the cherubim should be regarded."

[1] See Smith's Dict. of the Bible, s. v. "Cherub."

This is exactly the saving distinction between symbolism and idolatry ; that the symbol is fully understood not to represent to the eye that which it calls
to the mind. It may be like nothing in nature ; but
at all events it must be such an image or form as
never can be supposed to possess or contain an actual
supernatural presence. It is a visible sign of the
Invisible : pointing onwards to Him, for ever teaching things concerning Him, proclaiming itself not to
be Him. This is the principle of Christian symbolism, and it appears to be identical with that laid
down for Hebrew worship. No one would ever think
of worshipping the Vine or the mystic Fish ; even
the Good Shepherd is not represented as standing to
receive the worship of His people. He is always
engaged in this work for them, laying them on His
shoulders or bearing them in His arms, and the
figures only repeat His parable of Himself as the
King and Shepherd of His people : that image also
being Homeric and universal, probably from the
earliest days of Aryan herdsmen.

As regards the Cherub form, connected as it is with
the Apocalypse, it is useless and idle to attribute it
to actual existences. Though the prophet seems to
have recognized them in his vision as beings far
above man, his description conveys no definite idea
to man. No Hebrew or Gentile can ever frame or
record images in words or on canvas, which shall
give clear conception of the fourfold faces and wings ;
or of the wheels in whom was the spirit of the living
creatures, to whom was said, O Wheel. The great
cloud out of the north, the fire enfolding itself, the
shapes of fire and lightning, the firmament above as

the terrible crystal, the brightness of amber and flame, the likeness of a throne and One sitting thereon— these are the expressions of a man who, having seen the glory of God, finds his powers of conception and expression, the thought of his brain and the language of his fathers, all fail him together; and if speech failed the prophet, the language of art may well fail also. Seldom, and rightly but seldom, has this sub- ject been attempted. Raffaelle's attempt at the subject confesses the inadequacy even of his gifts; it is not a failure of power—it is a misapplication of power; and one feels it to be beside the mark, a wondrous thing of nought. One other attempt we remember, strange and archaic, to many eyes probably too contemptible for notice, the work of a Syrian ascetic of 1200 years ago. It is in the great Medici or Laurentian MS. of Florence, known by the name of its copyist, as the MS. of Rabula the monk, dated 587.[1] We have to refer to it frequently; and quaint and extra- vagant as the Ascension woodcut in this volume may be, it gives, like all the other illustrations in the MS., a very strong sense of the author's originality, of his intensity of conception, vigour of thought, and graphic power of expression, which anticipate, not only the best MS. work, but the highest art of Europe. As is observed in our Chapter on Mosaics, this MS. is the type and highest example of the genius of Eastern- Greek or Byzantine work, where it possesses any genius. No one can doubt the connection of Byzan- tine work and thought with Orgagna's; nor of Or gagna's with that of Michael Angelo.[2]

---

[1] See Assemanni's Catalogue of the Laurentian Library and woodcut facing Index.   [2] See Crowe and Cavalcaselle, i. p. 447.

It seems that safety is only secured in religious art when this rule is made absolute; that pictures shall be symbolic and not representative; that they shall point to that which they do not resemble; shall suggest but not portray; shall appeal to thought, and not to emotion. Dean Milman's view, quoted in Chapter III., points to a rule of this kind. He looks forward with hope to a time of greater intelligence and greater faith and reliance on God's written Word, when illustrations of it in form and colour shall be no temptation; when the artist shall be able to appeal to all the emotions which the sense of beauty can give the soul, without misleading or confusing the soul. And he most rightly looks to the prospect of an improvement, an elevation and purification in art, which may conduce to this. To follow the line of thought thus indicated, is in great measure the purpose of this book. What seems best to say in a popular work on the subject is said in its last chapter. For the present—and speaking very briefly—there is no doubt that religious painting (symbolical or historical, for under these two heads we include all right church decoration) ought at its best to be a kind of artistic preaching, a proclamation of truth in Christ. It is felt to be always an appeal from the spirit of the painter to the spirit of the spectator. And if there has been true desire of the glory of God in the painter, it will somehow be felt by the spectator; he will understand, that is to say, that a man gone before him has devoutly sought to serve God by his art: and that feeling ought to be the chief value, if not the chief beauty, of the picture to him. This is the true emotion of religious art, the sense of the earnest self-dedication and faithful work of the painter or preacher. Like everybody else's faith and devotion, it admits endless mixtures of motive, and is thwarted by a thousand peculiarities and frailties; but if the spirit of devotion to God's service be in the painter, he will some way or another show by his picture that he was doing his best in that service. He will have a definite purpose and a determinate idea; he will tell his tale and express his idea faithfully,[1] and not be always appealing, straightforward or sideways, to the critic's emotions about loveliness. The essence of sacred art is not to work on the spectator, but at the great Subject. It is well in all art to forget oneself, but in this department it is indispensable. The self-consciousness of learning, and natural egotism of delight in his own skill, vitiate all the later works of Raffaelle, or indeed he fails in earnestness of motive altogether. Laborious pride of science, and half-conscious, unavoidable, incessant rivalry with others, infected and harassed Michael Angelo through all

[1] The latest confusion in which the words Idea and Ideal have been involved seems to consist, first, in making Ideal excellence of painting identical with technical excellence. Pictorial "nocturns" and "symphonies" mean nothing, but are technically admirable in the highest degree. Still, do not let us confound the ideal with the unmeaning. We have somewhere seen Mr. Whistler's beautiful studies of colour called ideal, whereas we should be inclined to call them charming, but to say they contained no intellectual conception or idea whatever. One hears, again, of ideal style or manner of painting and the like, meaning for the most part, that the painter in the given work realizes his fancies in a charming way, like Sandre Botticelli in his Spring or Aphrodite, or Mr. Burne Jones, or Mr. Spencer Stanhope. In this case the word ideal seems to be in collision with the word imaginative, or even passionate. At all events, Holbein's portrait of Wyatt, with all its literal resemblance to an actual and most practical description of man, is as *ideal*, in the wider sense of suggestive or expressive of spiritual fact, as any picture that ever was painted.

his long and glorious labours. At least, it is only in Florence, and particularly in the great works of the Medici Chapel, where he was undisturbed by competition, that his highest spiritual powers are seen in purity.

In many pictures, of the Madonna and St. John in particular, all higher aims are sacrificed to beauty, with disastrous effect. The work ceases to be sacred at all, even in the eyes of the most ignorant or simple. The painter has obviously no religious intention in what he calls a religious work, and his work becomes therefore not only neutral, but irreligious. And it is really this which accounts for Goethe's celebrated saying, that miraculous pictures are generally ill-painted. He had learnt to think that no well-painted picture could produce devotion, or conduce to belief in miracle. His idea of good painting was probably formed on the works of Raffaelle or his immediate followers in Germany or Italy: and his remark is correct enough. Those who are capable of believing in winking pictures, are persons for the most part unable to appreciate Raffaelle, and there is no special connection between beauty and super-stition. A picture painted simply as a piece of good painting falls short of high motive and inspiration, and is not likely to awake emotion, or raise influence of any kind. Those who can understand its technical merits will consider them its main object and purpose: those who cannot will have no sincere feeling about it; and its proper place is a picture-gallery, and not a place of worship. It is not our business now to consider what may be the qualifications of miraculous works of art; we are rather concerned that no objects of the kind should ever appear, by any accident or circumstance, within the disciplinary range of the Church of this country. Nor yet do we wish to pass any sentence on artists who paint secular pictures, or who even treat sacred subjects in a technical or academic spirit. For the former, as every act of right-doing is also an act of well-doing, their work is right and honourable, and may probably be done in zealous service of God. There is room for much casuistry in the matter, and one finds some difficulty in accepting Etty's conviction of the sacredness of his displayed beauties as exhibitions of the fairest divine work on earth. But the faithful purpose to work with honest exertion of power, and with sense of the workman's honour, is enough to make any picture a good work, in the most important sense. But he who has gone through the usual artistic training of the school of this country, —now a tolerably severe one—and who faithfully gives himself up to realizing a subject from the Old or New Testament, believing or desiring to believe in his subject, and wishing to impress it on others, is attempting a higher thing: and he is likely to have success, whether he sees it or not, and whether it is accompanied by personal applause and profit or not.

But there is another danger, or dangerous tendency, in the use of symbolism, which we trust, for our own Church and period, may be considered historical rather than actual. Yet it is a risk the recurrence of which is possible. It is true that symbols, in the second or some subsequent generation, are apt to become first conventional realisms, then personifications, then idols. It is well known, for instance, that at one time in the Middle Ages, the Cross became a personification and object of worship in itself, instead of the Symbol of the Death of Christ for man. The names of St. Cross and St. Sepulchre bear witness to this in our own country, as the Dean of St. Paul's observes. The popular, or Gentile Cherub —the "wise" or "mighty one," in all its varieties of combination—aquiline, leonine, and human—may have been originally a pure symbol of Divine Attribute. Next, and by easy transition, the composite is supposed to have a real existence corresponding to it, and resembling it, in the visible or invisible world. It gets personified. From this may follow—indeed, by the worship of the calves at Dan and Bethel, it seems that there did in this instance follow—actual worship of the graven image : still of the God of Israel, but by means of prayer addressed to a Personified representation of Him. There is a kind of Pagan's Progress, from the sign of Divine Attribute to the fetiche or image worshipped for its own sake. It has been too often made even in the Christian Church, and it may be observed in full completion in our own days. It seems to belong to all religious systems in which a caste in any form is retained or sought after ; where the priesthood are definitely and absolutely separated from the people. The real nature of the Symbol may be indeed remembered and understood by an initiated caste, or by an educated or privileged class of persons. In Egypt, the hieratic body retained a sense of the One God, leaving the people to gross idolatries. In Greece, under happier auspices, a philosophic laity, and a national temper alike speculative and hard-headed, may be

thought to have clung to the idea of a greater and
perfect Zeus, who was identical with Fate, and the
true Lord and Restorer of all things.[1]   There is no
doubt, that to the educated priesthood, and perhaps
laity, of the Roman Catholic Church, the distinctions
of worship, service, and devotion, are intelligible
enough. They are probably an after-thought, a series
of differences set up to explain or palliate an evidently indefensible state of things.   There is no particular comment to make on them ; except that worship or Appeal of Prayer for help in need can only be
made by the soul to one object at a time ; and that,
consequently, to entreat a saint or saints to mediate
for us with Christ the Lord, is to refuse worship or
personal appeal to Him. Well-trained and thoughtful priests or laity may possibly be able to maintain
such distinctions, and to keep the unseen Beings of
the spiritual world in some right relation to each
other in their creed.   It may have been so under the
hieratic despotism of Egypt; possibly afterwards, with
the higher and better spirits of the sophist or philosophic teaching of ancient Greece. All these alike,
on close examination as to what the idol or image
was, before which they knelt, might perhaps have
answered, that to them the idol was nothing at all ;
nothing Divine, no Hearer of Prayer to Whom all
flesh should come. Yet there can be no doubt of the
absolute and degrading idolatry of the mass of the
town population of Egypt, Greece, and Rome ; or that
the personified and representative Image did really
receive worship and aspiration due to God, and

[1] See Dr. Zeller's Essay in "Contemporary Review," vol. iv. p.
359 ; and compare Prof. Ruskin's "Queen of the Air."

debase the minds of the worshippers. We have already referred to Prof. Müller's Brahmin, who defends Hindu Iconodulism, and asserts the use of images as portraits, disclaiming all fetichism or belief in the efficacy of the wood and stone itself. As an excuse for the untaught, as a consolation to the Christian mind—sad because of the heathen, and living in the hope of our Litany that it may please God to have mercy upon all men—this justification is weighty and most valuable. But it could only be addressed to educated and thoughtful people, and it is only true when said of or by the educated and thoughtful. It is excellent *ad hominem*; it puts the Christian on his charity, and reminds him that he is not to condemn the heathen. But in the first place, to acquit our neighbour is as much an act of judgment as to pronounce him guilty; and we can but state his case as it appears to us, and leave it to the Judge of all the earth. And the plea is open to this exception, that the portrait is a record of the appearance of somebody who has been seen of men with eyes, whereas no man hath seen God at any time. If any authentic likeness of Christ the Lord remained on earth, we cannot suppose that to look on it in prayer to Him would be an act of idolatry. Having been manifest in the flesh, He had a human body and likeness. It is doubtless part of His scheme and care for men, that no such image should ever have existed; that His people may learn to face the life-long difficulty of walking by faith and not by sight. But a portrait of the Invisible Father of Spirits is a contradiction in terms. If the Hindu really believes in a hundred-headed being in the heavens, bearing dagger and axe, hurling quoits, and brandishing skulls, and "wielding all weapons in his countless hands"—his worship of the monstrous portraits of that Being can hardly be such as we can be satisfied with; we cannot leave him in it without such protest as is possible, and such attempts at better teaching as we can make. When the religious symbolism of a highly intellectual race is very rude and degraded, a natural suspicion arises that it is kept so for the poorer and less informed by some governing class who know better. It is clear that a man who could speak thus of the quasi-symbolic idols of his race would be able to dispense with their use himself in prayer; while the vulgar would continue to worship in abject fetichism. Would he say that a large proportion of the Hindu population of India understood the matter as well as he understood it himself? In short, the plea of symbolism may excuse the idolater, but it does not justify idolatry. As soon as the symbol is looked on as anything more than an assistance to thought or understanding, invented by man for man's convenience, without actual likeness to God, it is on the way to become an idol, whether it be set up in a Heathen Temple or in a Christian Church.

A brief account of the symbolisms most freely used in the primitive Church may close this chapter. They seemed to have been used entirely for instruction or suggestion of thought, and the beginnings of idol-worship are to be traced, not to them, but to the portraits, or supposed portraiture, of saints in the various churches, especially of Rome.[1]

[1] See Chapter on Mosaics. For permitted symbols, Clem. Alex. Pædag. iii. c. 11.

As has been already so often observed, the Vine, the Dove, the Lamb, the Good Shepherd, are the most ancient emblems ; together with the Monogram of the Lord's Name, the Fish in both its senses, and probably the hastily-inscribed or engraved palm-branch of the Martyr's or confessor's grave. The first four were sanctioned or virtually prescribed in Holy Scripture itself, and the others are sufficiently obvious images. Thus the Fish, as an anagram, represents the Lord Himself, and, as a symbol, the believer, according to the parable of the net ; the Dove and the Lamb are used both as signs of the Second and Third Persons of the Trinity, and also to represent His faithful followers. All these forms are found in the earliest cemeteries and catacombs, sometimes with the most archaic and barbarous treatment. In a few cases— and those, of course, the most ancient—they are in beautiful Græco-Roman fresco or stucco, admirably composed in decorative patterns, and so well executed, with scientific preparation of the wall-surface beforehand, as to have lasted better than much more recent work by less skilful hands. Such works are the paintings in the tomb of Domitilla and the catacomb of St. Prætextatus.[1] The probability of their having been executed by heathen hands is generally recognized ; and, as has been suggested above, it seems not unlikely that the Christian community accepted the decorations of the halls and rooms in which they met, simply as they found them ; and then began to make special choice of ordinary subjects, as vines and doves, which spoke a double language, and reminded them of events in the Gospels or of words from the Lord's mouth.

[1] See Chapter on Catacombs.

Other emblems more rarely found, and not immediately derived from Holy Scripture, the ship and chariot, the anchor and lyre, the dolphin, phœnix, peacock, and pelican, are all used on Christian sepulchres. From Scripture, the cock, stag, lion, dragon, and serpent occur in various relations. The olive, fir-tree, and fig-tree are rarely seen; the palm is found on all tombs, and on the sarcophagi it accompanies the subject of Our Lord's Entry into Jerusalem. The various symbolic or parabolic events are mentioned in the Chapters on the Catacombs and on Sarcophagi and Christian Sculpture, and in the index of our subjects. The principal ones are the Agape of bread and fish, or the Fish carrying loaves; Adam and Eve with the Serpent; Noah in his square *arca* or chest; the sacrifice of Abraham; Pharaoh and the Red Sea; Moses and the rock; Elijah in his chariot; Jonah with gourd or whale; Daniel with the lions; and once[1] administering the balls of pitch and hair to the dragon, according to the narrative in the Apocrypha. To these may be added, from the New Testament, the adoration of the Magi, the miracles of Cana and of the Multiplied Loaves, and other miracles of mercy — in particular, the Cures of the Palsy and of the Issue of Blood. These, however, are historical rather than symbolical, and records of actual events rather than suggestive of the future.

Various attempts at setting forth the imagery of the book of Revelation are spoken of in the Chapter on Mosaics. The increasing alarms and distresses of the declining Empire from the end of the fourth

[1] Bottari. i. tav. 15.

century naturally inclined men to think of the latter days of Imperial Rome as indeed the beginning of the world's end. It is no wonder if workmen, whose style was formed in so stern a school as the Byzantine period, should look willingly at the future world rather than the present, and dwell in imagination on spiritual hope; being hopeless in this life. Still, within a period of ten centuries there are no anticipations of judgment in authentic painting or carved work; the rejoicings of the saints in and with Christ, in open vision in Heaven, are not as yet contrasted with the torments of the lost: only with the state of the faithful as sheep on earth, on the other side of the mystic Jordan.

The most commonly-used symbolism of the Apocalypse, if we except the mystic Lamb, is of course the fourfold sign of the Evangelists—the Tetramorph, as it is called—when, as frequently happens in ancient art, the four are combined in one form. They thus involve a peculiarly impressive connection between the beginning of the visions of Ezekiel and the first unveiling of heaven to the Beloved Disciple. It cannot be mistaken, though in the prophet's vision the Living Creatures were not only four in number, but each was fourfold in shape. "They four had the face of a man, and the face of a lion, on the right side; and they four had the face of an ox on the left side; they four had also the face of an eagle:" while in the Apocalypse "the first beast was like a lion, the second was like a calf, the third had the face of a man, and the fourth beast was like a flying eagle." This connection is said by Mrs. Jameson[1] to have been noticed

[1] "Sacred and Legendary Art," p. 79.

as early as the second century, though no representations are found till the fifth; nor is it till the fifth that the four creatures were taken to represent the four Evangelists. It was not, indeed, till long after that each was separately assigned to each writer. The united Tetramorph connects them more closely with the vision of Ezekiel, and is represented (evidently with that connection present in the mind of the workman) in the great MS. of Rabula. (See woodcut.)

But the original emblem of the four Evangelists [1] is the four rivers of Paradise. These are found in some of the earliest specimens of certainly authentic Christian decoration, as in the Lateran Cross.[2] The four books or rolls are also found in early art. The stag is generally placed by the four rivers, especially when they are united in the one Jordan and combined with baptismal imagery; as so frequently happens.

The upraised hand of blessing, as a sign of the presence of God the Father, is constant in the early mosaics of Rome and Ravenna. Some account of this and other Christian emblems will be given in describing the places where they occur, as of the Orantes or praying figures so often found in the Catacombs.[3]

It is difficult to lay down, or rather to suggest, any rules or limitations for the use of symbolism in the Anglican Church, nor would they probably have much authority with any builder or decorator of any sacred building, nor obtain much attention from that

[1] See Aringhi, vol. ii. p. 285.
[2] See Chapter on the Cross and Sacramental Emblems.
[3] See Index.

section of our clergy or people whose minds are most employed on the æsthetic part of Christian worship. But it is correct, at all events, to say that Scriptural subjects, and those alone, contented the Church of the first five centuries. It is not that others were forbidden, for Christian Church ornament either began, or was from the first mingled, with the deco rations of Pagan halls and Pagan cemeteries. But in those days the Christian imagination could dwell contentedly and continuously on a prescribed series of images, within the ample limits of Scriptural illustration. We earnestly desire to restrict Anglican decoration within the same bounds as those of the primitive Church, and may fairly ask if the histories, emblems, and parables of the Old and New Testament are not, after all, enough to employ the mind of an English worshipper in the intervals of church service, or at times of private meditation in church? And, setting aside for a moment all the vast mass of historical subject which invites the artist—and has quite vainly invited the English artist, till very lately—it may be said that Scriptural symbolism will find quite subject enough to call out and to reward the greatest efforts of the greatest man— that is to say, of the greatest believing man; for it is not desirable that our sanctuaries be adorned with the paintings of men who do not believe what they paint, and who despise their own labour; or even with works whose technical excellence is their only appeal to thought. Earnestly as we may admire Michael Angelo and his great deeds, none of us can wish (if such a thing were possible) ever to see another Christian Church adorned entirely like the Sistine, where glorious histories and mighty ideals of Prophet, Apostle, and Sibyl, are mingled everywhere with problems in Titanic anatomy. If a poet wished to form an idea of the noblest imagery conceivable, and of its expression in the mightiest words, he would at least see it in the prophecies of Isaiah or Ezekiel. The words and diction should enter into him, and be an element of strength to him, though he would not think of imitation. The thoughts and expressions, ever so imperfectly understood, will certainly take possession of the reader, and feed his imagination with ideas. The Scriptures are to afford, as Mr. Arnold most weightily and pithily tell us, the whole and sole intellectual culture of large masses of the people ; and they are a part of it which no class of the English people can spare, because they appeal with matchless power to the imagination, which requires more culture than any other spiritual faculty in our own race and time. That which inspired the mighty poet, may fill also with inspiration, with hope, and faithful imaginings, the brains of poor men and women, pupil-teachers and school-children. It may inspire the painter also; and the best men of our day have known how to drink at the source of all this strength. In short, the range of human imagination working on God's Word is vast enough to supply any painter or number of painters with happy work for life ; if they be fit and willing men to undertake any sacred subject at all.

VINE NO. 2.—CHAPEL OF GALLA PLACIDIA.

CHAPTER III.

ICONOCLASM AND CREATURE-WORSHIP.

THE subject of pictorial or other representative ornament in Christian churches has been made specially difficult by the controversies of so many centuries. It has probably been debated in one form or another from the earliest times of patriarchal worship; but it would seem that the Church of the first three centuries suffered as little from it as any assembly of devout persons could possibly do. Their art was artless and unexciting: their faith was both art and poetry to them, because it kept continually before their imaginations the highest subjects which they could possibly aspire to.

The Hebrew and the Greek element in the Church may have differed somewhat in this matter; but it seems very probable that symbolic ornament was used in the earliest catacombs, even while the strongest feeling against representative images, or forms set up in church to assist devotion, was felt and expressed on all hands. For the present it may be said; that as (A.D. 180) Irenæus[1] urges it against the Gnostics that they made use of pretended portrait-images of Our Lord; while Celsus urged it against the Faith[2] that Christians endured neither altars nor images;—the practice of image-worship, or addressing any visible form in prayer, is contrary to the theory and practice of the primitive saints. But painting and sculpture may have been used for instruction, and may have aided sermon and catechism, if not prayer. We cannot say what was the date of the first Good Shepherd, or Vine—both existed in heathen art, and were adopted symbols, in which Christians recognized the words of their Lord written in colour by heathen hands. Tertullian[3] (A.D. 300) speaks of a Good Shepherd on a chalice: and the sign of the Cross[4] was used from the very first, as a badge of Christ's followers, though it may have originated in

---

[1] Adv. Hær. i. 24 ad f., 25 ed. Migne.
[2] Origen contra C. viii. pp 396 Lat., 400 Gk. ed. 1605.
[3] De Pudicit. c. 7. "Ovis perdita a Domino requisita, et humeris Ejus revecta. Procedant ipsæ picturæ calicum vestrorum," &c., &c. The longer passage which immediately follows, seems to apply to heathen imagery and its consequences. There can be no doubt, either, of his view as to the use of images for devotion in churches; but he lets Scriptural symbolism pass without comment. Origen argues on the side of spiritual worship against Celsus, who seems to have raised the same artistic objections against Christianity, for not having produced a Phidias, which have been urged covertly or openly ever since. He says man is made in the image of God, and is His best Agalma. Man is the temple of the Holy Spirit, and His fittest abode.
[4] See p. 6.

the Monogram.[1] So that, for a time, perhaps for nearly 300 years, Christian worship and Sacraments may be thought to have been conducted in spirit and in truth, so far that the faithful needed no stimulus to their devotion, and sought no other sign of God's presence with them than the Sacraments of His ordaining.

The first public sign of alarm, or rather of precaution, appears in the Council of Illiberis (Grenada) in Spain, about 305.   One of its canons ordains that no picture shall be in the church, lest that which is worshipped or adored be painted on the walls. At the end of the fourth century we find Paulinus of Nola ornamenting his church of St. Felix, and painting a catacomb with Scriptural histories, and with pictures symbolic of the Holy Trinity.   Nor does he seem to have raised alarm, though it must have been "nearly at the same time," says Bishop Harold Browne,[2] " or a little earlier, that Epiphanius, going through Anablatha, a village in Palestine, found there a veil hanging before the door of the church, whereon was painted an image of Christ, or some saint, he did not remember which.[3] When he saw in the church of Christ an image of a man, contrary to the authority of Scripture, he rent it, and advised that it should be made a winding-sheet for some poor man." This would scarcely have happened in Italy; and indeed the distinction between history and symbolism on the

---

[1] Minucius Felix, quoted in Chapter on the Cross.

[2] Exposition of xxxix. Articles.   Art. xxii. p. 507.   Epiphanius' letter is in Jerome.   Ep. 60.

[3] Epist. ad Johan. Hierosol. Bellarmine and Baronius dispute this passage as an Iconoclastic interpolation, but it is acknowledged by Petavius.   See Bingham, book viii. chapter viii. 6, 7.

one hand, and emotional idolatry on the other, is somewhat fine, though perfectly real; and has often been sternly rejected in the East. The use of pictures depends, for good or evil, on the characters of the people who use and the artists who supply them; a growing superstition in demand leads infallibly to a supply of more and more dangerous decorations.

In the fourth and fifth centuries, the instructive use of pictures must have begun to be mingled with picture-worship, as the tendency to adoration of saints and martyrs declared itself. St. Augustine says[1] there were many worshippers of tombs and pictures in his day: that the Church condemned them and strove to correct them. Chalices and patens, he says, are gold and silver, the work of men's hands; there is no fear of their being worshipped; it is the lifelike form which has power to make itself adored. And at the end of the fourth century, Bishop Browne concludes, both historical pictures, and, soon after, commemorative portraits of Apostles, saints and martyrs, and even of living kings and bishops, were hung up; and the use of statues followed. In the sixth century there is evidently serious alarm among bishops and thoughtful heads of the Church at the popular devotion to these visible forms; and Serenus, Bishop of Marseilles, seems to have ordered all the images in the churches of his diocese to be broken; on which Gregory the Great writes to him to say that

---

[1] " Novi multos esse sepulcrorum et picturarum adoratores quos et ipsa (Ecclesia) condemnat," &c. (Aug. De Moribus Eccl. .l. c. 34, 74, 75).

he altogether approves of his forbidding image-worship; but blames him for breaking them, as things harmless in themselves and useful for instruction. St. Gregory clearly looked on them as historical pictures of events, not as Personifications of the Creator.[1]

A superstition resting on foundations so deep and wide as the human longing for a sign from God could have only been coerced by the determined efforts of the whole clergy and conventual orders. The latter in particular were the last persons to make any attempt of the kind; and the lamentable struggle of Iconoclasm and Iconodulism in the eighth century was a contest between military and monastic power, which anticipated in the East the papal contests with the House of Swabia in the West. It is not here necessary to follow its course historically.[2] Leo, the Isaurian, and his son Constantine Copronymus were the great Iconoclast emperors; the Empress Irene lived to undo their work. The Council of Constantinople in the reign of Copronymus, A.D. 754, is called by the Greeks the Seventh General Council; but it is rejected by the Latins. It condemned all worship and use of images. Thirty years after, in the reign of Irene, the Second Council of Nice reversed its decisions, ordaining that images should be set up, but not adored with the worship of *latria;* which John Damascenus vigorously protests had never been paid them. Charlemagne and the Gallican bishops replied to Pope Adrian, who sent

[1] Epp xi. 13. p. 1127 vol. 77 ed. Migne. 1849.
[2] Alt's "Heiligenbilder," Leipsic, 1845. This work, with Dr. Piper's "Einleitung in die Monumentale Theologie," Gotha, 1867, are complete and exhaustive works.

them a copy of this decree; allowing images for ornament and history, but condemning all worship. Their formal reply is called the Libri Carolini, and was published by Charlemagne A.D. 790.

The British bishops fully confirmed this in 792, abhorring the worship of images; and Charlemagne, two years after, assembled the Synod of Frankfort, consisting of 300 bishops from France, Germany, and Italy, who formally rejected the Synod of Nice, declaring it not to be the seventh general council; nor was it received in the Western Church, except in churches specially under Roman influence, for five centuries and a half.

It is clear that the distinction between decorative or even historical painting or sculpture, and use of idolatrous objects for worship, was perfectly well understood in the primitive Church, though there was no necessity for express statements on the matter. Tertullian's language [1] seems sweeping and violent; but he is addressing himself to Pagans or their imitators, or, as it seems, to Christians in the artistic employments, who were in danger of being led to seek gain by sculpture and painting of heathen subjects.

" There was a time long past when the idol did not exist; the sacred places were unoccupied, and the temples void. . . But when the devil brought in makers of statues and images and all kinds of likenésses on the world, all the raw material of human misery, and the name of idols followed it. And ever since then any art which produces an idol in any way is the source of idolatry. It makes no

[1] De Idolatria, c. iii.

difference whether the workman makes it in clay, or
a sculptor carves it, or if he weaves it in Phrygian
cloth, because it is of no consequence as to the
substance an idol is formed of, whether it be plaster,
or colours, or stone, or brass, or silver, or canvas."[1]

Such is his trenchant and inclusive comment on
the pictorial or other representation of any human
form, and in his next chapter he adopts the language
of the second commandment, and seems to apply it to
the whole range of art; nothing is to be represented
at all. As he proceeds, however, on the grounds of
the Hebrew Law, he is reminded of the Brazen
Serpent; and at once ·justifies it as a symbol or
type of the coming Redeemer Who should be lifted
up for mankind. Without seeming to be aware of
the logical bearings of the important exception he
has made, he returns to the charge to show that all
employments connected with idolatry or the temples
are forbidden, and then (ch. viii.) suggests various
trades or crafts to which the artists of his time (who
seem to have been numerous) might apply themselves. They may become painters and glaziers in
the literal sense—at most they can find other ornaments to paint on the walls than "simulacra"—
likenesses of human or animal life. It is pretty

[1] "Idolum aliquamdiu retro non erat," he exclaims; "sola
templa et vacuæ ædes. . . At ubi artifices statuarum et imaginum,
et omnis generis simulacrorum diabolus seculo intulit, rude illud
negotium humanæ calamitatis, et nomen de Idolis consecutum est.
Exinde jam caput facta est Idololatriæ ars omnis quæ Idolum quo-
quomodo edit. Neque enim interest, an plastes effingat, an
cælator ex(s)culpat, an Phrygio detexat; quia nec de materia
refert, an gypso, an coloribus, an lapide, an ære, an argento, an
filo formetur Idolum."
The sentence of the Apostolical Constitutions on this matter, as
Alt remarks, is brief (viii. c. 32), Ἐιδωλοποιὸς προσιὼν, ἢ παυσάσἴω
ἢ ἀποβαλλέσθω. "Heiligenbilder," p. 45.

E

clear that Tertullian meant to make the same
Eastern protest against all representative art which
Islam made after him.[1] Such arts had been
abused, therefore they were to exist no longer.
The fiery Father, in short, represents the views of
the remnant of the Hebraic party in the early
Church on this matter.[2] His idea is simply to

[1] Koran 22, 31. "But depart from the abomination of idols * *
being orthodox towards God and associating (no other God) with
Him." Also ch. 25. See, however, *infrà*, note 1, p. 16.

[2] The expressions of Augustine, De Fide et Symbolo, vii., seem to
refer to images of God the Father. See p. 102, ed. Frob. Basle, 1528.
He is speaking of the Lord's Place,at the Right Hand of God :—"Nec
ideoquasi humana forma circumscriptum esse Deum Patrem arbitran-
dum est. * * Tale enim simulacrum nefas est Christiano in templo
collocare, multo magis in corde nefarium est." This might seem to
throw serious doubt on the propriety of representing our Lord at
all in portrait-images, as if it would amount to a breach of the
second commandment; but Augustine still (De Trin. book viii.
chap. 4) mentions the numerous and varied representations of Our
Lord without blame; and acknowledges the universal tendency of
thought to picture to itself persons and events by imaginative effort.
It seems as if he recognized the distinction between symbolic likenesses of the Lord— not supposed to resemble His earthly features,
but necessary impersonations in pictures representing His acts and
life—and portraits intended to stimulate devotion by means of
beauty or otherwise. The argument in Damascenus and elsewhere,
that as He appeared in the Flesh His Flesh may be represented,
seems to hold good. His real likeness being unknown, the portrait
is after all but a symbol of His Humanity, and an acknowledgment that He is real though unseen. "The likeness of our Lord
in the Flesh," says Augustine, De Trin. viii. 5, "is variously
imitated by diversity of innumerable minds; but still it is what it
actually was." He is reasoning about the difficulty of believing
that things *are*, or have actually *been*, without an idea of what they
are or were *like*. Of St. Paul, or Lazarus, or Bethany, he says,
we may have wrong mental pictures, but the places are real, and
the mental picture is essential to our feeling of their reality. Clemens
Alexandrinus, Pædagog. I. iii. cap. 1 (ap. Molanum, cap. 49) thus
enumerates the Christian symbols in use in his time. "Sint nobis
signacula columba vel piscis vel navis quæ celeri cursu a vento
fertur, vel lyra musica qua usus est Polycrates, vel ancora nautica,
quam insculpebat Seleucus. Si sit piscans aliquis, meminerit
Apostoli, et puerorum qui ex aqua extrahuntur. Neque enim
idolorum sunt exprimendæ facies, quibus vel solum attendere pro-
hibitum est. Sed nec ensis nec arcus, iis qui pacem persequuntur;
nec pocula, iis qui sunt moderati et temperantes."

lay the axe well to the roots of the system of Pagan worship and its abominations. It is strange that the subsequent history of the Brazen Serpent and its destruction by Josiah should not have led him to consider that even things once ordained by immediate revelation of God are capable of abuse through lapse of time. It was Josiah's duty to destroy the image which was one of the most important monuments of the long wanderings of the fathers in the wilderness. But that does not prove that it never ought to have been made by Moses in the first instance.

The mind of Tertullian seldom rejoiced in distinctions. He knew what idolatry had been, and what it was; and felt that it was no time to talk of art and beauty, when the charm of the graven image was on the side of persecution. Men who had seen their brethren and children tortured, not accepting deliverance, before some indifferent Pallas severely fair, may be excused for not appreciating the artistic devotion of Cæsarian Rome; though, St. Paul had charity, and on Mars' Hill, suggested hope for the art of ancient Athens. Nor would the beauteous scorn of the bow-lipped Apollo give any comfort to those whose kindred were flogged to death because they would not burn incense before him. In the very earliest days of Christian art, it is true, there seems to have been little severity of feeling. But as the times waxed more evil, and trial deepened, and the Lord delayed His coming, it is no wonder if men's souls took a despondent turn. The monuments of that special tendency in the early Church are the hermitages and caves which now honeycomb the rocks of Quarantania and Mar Saba; and the grim mosaics which give us our popular notion of the art called Byzantine.

The Iconoclastic controversy, in fact, has never ceased; at all events since the earliest form of patriarchal worship and communion with the Creator has been lost to mankind. Ever since the open vision of God and certain consciousness of His Personal presence, in vision or otherwise, has been withdrawn, man has unceasingly sought to find God, and to be found of Him. And as a natural consequence, men have always sought to be persuaded that they have found their God in this world of sense; have sought after signs of Him; and finally have sought to make to themselves signs of Him; and indeed the word *signum* is Latin for statue or highly relieved image.[1] More speculative or spiritual races have been contented with symbols, which appealed to their aspirations by the way of their intellect—not desiring to see God, His image or His shape, yet nourishing and illustrating their thoughts of Him by the analogies of visible things, and setting forth those analogies in visible forms and colour. So undoubtedly did the Church of the earliest ages. No one, probably, ever knelt to worship in the catacombs before the figures of the Good Shepherd or the Vine; the remaining portraits of the Lord there are not earlier than the seventh century;[2] in any case the use of His portrait-image in churches seems to have been unusual till the sixth. But in all ages the more creative, active, and energetic races of men

[1] Virg. Georg. ii., "Stabunt et Parii lapides, spirantia signa."
[2] See, however, Chapter on Catacombs.

have desired to possess some visible and beautiful object of adoration, and not merely sought for abstract beauty as an aid to the act of adoration.   This is the inner principle of Greek image-worship; and the contest between Iconoclasm and Iconodulism is in one sense a contest between the Hebrew spirit and the Greek spirit.   The Symbol is felt by its authors, and their generation, to be a confession of human infirmity, an acknowledgment that language fails in things unspeakable; it directs the mind of the spectator onwards to greater things, for which it is substituted for the time.   It may become to other races an Idol; a thing of man's work in which supernatural virtue is believed to reside.   The word Image (Imago), a form, is taken in this book as corresponding with the Greek Icon, or likeness; and is meant to convey no disparaging idea, but to be the harmless title of a harmless object.   Every visible representation is, in our sense, an image, or combination of images.   It seems that the symbolic image becomes an idol, or in the lower degradations of thought about it a fetiche, whenever local and personal virtue is supposed to reside in it, so that the mind of the worshipper rests in it and goes no farther.   While no feeling, or aspiration, or hope in prayer is intercepted by the visible object, it may give comfort to the worshipper, and he may be borne with in using it.   Even then his use of it is a confession of weakness, to be borne with, perhaps, but not without renewed and sustained explanation and protest.

On this subject, as on so many others, the massive learning and careful impartiality of Dean Milman are of the greatest value.   On the one

hand, he points out the danger of refined distinctions, the incapability of untaught and busy men to
understand them, and the certainty that those who
begin by worshipping through an image will end by
worshipping the image itself; appealing simply to
the undoubted facts of the History of the Early
Church.   On the other, he observes, with equal
truth, that the evil and abuse of Iconodulism arise
from the fault of the worshipper, and not of the
images; and that the Church cannot break with the
fine arts as means of instruction, or repudiate appeal
to the human imagination of truth.   Finally, and
with what appears to us great insight and true
wisdom, he says—half apologizing for the words as
for a paradox—that the reconciliation between Religion and Art really lies in Art; that is to say, in the
artist, and in the greater learning, refinement, purity
of spirit, and singleness of aim of those who represent the graphic powers of an age.   The following
extracts from " Latin Christianity "[1] will be found
to bear on this matter with particular force and
clearness ·—

" This question, thus prematurely agitated by the
Iconoclastic emperors, and at this period of Christianity so fatally mistimed, is one of the most grave,
and it should seem inevitable, controversies arising
out of our religion.   It must be judged by a more
calm and profound philosophy than could be possible
in times of actual strife between factions.   On the
one hand, there can be no doubt that, with ignorant
and superstitious minds, the use, the reverence, the
worship of images, whether in pictures or statues,

[1] Vol. ii. p. 343, ed. 1867.

invariably degenerates into idolatry. The Church may draw fine and aerial distinctions between images as objects of reverence and as objects of adoration; as incentives to the worship of more remote and immaterial beings, or as actual and indwelling deities; it may nicely define the feeling which images ought to awaken; but the intense and indiscriminating piety of the vulgar either understands not, or utterly disregards, these subtleties: it may refuse to sanction, it cannot be said not to encourage, that devotion which *cannot and will not weigh and measure either its emotions or its language.* Image worship in the mass of the people, of the whole monkhood at this time, was undeniably the worship of the actual, material, present image, rather than that of the remote spiritual power of which it was the emblem or representative. It has continued, and still continues to be, in many parts of Christendom, this gross and unspiritual adoration; it is part of the general system of divine worship. The whole tendency of popular belief was to localize, to embody in the material thing, the supernatural or divine power. The healing or miraculons influence dwelt in and emanated from the picture of the saint—the special, individual picture. Where the image was, there was the saint. He heard prayer, was carried in procession to allay pestilence, &c. He smiled or stretched his hand from the wall. One image of the same saint rivalled another in power.

"On the other hand, is pure and spiritual Christianity implacably hostile to the Fine Arts? Is that influence of the majestic and the beautiful, awakened by form, colour, and expression, to be altogether

abandoned ?   Can the exaltation and purification of
the human soul through Art be in no way allied
with true Christian devotion ?   Is that aid to the
realization of the historic truths of our religion, by
representations, vivid, speaking, almost living, to be
utterly proscribed ?   Is the idealism of Reverence to
rest solely on the contemplation of pure spirit ?
Because the ignorant or fraudulent monk has ascribed
miraculous power to his Madonna or the image of
his patron saint, and the populace have knelt before
it in awe undistinguishable from devotion, is Christianity to cast off Raffaelle and Correggio ?   *   *   *
Religion must either break off all association with
these dangerous friends, and the Fine Arts abandon
their noblest field ; or their mutual relations must be
amicably adjusted.   *   *   *   The causes which may
be expected to work this sacred reconciliation may
be the growing intelligence of mankind; greater
familiarity with the written Scriptures ; and, para-
doxical as it may sound, greater perfection in the
arts themselves, or a finer apprehension of that perfection in ancient as in modern art."

It is in the Church of England, if anywhere,
that some practical adjustment of this great controversy must be worked out; and it may be a
sufficient apology for so long a quotation that it
contains or implies the principles on which this
may be done.   It cannot be done by a Puritan,
or indeed Mohammedan, prohibition of all use of the
representative arts, which is simple Iconoclasm; nor
yet by allowing creature-worship in any form whatever.   It is on the license of addressing prayer to
some saint gone before, because he is supposed to be

nearer us than his Lord and ours, that Iconodulism stands. Some distinctions the Church must draw, and if possible they must not be too fine or aerial. That between the *cultus latriæ* and lower degrees or intensities of devotion never can hold long, if indeed it is intelligible at all. It is the refinement of learned and subtle-minded persons, called upon to justify a state of things on which their whole personal power rests; a system which they have been born into, and have not themselves created; a system, as it seems to them, based on truth, because based on devout and noble feeling; a system, as it seems to them, beneficial in its working, because it makes devotion and obedience easy to the poor; and because, if it does not teach absolute truth, it seems to make instruction unnecessary. The distinction was intelligible, yet the multitude might be trusted not to understand it. "It is one thing," says John Damascenus, "to set forth service of actual worship; another to proclaim persons as possessors of some dignity, for honour's sake." This is true; and had the chief advocate of Iconodulism held by his own distinction, and had all the monks and preachers on his side faithfully impressed it on the people, the Iconoclastic controversy would never have arisen, and the course of the history of the faith would have been altered for the better. But the plea is evidently meant *ad hominem;* it is addressed to argumentative opponents, and was never meant to moderate the zeal of fanatic supporters; and from his age to our own, the same use has been made of the same refinement. Damascenus himself argues in his next oration, that it is manifestly absurd[1] to make our Lord the sole object of portrait-images in church. It is an act of confessed hostility to the saints; if they suffered with Him, they are to be glorified with Him, &c. His work, in fact, is full of the unconscious Jesuitry of a difficult argument addressed alike to unquestioning followers and un listening adversaries, in defence of a system which, to his mind, ought never to have been questioned, so that any answer seems good enough for the questioner.

Dean Milman's observation that the Church may draw aerial distinctions in vain, seems at variance with what he himself says[2] of the virtual and final compromise of the Eastern Church between pictures and statues. He there explains that the more contemplative and refined intellect of the East would see, and be content with, the distinction between the painted image on a plane surface, and that which possesses projection, and solid or quasi-personal form. Subtle as it may seem, this difference is felt and acted on with the greatest strictness by the Eastern communions.[3] The fact is, that any distinction, faithfully dwelt on, and expounded for what it is, will be made intelligible at last, and must then stand or fall on its merits. The reason why the *cultus latriæ* in the Western Church is not practically distinguishable from lower degrees of reverence is a plain one—because the distinction has never been

---

[1] " O hominum absurditas! nonne animadvertitis, vos plane Sanctorum inimicos confiteri? Domini exercitus sancti sunt," &c. De Imaginibus, Or. 2.

[2] " Latin Christianity." Book xiv. chap. 9, quoted *suprà*.

[3] See Chapter on the Crucifix.

-enforced. We ourselves recognize a difference between Prayer and Reverence, because it is proclaimed and taught to all English people. But
in the Church of the seventh century, the *idiotes*
or unlearned person, was encouraged to call on
the saints for all he wanted, and to put them
in the place of the One God, Whom his instructors
nevertheless proclaimed they held the sole Object
of prayer. "Thou that hearest prayer, unto Thee
shall all flesh come." This is one of the great texts
or standards of Monotheism—the appeal to One
Will, Omnipotent, Omniscient, and All Merciful.
Reverence for the memory of a departed saint, the
communion in which we believe between the Church
Militant and Triumphant, are ideas quite consistent
with the view that God rules and hears prayer in
person, and draws all men personally to Himself,
that they may know Him and be His.

The principle of Instructive Decoration, to which
we shall appeal, is well set forth by John Damascenus. Gregory II. also urges it in his Epistle
to Germanus.[1] The Eastern Father's argument is
contained in the words already quoted :[2] Pictures are
poor men's books. To treat pictures as books, and
to take them for what they mean, is a principle easy
to enunciate. But religious pictures will always
be taken for all which they can be made to mean.
It is the duty of a clergy who make use of painted

---

[1] "Enarrent illa et per voces, et per literas, et per picturas."
A favourite authority was Basil's ἃ γὰρ ὁ λόγος τῆς ἱστορίας διὰ τῆς
ἀκοῆς παρίστησι, ταῦτα γραφὴ σιωπῶσα διὰ μιμήσεως δείκνυσι. So
J. D. ὅπερ τῇ ἀκοῇ ὁ λόγος, τοῦτο τῇ ὁράσει ἡ εἰκών. Note,
Milman's "Lat. Ch." ii. 348, ch. iv.
[2] Picturæ sunt libri idiotarum.

images to take care that they convey no lessons except those of the Faith. The most thoughtful commentator will from time to time read his **own** meanings into the text he expounds, and that more probably if he is himself appealing to emotion rather than to conviction. And this is the differ- ence between pictures and books—that the appeals to feeling made by the former are alike more subtle, more forcible, and more popular. This is nearly as much so in our own impatient days, when real attention to a carefully expressed meaning is so hard and rare to obtain. At times like those of the first Gregories, and in conditions of society like the lower strata of our own—at all events in the schools of many missions [1]—pictures may be valu- able books to convey ideas, and powerful means to im press them. The more reason why a living and teach ing Church should have a standard and a system for their use, and should prevent their misuse. Symbols which assert the doctrines of the faith, historical paintings which describe the history of the gospel, are pure narrative teaching; the isolated figure of the saint may be a harmless commemoration of his work in the Lord; but it is open to vague alarm and objection, which will never apply to him if he be represented *engaged in* that work; if some real and true event or action of his life be set up to commemo- rate him, and God's work in him be made his monu-

---

[1] The author was long ago requested by the Bishop of Nassau to endeavour to make or collect a set of symbolic and historic illustra- tions of the Apostles' Creed, to be used in oral instruction, and form, as it were, a basis for realization in the barbaric mind. The use made of art by Methodius in the ninth century, and his conversion of Bogoris, king of Bulgaria, by the terrors of a picture of the Last Judgment, are not disputed, and may be historical facts.

ment; instead of an imaginary portrait, totally unlike him, done for the artist's pleasure, in robes which he may never have worn, and surrounded by landscape which his eyes never beheld.

Let the picture-book in form and colour obey the strict rule of truth, to which all books are bound which are without those attractions; and let us especially beware of error or falsehood, if conveyed in the most delightful form. We do not rehearse the Legends of the Saints in church, and the Apocrypha is read with a certain protest. It is hard to say why, after all, our church decoration should not be limited to Scriptural subject, historical or symbolical. Our artists can hardly ask for a wider range than the History of the Redemption of Man in the Old and New Testaments ; or for deeper thoughts to express than those which fell from His lips, Who spake as never man spake. The fact is, that the great events of the Old Testament are as yet most incompletely represented ; hardly attempted, as history, since Raffaelle's Vatican paintings, and the more forcible work of Holbein. Historical pictures are painted, frequently good ones—sometimes great ones ; but they are scarcely read like good or great books, since copies of them cannot be multiplied, and easel pictures are sure to vanish, far too soon, into the mausoleum of some great private gallery. Years and years ago, two of the best painters in England, Messrs. Watts and Armitage, desiring, as it seemed, to dedicate or do sacrifice of their great talent to God Who gave it, brought this subject before the English public, desiring employment in sacred work, virtually as lay-preachers. Their offers have been but scantily

accepted, though we may hope that the decoration o
our great city Cathedral may lead to the formation of
a school of fresco, or rather of broad though severe
mosaic.   But on this question, as on all others connected with religious doctrine, the chronic anxieties
and disputes of doctrine are brought to bear ; and
some degree of unnecessary alarm and suspicion of
mediæval treatment and Iconodulism seems to pre
vail.   Let us hope for better things and thoughts.

If the present writer must express his opinions as to
the position and principles of the Anglican Church
in this world-old controversy on the walk by faith
and the walk by sight, he does so with a diffidence,
which is none the less or less sincere because he
has no space to dilate upon it.   This is hardly to be
desired; for long study of ancient chronicle and
rhetoric seems to show that the most energetic
and voluminous professions of unworthiness and
self-condemnation are often the prelude to excessive
violence of statement, not unmingled with occasional
Jesuitry.   It is the honourable distinction of the
best Anglican writers, to be tolerably free from
these last faults ; at all events those who on principle
avoid extremes should avoid extreme statement, and
a Church of moderation should use moderate language.
We are so continually reminded of this by those
who advocate our absolute extinction as a Church,
that one may hope in the far future for some re-
laxation of their intense bitterness of expression.
In any case, the Church of Christ in England
appears to stand in an unpopular position on this
question, as on all others which are argued by
popular advocates ; inasmuch as she leaves much to,

and consequently charges much upon, the individual consciences of Christian people, and frequently refuses either to commend or condemn.   Much of the language of Tertullian may be rightly adopted by her teachers ; for were Tertullian here at this day he would be venerated and obeyed, if he could be induced to restrain the passionate energy of his language and logic of condemnation.   And nearly all the expressions of John Damascenus might pass in modern discourse or writing, were he present, and willing manfully to declare his own adherence to the worship of the Holy Trinity alone.

The appeal of the English Church is not to popular clamour, and it is not easy to adjust her usages to the needs of the hour or the day.   It has been said of her that she is at least silent on things unspeakable.   And why ? Because as a part of the national system supported by the nation, she has never been forced, for her very existence, to take up popular cries, to encrust herself with petrified superstitions, or to tamper with the madness or the dulness of the people.   To this principle, that the faith cannot be altered to please the people, their representatives, or their organs, she has clung in act and in principle ; and her view of the modern iconoclastic question will probably be determined by its bearings on the popular creed ; that is to say, on the extent to which it affects English people in their holding of the Nicene Creed. In as far as it tends to withdraw the personal devotion of one Christian from the Holy Trinity— in so far as it tends to intercept and withhold from Christ the Lord that personal seeking and reliance which He will have from every individual Christian— so far His Universal Church has always forbidden it, so far her representatives in national Churches are bound to protest against it.

The history of the Church of Rome has often been favourably contrasted with our own, because she has always known how to employ vagrant energies, and never lost valuable servants for want of a sphere to employ and develop their powers. The Church of Rome would have known, we are told, how to keep Wesley, and Whitfield, and Dr. Newman. Had she refrained from anathematizing Dante, and known how to keep Luther, and England; had the genius and the devotion of Newman been treated with less systematic neglect; this remark would be still more effective. It is quite true that she has known when to adopt popular error, and stamp it with her sanction, and then, if necessary, to enforce it by all conceivable methods and severities: she has also, probably from real kindness and charity in her representatives, in all ordinary times and when no great interests have been concerned, known how to accept conformity without credulity; sometimes without faith. And as this last has been more openly done by the English Church (which at least never professed to smite either with the sword of St. Peter or the dagger of Ravaillac), laxity of doctrine is imputed to her whose unchanging appeal has been and is to the primitive faith. On the other hand, her representatives are sometimes invited or challenged to waive all definite doctrinal statements, and try the experiment of a fold without gate or fences. The same unsatisfactory answer has to be made—that the faith is a real thing and an unchangeable thing.

The more Puritanic section of the Church of England may be considered to have in great measure withdrawn its objections to church decoration within moderate limits. The question of admitting or not admitting pictures into our temples has long been virtually settled by the free use of stained glass. Altar-pieces of the events of the Passion were part of our church ornaments long before the Revival of forty years ago. And it really seems that the distinction which seems to have been in the mind of St. Augustine[1] and is sustained in this book—of using pictures for instruction, making them illuminations to the building, like illustrations to a book—might be a basis of agreement to all parties. No legislation or fixed rule on the subject can be thought desirable. It would hardly ever be effectually carried out, and the subject is one on which all sides alike would fret against control, and find every means of evasion; as indeed was done, *mutatis mutandis*, by the persecuted Church of the earliest ages.[2] But when religious pictures repeat Scriptural symbolisms, or are genuine historical representations of events, all is well. The former are no more than texts written pictorially, and where the motive is honestly to set forth to the imagination of the present God's dealings in the past, the human actors in those dealings are not presented as objects of worship to their successors.

[1] De Trin. viii.
[2] *E.g.*, In assigning a Christian sense to Heathen symbols and decorations. See Catacombs, Cross, &c.

The real objection felt by our people to the use of portrait-images, or visible personifications of any kind in church, is in fact inherited from the Hebrew dispensation. Nobody has any feeling against the Lamb or the Dove, or Vine or Palm ornaments, any more than the faithful Hebrew had against the Cherub. The Cherubs did not mislead the Hebrew; since their form was prescribed of God, and they were like no living thing. They were not the image of anything that is in the firmament, or on the earth, or in the waters under the earth; and they were not inventions of the mind of man, set up in the place of God. They were not, as Greek images were, gods in the image of very handsome men and women : and the subtle sin or danger of Greek image-worship appears to have been the connecting human flesh, beauty, parts, and passions indissolubly with the Creator and Invisible Lord. This was the evil of all use of images before the Lord's coming: that it made men think of the Invisible Deity as He was not, and as He would not be thought of. Since He, the Second Person of the Trinity, has appeared on earth as Man, there certainly can be no longer any reason for prohibiting representations of Him to those who desire them. This is John Damascene's first plea, and it carries conviction as far as it goes. But we cannot, as he does, extend it gratuitously to the hagiology of all saints. They may be represented in attendance on their Lord; the principles and practice of our own Church might permit the symbolized Heaven, or Glory of the Lord, which so often fills the apse and choir arch of a Byzantine church. It might be permitted, whether desirable or not : but we rather think when it is carried out in an English church, it should be the concluding picture, as it were the consummation, of a series representing the Lord's life on earth. It is thus in St. Mark's at Venice ; where, through indescribable splendour of material, and perfect beauty of execution, the principle of Scriptural illustration is faithfully adhered to. The following description will probably be for many years a standard and evidence of the powers of the English language in the nineteenth century; and may perhaps lead future ages to question that universal degeneracy which so many writers and thinkers of our time seem almost complacently to acknowledge.[1]

The author begins—by showing how the main lessons of the faith, the Apostles' Creed, and the Sacramental doctrines are practically inculcated in successive pictures which meet the eye of the newly baptized catechumen, or believer of mature age, on his entrance through the door of the baptistery,[2]— in words which linger in the memory like the passionate notes of a clear trumpet. All its imagery begins and ends with the Cross. "The contemplation of the people was intended to be chiefly drawn (in the main building) to the mosaics of the centre of the church" (the Ascension or final glory of the Lord in the cupola; prepared for by the Crucifixion and the Resurrection on a wall between the first and second cupolas). "Thus the mind of the worshipper was at once fixed on the main groundwork and hope of Christianity—' Christ is risen ' and ' Christ shall come.' If he had time

[1] "Stones of Venice," vol. ii. pp. 114-117.
[2] See p. 69.

to explore the minor lateral chapels and cupolas, he could find in them the whole series of New Testament history, the events of the Life of Christ, and the Apostolic miracles in their order, and finally the scenery of the Book of Revelation; but if he only entered, as often the common people do to this hour, snatching a few moments before beginning the labour of the day to offer up an ejaculatory prayer, and advanced but from the main entrance as far as the altar screen, all the splendour of the glittering nave and variegated dome, if they smote upon his heart, as they might often, in strange contrast with his reed cabin among the shallows of the lagoon, smote upon it only that they might proclaim the two great messages 'Christ is risen,' and 'Christ shall come.' Daily, as the white cupolas rose like wreaths of the sea-foam in the dawn, while the shadowy campanile and frowning palace were still withdrawn into the night, they rose with the Easter voice of triumph,—'Christ is risen;' and daily, as they looked down upon the tumult of the people, deepening and eddying in the wide square that opened from their feet to the sea, they uttered above them the sentence of warning,—'Christ shall come.' And this thought may surely dispose the reader to look with some change of temper upon the gorgeous building and wild blazonry of that shrine of St. Mark's. He now perceives that it was in the hearts of the old Venetian people far more than a place of worship. It was at once a type of the Redeemed Church of God, and a scroll for the written Word of God. It was to be to them, both an image of the Bride, all-glorious within, her clothing of wrought gold;

and the actual Table of the Law and the Testimony, written within and without. And whether honoured as the Church or as the Bible, was it not fitting that neither the gold nor the crystal should be spared in the adornment of it; that, as the symbol of the Bride, the building of the wall thereof should be of jasper, and the foundations of it garnished with all manner of precious stones; and that, as the channel of the Word, that triumphant utterance of the Psalmist shall be true of it,—'I have rejoiced in the way of Thy testimonies, as much as in all riches'? And shall we not look with changed temper down the long perspective of St. Mark's Place towards the sevenfold gates and glowing domes of its temple, when we know with what solemn purpose the shafts of it were lifted above the pavement of the populous square? Men met there from all countries of the earth, for traffic or for pleasure; but, above the crowd swaying for ever to and fro in the restlessness of avarice or thirst of delight, was seen perpetually the glory of the temple, attesting to them, whether they would hear or whether they would forbear, that there was one treasure which the merchantman might buy without a price, and one delight better than all others, in the Word and the statutes of God. Not in the wantonness of wealth, nor in vain ministry to the desire of the eyes or the pride of life, were those marbles hewn into transparent strength, and those arches arrayed in the colours of the iris. There is a message written in the dyes of them, that once was written in blood; and a sound in the echoes of their vaults, that one day shall fill the vault of

Heaven,—'He shall return, to do judgment and justice.' The strength of Venice was given her so long as she remembered this; her destruction found her when she had forgotten this; and it found her irrevocably, because she forgot it without excuse. Never had city a more glorious Bible. Among the nations of the North, a rude and shadowy sculpture filled their temples with confused and hardly legible imagery; but for her, the skill and the treasures of the East had gilded every letter, and illumined every page, till the Book-Temple shone from afar off like the star of the Magi. In other cities, the meetings of the people were often in places withdrawn from religious association, subject to violence and to change; and on the grass of the dangerous rampart, and in the dust of the troubled street, there were deeds done, and counsels taken, which, if we cannot justify, we may sometimes forgive. But the sins of Venice, whether in her palace or in her piazza, were done with the Bible at her right hand. The walls on which its testimony was written were separated but by a few inches of marble from those which guarded the secrets of her councils, or confined the victims of her policy. And when in her last hours she threw off all shame and all restraint, and the great square of the city became filled with the madness of the whole earth, be it remembered how much her sin was greater, because it was done in the face of the House of God, burning with the letters of His Law. Mountebank and masquer laughed their laugh and went their way; and a silence has followed them, not unforetold; for amidst them all, through century after century of gathering vanity and festering guilt, that white dome of St. Mark's had uttered in the dead ear of Venice, 'Know thou, that for all these things God will bring thee into judgment.'"

     *   *   *   *   *

The writer of this book speaks without authority to commend any practical course in Anglican church decoration. The rule of Scriptural subject, doctrinal and historical, is one to which he would gladly conform and see others conform, and he has given reasons why it seems best to him. Yet it will certainly be unsatisfactory to many whom he would gladly satisfy; and they will, perhaps, be little better pleased at being told that such a limitation to artistic church-work is in the spirit of the Anglican Church; or that the spirit and practice of the Anglican Church, in such matters, is in accordance·with that of the four primitive centuries, so far as we can judge from the examples which are left us. Yet it is not the same thing to lay down tentative rules and limits, as to pronounce judgment against those who transgress them; and, though he would rather not have any legendary subjects in an English church, he would bear with them without protest as an individual. There can be no doubt that there is license given in our Church as by law estab lished, on the positive side as well as the negative side. With the negative side, he is not concerned; but on the other, it seems indisputable that doctrines, and interpretations of doctrine, which may legally or rightly be held in the English Church —and legally and rightly are under present circumstances the same thing—may also be symbolized in her edifices and services. The Communion of Saints is an article of our Creed; and our sense of that Communion, our spiritual thoughts of our

elder brethren and sisters in the Church Triumphant, must needs be awed and reverent. It may
be so in the highest and deepest degree without any
creature-worship whatever; therefore it certainly
may be expressed in churches with the full strength
of all the arts, without really and logically tending
to creature-worship. It should not be forgotten that
the sudden violence, and ill-timed impatience of the
Iconoclast emperors both spread and intensified the
popular devotion to idols; because it blew furiously
on passions which already prevented men from hear-
ing distinctions, or understanding what they really
denied or upheld. The Church may make distinctions in vain in one age, as Milman observes; yet
they may be, after all, valid, and then another age
will be able to recognize them. Yet it seems that the
Communion of Saints may be sufficiently asserted
by representations of those whose names are written
in Holy Scripture. Many will repudiate such a
limitation just now, with the contempt of a rising
party which feels its own power, without having
held it long enough to have learned moderation in
its use. For these, there is nothing but patience and
some kind of mild caution as to the difference between
prayer to God and fraternal reverence for His saints;
which is at all events as easily recognized in theory
as it is overstepped in practice.

But from the artistic, or painter's side, it is really
worth our while to understand the importance of
getting the best workman and setting him to the
highest subject; and of seeking, wherever funds
permit us, to have works of enduring value in
our churches. In some situations and vehicles at
least, fresco is permanent—that is to say, with

careful gaslight arrangements. Mosaic endures with perpetual freshness. historic beauty, and the passionate appeal of colour to the colourist. Is it not better to spend less on flowers and robes and candles, and mere church furniture, for the sake of permanent works which may appeal to generation after generation, like the splendours of St. Mark's? We are not protesting against ritual, but urging its more thoughtful, and in fact more spiritual, forms—pressing the claims of art as against ceremonial. To say that the lower part of ceremonial exercises wider influence, is, in point of fact, to admit what the adversaries of all ritual say, that it is only for the weak, and so forth. It is not right, because ladies understand lace, to spend hundreds on copes and chasubles, when you ought to be carving or inlaying the articles of your creed upon the church-walls, and in that work developing perhaps, the genius of masters, certainly the talent of good workmen; calling Intellect, all the while, into her right place in the Sanctuary; that she may offer her incense also, along with the Angels of Knowledge. If candles and draperies and flowers are symbolic, they are so in a less important way than those histories or emblems of the faith which have been handed down from the first centuries, which ought to be seen in every temple of the faith. Let these at least come first. for they express the faith; when they are provided, the sacrifice of thought and imagination, of the aspirations of the soul and the cunning of the hand, will have been made to the glory of God; nor can we conceive of any more precious offering.

F

CALLIXTINE HEAD OF CHRIST.

CHAPTER IV

THE CATACOMBS AND THEIR PAINTINGS.

" When I was a young man, and was studying in Rome, I was
in the habit, on Sundays, of visiting the graves of the Apostles
and Martyrs ; and often did we enter those vaults, which are excavated deep in the earth, where the bodies of the buried are seen in
the walls on each side of the visitors, and all is so dark, that the
words of the prophet seem literally fulfilled : ' Let them go down
quick into hell '—where the gloomy darkness is seldom broken by
any glimmer from above, whilst the light appears to come through
a slit, rather than through a window, and you take each step with
caution, as, surrounded by deep night, you recall the words of
Virgil : ' Terrors appal thee thoroughly, above all terrible still-
ness.' "—Hierom. in Ezech xl. circ. A.D. 354.

THE Roman Catacombs may be said to be the
grave of Græco-Italian Art. Gentile or human
genius—what is called artistic power, be it what it
may—had culminated early in the great Phidian
school, and has never been surpassed ; yet its effects
have been always more and more widely spread.
And the emulous efforts of Rhodian, Ionian, and
Italian workmen, in successive ages, were at all
events of incalculable value to the culture and
life of the Græco-Italian world. We know sadly
little of the painting of the ancient Athenian schools,
yet it is certain that between the period of Poly-
gnotus and of Apelles—between the Athenian and
Alexandrian wars with Persia (say 450—330) the
graphic art was developed in such a manner as to

F 2

rival the successes of Greek sculpture. Those who would pursue this subject will do well, in the first place, to read Mr. Wornum's highly important article on Painting,[1] and to follow, if possible, the authorities there referred to. For ourselves, there is, and was, the same connection, and the same repulsion, between Greek and Christian art, as between Greek Nature-worship and the service of Christ, as God made Man. If, as the labours of Professor Max Müller and others seem to prove, the mythology of Greece is a grand phantasmagoria of some original Aryan worship of one God or Father, as recognized in the workings of Nature and Life; then Greek sculpture, in its noblest forms—Theseus, Demeter and the Koré —is the petrifaction of the grandest features of that phantasmagoria. These are the noblest imageries man could ever project before his fellows—of gods made in Man's image; in a way which was for-bidden to races favoured with Revelation or open Vision, but, as Saint Paul says, was "winked at," as the work of a time of ignorance. The heathen reli-gious sentiment, or spirit of prayer, undoubtedly did express itself in Greek sculpture and painting; and so far there is relation between Greek art and the religious art of Christendom.

Again, all the technical powers of Art—her gathered knowledge of colour and form, her vast inheritance of method and material—were derived from Greece through Rome. The capture and plunder of Corinth by Mummius in 125 B.C. is the point of transference, when the art of Greece, in a great degree plundered and destroyed, was trans-

[1] Smith's "Greek and Roman Antiquities."

ferred to Rome ; and, however brutal and barbaric the change may have been, when " the soldier was wont to break cups wrought by great masters, that his horse might be decked with gay trappings," it was then that Rome first applied herself to those arts, whose decayed fragments yet retained a suspended life in the Late Empire. In that state we call them Byzantine art. Drawing and sculpture, in short, came from Greece to Rome, and were adopted by Roman Christianity; and when the day of vengeance was come to Rome, when Alaric and his Goths rushed in at the Salarian Gate, and brought down darkness on her for 600 years, spiritual life and the seeds of culture survived, in the relics of Greek art; and in the mosaics of the great Churches, which succeed the Catacomb paintings as exponents of the Faith of their time. There is no doubt that the Christian faith owes great part of its means of self-expression to Greek art, in the same sense that it owes them to the printing-press. The Creed, and the Histories of the Old and New Testaments, meeting in Christ as type and antitype, have always been taught by means of art in some form or sense, and the revival of all art after the destruction of the Empire is as certainly due to the Christian Church, as the origin of Western art is due to Athens.

The repulsion between Greek and Christian art, again, is that of a higher and a lower morality. It is the contrast between the impurities of Nature-worship—which, as Mr. Disraeli said, " always ends in an orgie "—and the continued effort and appeal for deliverance from evil—that is to say, from one's own personal sins and impurity. The one side justifies indulgence, denies the existence of corruption, treats the world as very good against the facts, and fails accordingly; the other tends to asceticism, regards the world, first, as under curse and corruption, then as utterly accursed—and so becomes a yoke too heavy to bear. We must, if possible, return to this subject; for the present a short account of the Catacombs themselves will be useful before we go into the subject of the " Biblical cycle " of paintings therein contained—to use the admirable expression of the Commendatore de Rossi.

There are three standard works in particular on this subject, all founded on the labours of the indefatigable Oratorian, Cardinal Bosio, which will be found, we presume, in most public libraries. One or other of them, at least, must be in many private collections. A diligent use of any one will give the reader a good idea of the nature of the subterranean cemeteries, and of the character of the pictures which adorned so many of their chambers. They are as follows:—The book of Bosio, who died in 1600, completed by Severano; a translation of it into Latin by the Oratorian Aringhi; and the "Sculture e Pitture Sagre" of Bottari, 1737-54, in which Bosio's plates are used again. These three, or indeed one of them, with the learned work of Boldetti, the fruit of thirty years' labour, will give a perfectly good account of the condition of the cemeteries and paintings at their date. The magnificent " Roma Sotterranea " of De Rossi is a book of the same character and equal merit, and his work, as well as theirs, has the unspeakable merit of impartially

recording what is found, without endeavour to con-
struct more. The latter part of Dr. Northcote's
version of De Rossi's volumes is complained of, by
the late Mr. Wharton Marriott and others, as full
of attempts to read distinctively Roman doctrine in
records which are simply those of primitive Christianity, and do not contain it. This is, of course,
natural in a convert, and is one of several modern
instances in which propagandist zeal for a new-found
creed has somewhat disguised the real aspect of facts.[1]
The works of De Rossi, and the smaller but pre
eminently useful Dictionnaire des Antiquités Chrétiennes, by M. l'Abbé Martigny, are either perfectly
impartial and accurately honourable, or, which is
the next thing to it, are written with an avowed
and well-considered bias. Our references have been
confined, as far as possible, to these works, with
Mr. Parker's; but a few have been added to photographs in the portfolios of South Kensington. Mr.
Parker's photographs, and the accompanying text,

[1] Dr. Northcote displays an humorous daring, which does him
the greatest credit, in accusing Anglican inquirers of this frailty.
He instances an unfortunately ingenious guess about Pliny's doves
in mosaic, of an English describer who took them for a Christian
work, and thought they symbolized the admission of the Laity to
partake of the cup in the Eucharist! It certainly may have been
a mistake to consider the Capitoline Doves a Christian work, as
they can hardly be a copy; but there can be no doubt that
doves signify lay members of the Christian Church, or that
the symbol of two doves with a chalice, so frequent on the sarcophagi, has reference to the Holy Communion. One or two of
Dr. N.'s own statements are given, with elucidations, by Mr.
Marriott, and they seem rather worse than this. He will have
it, that all Oranti mean the Blessed Virgin, never mentioning that
there are male Oranti. He says the Orante is a *companion* to the
Good Shepherd, in an instance where four of them are found surrounding Him as central figure on a vault : he treats the Adorations
of the Magi as, in fact, portraits of the Blessed Virgin, "the
Infant being only added to show who she is ;" and so forth.

are a profoundly valuable addition to the literature of ancient Rome, Christian and Heathen. Their architectural department is the special work of the author, on his own subject. Mr. Vaux has undertaken the antiquities, and Professor Westwood gives an account of the few Christian statues, and the larger and more important subject of the bas-reliefs. Mr. Parker asked the present writer for some observations on the Catacomb-frescoes, and Church mosaics aboveground; and he has also had the kindness to allow him to repeat them, in great measure, in this book. In the course of his reading, the writer observes, with feelings of mortification, and also of satisfaction, that the Rev. Wharton Marriott's works have anticipated much information which he has himself exhumed in the course of study, and of which he could have wished to be a modern reproducer. In any case, he can now bring it forward with confidence.

One of the earliest names of visitors inscribed in the Catacombs, after their re-discovery in the fifteenth century, is that of Raynuzio Farnese, father of Paul III., in 1490. This is found in the Callixtine cemetery; its appearance seems to be one of the coincidences of that time of invention and discovery. The entrances to the subterranean passages had been forgotten, even by the clergy; and the attention of the world was not re-directed to them till late in the next century, by new lights from science and history. They had probably ceased to be visited for prayer, or meditation at the martyrs' tombs, late in the thirteenth century. Their generic name applies to one of them in particular, and is of uncertain derivation;[1] whether from κατά and *cumbere*, κατά and τύμβος, or the Spanish *catar* (to see), as Dr. Theodore Mommsen suggests. " The early Christian burial-vaults," he says (near the Porta S. Sebastiano), " in which, according to tradition, the bones of the Apostles Peter and Paul rested for a year and seven months before they were removed to the spot where the churches of St. Peter and St. Paul now stand, were designated as the vaults *ad catacumbas*. It was in the ninth century that this designation first began to be more commonly applied to other Christian burial-vaults; and the present use of the term gradually grew up." The earliest date in them, or rather on a sarcophagus most unfortunately removed from its proper place in them, now unknown, is A.D. 72. It is a consular date, and satisfactorily certain, about the fourth year of Vespasian. There are two consular inscriptions in St. Lucia of 107 and 110 A.D. " The Catacomb of St. Priscilla," says Mr. Hemans, " entered below the Salarian Way, and belonging to the mother of that Christian senator, Pudens, who received St. Peter—also those of St. Nereus and Achilleus near the Appian Way—have been referred to an antiquity correspondent with the Apostolic Age · and if those called after St. Callixtus were indeed formed long before that pope's election in 210 A.D., we may place them second in chronological order." With this, in great measure, agrees the view of Prof. Mommsen ; and those of the Commendatore De Rossi and Mr. J. H. Parker are at no great distance of

---

[1] Mr. Marriott says this derivation is unquestionably from a root traceable in the Greek κύμβαλον ; Lat., *cymba* ; Eng., coomb or hollow : Sansc., *kumbhas*, pit.

opinion on these leading questions. It is agreed in any case, that the Catacombs preserve for us some of the last efforts, the feeble and dying palpitations, of Græco-Roman painting and sculpture, adopted by the Faith of Christ, which could not breathe fresh vigour into them, yet retained the germs of their life, as seed from withering flowers. It is agreed that, whatever number of martyrs perished in Rome,[1] whatever exaggeration may have been attempted, they did perish in great numbers, and are frequently buried here: at times, possibly, with Gentile corpses also; with strange, scattered relics of secular as well as religious life; with the histories and memories, known to God only, of 350 miles of human sepulchres.[2] It is agreed that these vaults contain a Scriptural cycle of historic and symbolic paintings; and it is an object of this book to show that such ornamentation, based on Holy Scripture, and having for its end to illustrate the fulfilment of Old Testament type and prophecy by the historical events of the New Testament, is the decoration best suited to the Anglican Church; especially desirable at this time; and calculated to develop religious feeling and intellectual power. It cannot be alien or painful—it must be delightful—to the feelings of any man who believes that God in Christ lived and died for men, and that men and women were made strong to die for their belief in Him; to know, what all admit, that these relics of record of the martyrs' Faith still

[1] On this question see Milman's note to Gibbon, ch. xvi. fin. with references to Dodwell and Ruinart, &c.

[2] This is a low estimate of the length of the various passages of the Catacombs. Father Marchi thinks it amounts to not less than 800 or 900 miles. See Mr. Hemans's Essay.

exist in caves of the earth; that these men's minds
dwelt continually on the Lord's Parables concerning
Himself, as Vine of Souls and Shepherd of Mankind;
and that they insisted always on the ancient Law,
Prophets, and history of Israel as typical of Him; on
the miracles of mercy as representing His life, and
on the Cross which points to His death. Thus much
is, at all events, indisputably proved by the Catacomb
paintings and sculptures. And the creed of the Roman
martyrs ought not to be neglected by the Protestant
world, only because they were martyred in Rome.

It may be as well to explain a few words which
are constantly used in all writings on this subject.
Passing by the word catacomb, already discussed, we
come to cemetery (κοιμητήριον, *accubitorium*), the bed
or sleeping-place, in which it is promised that the
saints shall rejoice. *Cryptum* (κρύπτω) is the original
name for these graves, from which the modern Italian
grotto, and the adjective *grotesque*, appear to be derived. *A loculus* is a single grave; a larger one,
where the rock is hollowed into an apse, or half-dome,
above a sarcophagus, is called an *arcosolium*. *Cubicula* are square chambers, surrounded with tombs in
the thickness of their walls; and they were, no doubt,
places of worship, the Eucharist being generally
celebrated on the grave of a martyr. Here, then, the
skill of Christian painters, sometimes of Gentiles, was
employed to set forth the symbols of the Faith.

Other terms, like *columbarium, cella memoriæ*, and
the like, take us back to that connection between
Christian and Gentile burial, which is best dwelt on,
perhaps, by Dr. Mommsen; with whose views those
of Mr. Parker fully coincide, as we believe. The

columbaria, or pigeon-cotes, were the places in which
the ashes and burnt relics of the middle and lower
classes of the Romans of Christian ages were stored
in *ollæ,* or vases, along the shelves of subterranean
pits ; in small pigeon-holes, or cells, after which the
pits were named.   These were the receptacles of the
burned heathen—at least, of the middle and lower
classes ; and the Christians always preferred burial,
rejoicing in all the ideas of death as a rest, and of
the body expecting its resurrection. Yet burial was a
heathen custom also, although the high price of land
about Rome must have made burning more frequent,
as a convenience which superseded the ancient custom of burial.   A Christian writer, of the time of
Severus, says, with good reason, " that the Christians
did not hold the foolish belief that the burning of the
body was incompatible with its resurrection, but that
they preferred the older and better fashion of burial,
liking to consider the dead body as a tree, which
during the barrenness of winter still hides in itself
the hope of a spring to come."   But though burial
was a heathen, as well as Christian custom, public
burial with members of the same faith, and excluding
others, was a specially Christian custom in the primitive Church, as it had been a Jewish custom before.
At first, everyone, Christian or heathen, who possessed a piece of land was buried in it ; there his
mausoleum, or *cella memoriæ,* was erected ; and there
his descendants and friends assembled for solemn
funeral feasts, from which the Christian Agape, or
love-feast, was difficult of distinction—so difficult that
the custom had to be discontinued altogether.[1]   The

---

[1] See *infrà.*

chapels dedicated to the memory of the Apostles and martyrs were undoubtedly buildings of this kind, and the origin of the catacomb may frequently have been one of these burial-vaults, where some distinguished martyr or confessor was laid; and where many who had known him desired to lie around him, as round an accredited servant found faithful to the end.

Such a one is that of SS. Nereus and Achilleus, which Professor Mommsen chooses as an example of undoubted authenticity and antiquity. It will be described immediately; but before doing so it remains to point out that the catacomb, or underground cemetery, cannot have taken its rise from the mere sand, or puzzolana pit, in the first instance. The favourite soil in which these sepulchres were made is the soft tufa rock, or volcanic mud, cooled and hardened; and the beds of the puzzolana, or building-stone, are avoided, as too hard and difficult. So is all marshy ground, for obvious reasons. And the arrangement of these sepulchres is inconsistent with the idea of their having been puzzolana pits. The narrow passages, three-quarters or half a metre in breadth, and intersecting at right angles, cannot be quarried-out space from whence stone has been obtained; nor do they afford roads or wide passages for leading it in carts, when cut in the quarry. "These vaults have been devised for one object only, to get as much wall as possible, in a given space, of such depth as to admit of tombs on each side. In some instances, the real sand, or stone pits, have been found within the catacomb, very differently arranged, with broad passages and conveniences for carrying the sand to the surface; but these pits are evidently more ancient, and

either shut off altogether by the builders of the catacomb, or utilized for their purpose by intermediate
walls.   The enormous space occupied by the burial-
vaults of Christian Rome, in their extent not surpassed
even by the system of cloacæ, or sewers, of Republican
Rome, is certainly the work of that community which
St. Paul addressed in his Epistle to the Romans—
a living witness of its immense development." It
cannot, of course, be proved—nor is it very material to
prove—that no heathen graves exist among the masses
of Christian dead; but the Christian insistence on
common burial of all brethren holders of the faith,
so that the Ecclesia or Church of the Faithful on earth
might be continued and organized, as it were, among
the dead, would go very far to prevent heathens being
associated with it in death.   The heathen cultus of
the deceased members of families was a part of that
ancient hearth or household-worship which has been
lately described by M. de Coulanges in " La Cité Antique ; " [1] and we shall be reminded of it by details
connected with the early Agapæ.

It was simply the value of the ground, and the
nature of the ground, which gave the subterranean
system so great a development in Rome.   In Africa,
for instance, Christian burials took place in open
graveyards, or areæ.   Tertullian relates of the Car-
thaginians, in the reign of Severus, that in some
tumult against the Christians, the wrath of the mob
was directed against the Christian burial-places,
with the cry, " *Areæ non sint*," and Dr. Mommsen also
quotes an inscription from Cæsarea in Numidia :—

[1] See Translation by Rev. T. C. Barker, 1871.   Parker, 377,
Strand.

" A follower of the word gave this burial-ground, and built the chapel (*cella*), all at his own cost : he has left this memorial to the Holy Church. Euelpius bids you hail ; brothers of pure and simple heart, born of the Holy Spirit." At Alexandria, again, there are remains of catacombs, which the present writer has inspected ; and due reference will be made to those of Naples.

As has been said, Professor Mommsen's chosen example of an ancient burial-chamber, extending itself into a catacomb, or gathering subterranean additions round it till a catacomb was established, is that of the Cemetery of Domitilla, and the Catacomb of SS. Nereus and Achilleus, on the Appian and Ardeatine Way.

These vaults are attributed to a granddaughter of Vespasian, who bore the first of these names. She was accused of Christianity, as a Jewish superstition, in the reign of Domitian, A.D. 95, along with T. Flavius Clemens, her husband, or, possibly, her brother, the Consul of that year. He was sentenced to death, and his fate, of course, created strong excitement, and must have added very greatly to the influence of the faith; though he is said to have been a man of somewhat too retiring or indolent character. But St. Domitilla was sent, after his death, to the island of Ponza, where she probably ended her days in exile. The rooms she occupied there, says Professor Mommsen, were still visited by pious persons in the fourth century. He is not quite satisfied that Sig. Gianbattista de Rossi's opinion is clearly proved, that the burial-vaults near SS. Nereus and Achilleus were originally called Cœmeterium Domitillæ ; but

her name, ever since the time of Constantine, had
been connected with the traditions of the martyrdom
of Nereus and Achilleus.   He says, a heathen tomb-
inscription mentions Flavia Domitilla as the donor
of the burying-place.   In any case, the crypt which
Rossi ascribes to her is one of the oldest in Rome.
Dated tiles found there belong to the times of Hadrian
and Pius, 117–161: and Domitian was slain in 96:
so that the distance of time is not more than twenty
years from a Flavian Emperor.   "The vault," says
Professor Mommsen, " is no cemetery, according to its
original modest circumference—it is still a private
burial-place for the founder and his nearest relations.
The entrance to the later catacombs, though not
exactly concealed, is shown as little as possible.
The stone beds, or *loculi,* which peculiarly belong to
the later catacombs, do not appear at all.   On the
other hand, great niches are excavated in the walls
for the reception of sarcophagi.   At a later time,
narrower passages were certainly broken through the
walls, and stone beds in their side-walls ; but, as if
to mark their transition (from vault to catacomb),
these stone beds in the passages broken in the walls
are surrounded with a cornice, which gives them the
form of sarcophagi.   The remains of the frescoes,
*which clearly are of the same time as the original
building,* are the sole proof that this grave did not
belong to any of those heathens who abstained from
burning, but that it was really, from the beginning, a
Christian foundation.   They are, *especially in the
mere ornaments,* of rare beauty ; and no decorative
artist of the .Augustan age need be ashamed of the
vaulted roof in particular, with its exquisite garlands

of grapes, and the birds pecking at them, and the winged boys gathering and pressing out the fruit. There are also small landscapes, which are never found in the later Christian graves. The groups drawn on the side-walls are less perfect. Among those still preserved, the most remarkable are Daniel standing between two lions—the Good Shepherd— Noah's Ark, with the Dove—and the representation of a supper, which differs but little, on the whole, from the usual antique treatment of the subject. Two men are represented sitting on the dinner-sofa, &c., yet clearly showing the Christian influence in the bread placed round the fish on the dish. These are the beginnings of the ancient Christian graves."

We have thought it best to go the length of making a brief list, or index, of all the principal subjects of Christian decoration, to which we may refer in our descriptions of Catacomb-paintings. But a few words remain to be said about the materials and vehicles in which they were painted, though our statements will scarcely be of any importance. Still, it is better for readers not accustomed to the accurate use of terms in art, to explain that these works are called Frescoes, under limitation, and with doubt. Fresco means painting on *freshly-laid* plaster; with water-colour, and pigments not subject to injury by contact with the lime. The processes of early Christian art, as has been observed, are simply those of the later Græco-Roman period, and accurate information on the subject is greatly to be desired ; but it may be taken for certain that both fresco-painting on the wet and fresh plaster, and distemper, or tempera-painting on the dry coatings, were freely made use of. The latter method must have been, of course, employed in the various re-touchings or re-paintings, which have probably taken place from time to time since the days of St. Paulinus of Nola, and which throw doubt over the authenticity of some of the earlier decorations, considered as documents. The following extracts from Mr. Wornum's article in Smith's Dictionary of Classical Antiquities bear on this part of the subject.

"Fresco"[1] was probably little employed by the ancients for works of imitative art; but it appears to have been the ordinary method of simply colouring walls, especially among the Romans. The walls were divided into compartments or panels, which were called *abaci* (ἄβακες): the composition of the stucco, and the method of preparing the walls for painting, is described by Vitruvius (vii. 3). They first covered the wall with a layer of ordinary plaster, then three other layers of a finer quality, mingled with sand; above these still, three layers of a composition of chalk and marble-dust, the upper one laid on before the under one was quite dry, and each succeeding coat being of a finer quality than the preceding . . .

---

[1] A few technical words may perhaps be explained here. Starting from the popular and quite inaccurate use of the word fresco for *all* wall-painting—the distinctions branch according to the ground used *for* the colours, and the medium or vehicle used *with* the colours. Tempera means simply medium, and tempera-painting is the use of any medium with the colours, on old and dry plaster. Fresco proper is water-colours on wet plaster of silver-sand and lime. Gesso means simply chalk or plaster of Paris, and is used in all dry painting for canvases, tablets, walls; all alike are prepared with it. Intonaco is the last coat of surface on which the painting is done. Dry fresco is on old plaster, re-wetted. Distemper is on a dry wall, or with opaque colours, made up with size, egg, milk, or gum, in which last case it is called *guazzo*. Painting *a putrido* is when the egg gets bad.

Colouring *al fresco,* in which the colours were mixed simply in water, as the term implies, was applied while the composition was still wet (*udo tectorio*), and on that account was limited to certain colours, exactly as in fresco at the present day, where the artist is confined to the use of such colours as are unaffected by lime, &c." He goes on to say that the care and skill required to execute a work in fresco, and the tedious and expensive process of preparing the walls, must have effectually excluded it from ordinary places. The majority of the walls in Pompeii are in distemper; but those of the higher class of houses, especially if they were intended to be the grounds of pictures, were in fresco, both at Pompeii and in Rome. "The pictures themselves, on the coloured grounds thus prepared, are apparently all in distemper of the highest kind, in what is called *guazzo,* or gum-medium, &c. &c. Distemper, it need not be said, implies the use of a glue or size-medium with water, and is one of the most ancient methods of painting in existence, many of the Egyptian bas-reliefs of early date being so coloured."

The special advantages belonging to modern fresco, of figures approaching to the life-size, were not thought of by the early Christian artists; and could not have been obtained in subterranean galleries, or cubicula, by any method of work. They all centre in the luminousness and imperishable nature of the painting; but the fresco grounding, with designs in distemper, painted on it when dry, would have answered all the purposes of the Primitive designers. As soon as they obtained countenance, and were freely supplied with means, mosaic (*musivum opus*) seems to have

been their favourite work.[1]   This seems-to have been
a natural preference on the part of men who had
been accustomed either to subterranean paintings
seen by torchlight, or to small cells or mortuary
chapels on a level with the soil, from which
light and heat were somewhat closely excluded;
as the gold or white-glass grounds of the inlaid
work introduce light into dim cupolas and vaultings.
The highly-prepared panels inserted in the walls
of the richer houses of Pompeii, and bearing, as has
been said above, nine or ten coats of variously
compounded covering, or ground, are not found in
Christian subterranean decoration to our knowledge.

Several examples occur to us of the earliest
Vine-paintings, which may be compared, with great
advantage, with those of the Domitilla vault.[2]
The first is of almost equal antiquity, the Vine-frescoes
of the Catacomb of St. Prætextatus.   Then comes the
great Vine of the Callixtine, which surrounds the
" Dispute with the Doctors" (Bottari, vol. ii.).   In all
these the style may be called simple naturalism of
the highest kind ; the vines being simply and ably
drawn, to the best imitative power of the workman,
yet bent arbitrarily into decorative shape.   Next to
these, with the same naturalism, but somewhat inferior grace, come the vintage-mosaics of St. Constantia in Rome, described in the chapter on Mosaics.
Of intermediate date, near the end of the second
century, as we should conjecture, are the very
beautiful stuccoes described and illustrated by Bot-

---

[1] See Mosaic.
[2] The latter are represented in woodcut, and fully described in
Dr. Northcote's book, and may be taken as the standard example.

tari.[1] If they are compared with the Callixtine Vine,
or that of the Domitilla tomb, it will be seen that,
though the leaves, grapes, and boys are as freely
and beautifully drawn, the branches are more severely
twisted into an S form, and a more arbitrary arrangement prevails.   Lastly, the fifth-century vaulting of
the Church of Galla Placidia bears a vine in which
Græco-Roman art has reached the Byzantine stage
of high conventionality, still retaining great beauty;
and the same degree of subordination to decorative
pattern may be seen in the mosaic of the Vine on
the front of St. Mark's at Venice.[2] There is little
doubt that these vine-pictures, and many others, were
adopted by Christians as repetitions of the Lord's parable of Himself, and the more freely because heathen
eyes were accustomed to them, and they awakened
no special attention.   And it seems, certainly, that
it was not till the fifth century, at least, that the
stiffer and more ecclesiastical figures now seen in the
Catacombs made their first appearance. The unmis-
takeably early works of St. Domitilla and St. Prætextatus, the Vine of St. Callixtus, and so on down to
those of St. Constantia for the fourth century, are
enough to prove, when compared with Gentile decoration of the best or Augustine period, that the
ruder and more barbaric works of the Catacombs
are of later date : however confusing it may be
to compare the rudest work of a good artistic time
with the comparatively careful and earnest work of a
later and bad time. Some of the late work, indeed,
gives an idea of wilful carelessness or indifference.

[1] Vol. ii. pp. 92, 93.
[2] "Stones of Venice," vol. ii. ; plate, "The Vine, Free and in
Service."

There can be no doubt that the recent photographs taken and published by Mr. Parker give
evidence of re-touching on many of these paintings.   Stronger and less correct markings occur over
fainter and better forms.   Of course, no imputation
of deceptive intent need, or ought to be made, on the
repairers, from the time of John or Paschal I. to
the present day.   When a painting has reached a
certain point of decay, it must vanish, so far as the
handiwork of the original artist goes: but the record
of its existence ought to be preserved, and that is
best done, on the whole, by faithful restoration,
which really amounts to no more than an attested
inscription on the wall, giving careful account of the
original fresco.   This has been done, from time to
time, in the Catacombs — from the most ancient times,
probably, to the present.   Had it been done by dis-
honest hands, or in a spirit of imposture, the ancient
re-touchings, often in themselves venerable, though
often grotesque, would have had a far different
appearance now.   Even modern restorations are
justifiable; but they should be avowed and regis-
tered.   One or two will have to be referred to in
this chapter, certainly without thought of blame.
Whatever any of us may think of the present state
of the actual documents, which is only to be seen
in the photographs, there can be no doubt that the
Vine and the Good Shepherd were continually before
the eyes of the Primitive Church, as symbols of her
Lord; that Noah, Daniel and Job, Abraham and
Jonah, Moses and Elias were always set forth as
symbolic representatives of Him; that His miracles
of mercy were carved on the sarcophagi; that the

Monogram of His name faced the spectator every-where, with His nativity, His manifestation to the Kings of the East, His portrait-image in bas-relief, with an occasional ideal of His features in painting; that The Three Children encouraged the spirits of His martyrs; or that a long list of sym-bolic objects pointed to Him and the Word He taught. The Agape, too, repeatedly bade His fol-lowers, then as now, remember His last Supper with the Apostles, representing more immediately the last repast at the Lake of Tiberias—for it must always be uncertain what further eucharistic mean-ing it may have conveyed. The Bread so frequently seen must refer to the Bread of Life, and the sixth chapter of St. John. The unique picture of the Fish bearing Loaves, in De Rossi and Mr. Northcote, is of the greatest interest in this connection; but it is necessary to have an exact *fac-simile* of it in its present state, if we are to assert with these gentle-men and Abbé Martigny, that a vial of wine is represented in the basket. No Anglican need have any theological objection to its doing so, and a certain record would be a subject of congratulation. These subjects, and others of the same kind, form the Biblical cycle of the Catacombs. It is to be remembered that the photograph, taken with magne-sium-light on the spot, gives, in all probability, quite as accurate an idea of the real record, as it now is, as ordinary inspection on the spot, amidst flicker-ing and smoking torches and tapers, in uncertain lights or darkness visible. Mr. Parker adds to his collection of photographs many specimens of secular wall-ornament of the best ages, from

Pompeii, from the newly-discovered works at the Doria Pamphili Villa, the Villa of Hadrian, and other places. They are not only beautiful in themselves, but of the greatest value as standards of ancient ornament. They strongly resemble the St. Prætextatus frescoes in their correct realism of bird-and-flower drawing, which they combine with careful subjection to pattern. It is, of course, the perfection of decorative-painting, that everything should be placed where the artist wants it, for contrast, harmony, and proper subordination to architectural structure; while at the same time the decorative objects are not only in their right places, but rightly painted from nature. In these works, boys, birds'-nests, and grapes are charmingly and vigorously done, without any of that gloomy indifference to nature which is so prevalent soon after, marking the long coma of the arts up to the time of the early Florentine and Pisan Renaissance. One rather favourable characteristic of the Roman middle classes seem to appear in them—a great taste for domestic pets. It would be difficult to find better animal-painting in a simple way than the half-erased porcupine, crocodile, and palm-tree, the pheasant and spoonbill.[1] The Pompeian frescoes are generally square or oblong pictures, of more or less merit, painted on the wall, without much attention to display of architectural forms. It is probable that the beautiful series of painted stuccoes from the sepulchre of the Via Latina, in Mr. Parker's work, are of the same class and period with the Good Shepherd and Vine stuccoes in Bottari,[2]

[1] Parker's Photographs 2,700, 2,703, 2,705.   [2] See ii. t. 22.

which are said to be copied from one of the same tombs.   If this be the case, the interest of the latter is very great, as the photographed examples cannot be later than the early second century.   But, as has been said, their severer subjection to intricate pat terns inclines the present writer to think they must be as late as the end of that age.

One remark has to be made on the subject of the frescoes of St. Clemente in Rome, which have recently attracted so much attention.   That of the Assumption of the Virgin in the subterranean church is fully ascertained, by its inscription, to be of the date of Leo IV. (845–855), if not of Leo IX. (1048–1054).   Some of the figures are tonsured, which puts their date into the sixth century ; the square nimbus of one is quite mediæval ; and they also differ absolutely in style alike from the mosaics and the earlier frescoes, having much more Gothic quaintness and singularity.   Large numbers of photographs are circulated by propagandist members of the Roman Catholic Communion, taken from restorations of these frescoes—that is to say, from carefully-made copies, in which the ravages of time are repaired.   So far all is well, and these transcripts are exact enough ; but we think they ought not to be vaguely described, as at present, as *Imagines Vetustissimæ* ; as this tends to induce simple people to think such late works the work of primitive ages, and imagine that the vestments and functions represented in them are of the first four centuries ; which is contradictory to the whole art and litera ture of the Catacombs.

These cemeteries, in fact, with their sarcophagi

and inscriptions, contain a body of primitive doctrine, set forth in symbols of form and colour, earlier
than any others, and distinct from all others.   The
mosaics at Rome—scarcely those at Ravenna—
point to a period of development, of indulged popular opinion and emotion, leading towards Iconodulism and the deification of the Saints.   Had the
sarcophagi and inscriptions which now adorn the
Roman´museums been left in their places, and not
been arranged arbitrarily by the guardians and
literati of different times, the Christian world of the
nineteenth century would have been greatly assisted
in understanding the minds of Christian people of
the third and fourth, perhaps of the second.   But,
even as it is, the Scriptural cycle of ornament
has been most wisely and honourably set apart by
De Rossi from any other.   Its range in symbolism
and history alike is very wide; and it would be
matter of great rejoicing to the present writer to
think that it should become an order of decoration
for the Anglican Church, and that its objects should
be multiplied in many of her temples, calling out the
skill of believing artists in silent lay-preaching of
their belief.   To this subject he must return, well
aware as he is of the general futility of all counsels
of moderation, caution, or mutual respect or indulgence, between the very active organizations
which now divide Anglican opinion and practice
between them.   Mild talk only irritates both parties,
" Lambs' bleating makes wolves keen." [1]   Still it
is true, that in the Catacomb-paintings is found
an exposition of the facts most earnestly believed

[1] " Acuuntque lupos balatibus agni."

by, and considered by, the Church most essential to the faith of the great mass of martyrs and confessors.

The definition or development of Sacramental Doctrine is represented in the Catacombs by the various Agapæ, or Love Feasts ; by representations of the Lord's Baptism ; and (probably at a date as early as most of the subterranean paintings) by various Baptismal Crosses, of which the Lateran Cross, so called, is the great surviving specimen.[1]   The Catacomb of St. Pontianus on the Via Portuensis contains a regular Baptistery, with two of the most frequently-examined portraits of Our Lord ; and a representation of His Baptism, which is of exactly the same type as those of Ravenna, and their many successors, and as that in the celebrated MS. of the library of St. Mark, at Venice. It is probable that the fresco, *in its present state,* is considerably later than the Ravennese Baptisteries, as Anastasius[2] records the restoration of the Catacomb by Pope Adrian I. A.D. 772—775 ; and the character of the work agrees with his statement. On carefully inspecting one of Mr. Parker's photographs, it appears to the present writer that the harsh outlines of the upper part of the Baptist's arm and shoulder are drawn over a more careful and correct figure.   The biceps, deltoid, and pectoral muscles seem to have been quite clearly and properly marked in an older underlying picture of the same subject ; and they are neglected in the outline of the restoration.   The stiffness of the present picture, the white eyes of the figures, and

[1] See chapters on Cross and Crucifix.   [2] In St. Adriano, § 336.

their heavy, incorrect drawing, point to a date as late as Nicolas I. or Adrian I. The treatment is familiar to us by countless repetitions. Our Lord stands half immersed, as the Baptist performs his office, with the Holy Dove hovering above Him ; an angel holds the Lord's robe ; and the stag, which represents the Gentile Church, is drinking of the waters of Baptism below. The Head of Christ in this Catacomb (St. Pontianus) is said by Abbé Martigny to be a reproduction of the time of Hadrian I.; and Boldetti, he says, found a similar picture in the Callixtine cemetery, which fell to pieces when an unfortunate attempt was made to remove it from the wall. We have already regretted the distressing taste for removal; but this must be remembered, that it was forced on early Popes by fear of the Lombards, devoted as the latter were to "relic-conveying." No attempt seems to have been made to preserve any part of these cemeteries in its original state ; and Dr. Northcote remarks strongly on the destruction which has been wrought in frescoes since Bosio's time, in which even D'Agincourt seems by no means blameless. The loss of these later ideals of Our Lord's appearance— for they can be no more than traditional ideals— is, of course, no vital matter, yet is greatly to be regretted; and still more is it to be lamented that the more ancient portrait in the 4th cubiculum of the Callixtine,[1] attributed with great verisimilitude to the second century, should be now lost. It represented Our Lord on a medallion ; and, if Bosio's plate be correct, as is most probable, was a finely-drawn head and shoulders, with the long hair, oval face, fine

[1] Bosio, p. 253.

beard and moustache, arched eyebrows, and regular features, which have been repeated throughout Christian Art to this day. The face itself must have worn a look of gentleness and melancholy, but it seems to have been placed on a neck and bust of somewhat massive and athletic proportions. Whether, and in what sense, the portrait of Our Lord was used at all in the first three centuries must be held doubtful, even in spite of this beautiful work, which may, no doubt, have been of the same date as the enlargement of the Catacomb.[1] Stamped bricks of Marcus Aurelius, A.D. 161, 180, have been found in it.

But the well-known passage in Augustine[2] proves distinctly that no actual transcript, even from memory, of the real appearance of Jesus Christ, both God and Man, existed in his day. Had there been a record-portrait, entitled to the least attention, the fact must have been known to the Father; and it would certainly have changed, not only the words, but the whole drift of the passage. It is quoted in a note to the chapter on Iconoclasm in this book, where reference is also made to an illustrative passage from Irenæus, relating to Gnostic portraits of our Lord, which were said to be copies of a supposed likeness taken by order of Pontius Pilate. These frescoed heads in the Catacombs,[3] of which

[1] This is one of the earliest of the Catacombs, and the upper part of it must be of great antiquity; Mr. Parker thinks probably of the first century. The staircase and lower part of the Catacomb were an enlargement. "De Rossi found both Pagan sarcophagi and Pagan inscriptions in this Catacomb, in excavations made under his own eyes.—Rom. Sotteran, vol. ii. pp. 169, 281, 290." Parker, "Antiquities of Rome," Catacombs, p. 17, note.

[2] De Trinitate, viii. 4, 5.

[3] The spurious letter of Lentulus, describing Our Lord as fairest of the sons of men, is an expression of this ideal.

the lost one in St. Callixtus must have been the most ancient are clearly ideals, as must be the painting on ivory of the same type in the Museum of the Vatican, which De Rossi considers most ancient of all representations of the Lord.[1] The portraits mentioned by Eusebius,[2] as probably derived from the image at Cæsarea Philippi, must have been matter of the imagination or skill of the artist. "The outward appearance of the Lord's person." says St. Augustine,[3] "is variously represented by the diversity of conceptions without number." And it appears as if two classes of these ideals existed, until the period of darkness after the eighth century, when sculpture and fresco alike were lost, and even mosaic suspended for awhile. The religious imagination takes one of two turns, according to individual character and circumstances : it pictures facts to itself with pleasure or with pain, in joy of heart or in sorrow. In the first case, it takes the view of the religious artist ; in the second, that of the ascetic. As Dean Milman says, "the Christian Faith is its own poetry" in ages early and late—and in a sense also it is its own painting : for the habitual use of devout imagination goes on with the same vigour in high-wrought spirits, whether they ever look at a picture or not. There can be no doubt that if the spirit of a thoughtful person dwells passionately on the actualities and details of any subject, ideas on that subject will pass through his brain ; and in many

---

[1] See the valuable chapter by Messrs. Crowe and Cavalcaselle, "Hist. of Modern Italian Art," vol. i. See also Martigny, "Jésus Christ," with woodcut.

[2] Hist. Eccl. vii. 18.

[3] "Dominicæ facies Carnis, innumerabilium cogitationum diversitate variatur et fingitur."

cases they will be so vivid as to be like pictures, and to crave, as it were, for pictorial representation. And hence arose a twofold ideal of the bodily appearance of Him Who is our Lord. One invested Him with every possible attribute of human beauty, not excepting strength of body—for this, too, has been made His repeatedly, from the Callixtine Catacomb to Michael Angelo;—the other dwelt on the words, " He hath no form or comeliness," as the former on " Thou art fairer than the children of men."[1]   This inquiry, which is not, in fact, very useful or edifying, certainly need not occupy us now.   There can be no doubt that the distresses of Italy during the period from Alaric to Attila, and again to the settlement of the Lombard race in the northern plains, were great enough to give a specially ascetic turn to the thoughts of the monks and cloistered clergy, who alone were able to keep up the practice of any branch of art. The ascetics who looked forth on the ravages of Alboin had little spirit of enjoyment or thought of corporeal beauty, even when Alboin spared their lives and convents. Generation by generation, they thought less of beauty, because of anguish of spirit and cruel bondage : it seemed to them partly a snare, and they often lost both the wish and the power to produce it. And as they looked more and more for the day of the Lord, when He should come to end the fury of the oppressor,

[1] The Fathers are divided on this point.   Justin and Clement of Alexandria. (Dialog. cum Tryph. 85—88, and Pædagog. l. iii. c.1.), Stromata (l. iii.), Tertullian (De Carne Christi adv. Jud. xiv.), SS. Basil and Cyril of Alexandria—are for the uncomely ideal. SS. Gregory of Nyssen, Jerome, Ambrose, Augustine, Chrysostom, and Theodoret, are on the side of beauty. (Molanus' Hist. SS. Imag. p. 403, &c.)

they thought of Him more and more as an Avenger and unsparing Judge. His face, they thought, could not but have resembled the worn and piteous—often, perhaps, the ill-favoured and austere countenances of the brethren they knew. Their hearts were failing them, for the Faith seemed at length to be falling like a divided house. Conventual severities, too, deprived their own bodies of all sacredness or beauty in their eyes. So that Christian art seems for centuries (at least in painting and mosaic) to shrink from representing our Lord as fairest among men. His face grows more severe; He is the Judge and Avenger only. The mirror of the world is too dark for men to see Him in. "After the tenth century," says Mr. Lecky, "the Good Shepherd which adorns every chapel in the Catacombs is no more seen; the miracles of mercy are replaced by the details of the Passion and the terrors of the Last Judgment. From this period Christ appears more and more melancholy, and truly terrible: He is indeed the *Rex tremendæ majestatis* of a *Dies Iræ.*" Those who are able to consult Mr. Parker's photographs will have no difficulty in tracing this change from the Catacombs, and through the Church-mosaics, to the ninth century. The vast images, awful in their expressionless abstraction, which fill the tribunes of Pisan and Florentine, Sicilian and Venetian churches from the eleventh century, are derived from, but do not really resemble, the works of the Roman decadence or bathos of art: there is all the difference between them in feeling and character which one observes between evening twilight and morning twilight. These we must pass by; but the Roman churches of SS. Cosmo and Damian, St. Prassede and others, furnish examples of the ascetic and for bidding treatment in its maturity,—examples not ignoble or ordinary, but full of severe feeling; while the works at Ravenna, from the fifth to the seventh century, illustrate the gradual transition from beauty to repulsiveness. The Christ of St. Apollinare Nuova, in particular, Who sits to receive the long procession of Saints presenting their crowns to him, has a face, large-eyed and sad indeed when closely inspected in a photograph, but gravely beauti-ful in the original as seen from the floor of the church. And the Good Shepherd of a century earlier, in Galla Placidia's chapel, is a work of great splendour, where vigorous and successful efforts have been made at personal beauty of face and form. In many cases, in fact, the ascetic transition seems to be simply barbaric.

The Callixtine Catacomb is the one most frequently visited in modern Rome. From dated bricks of the time of M. Aurelius and of A.D. 161–180, in addition to the original vaults, it must have existed before 161. Callixtus, Bishop of Rome in 117, is said to have been entrusted with *the cemetery* by Zephyrinus, his predecessor, before he himself became Pope or Bishop; the cemetery including, probably, all Christian burying-places and rites. Pagan inscrip-tions have been found there, some evidently brought by Christians, as old marble to be used as palim-psests, others as original parts of sarcophagi belong-ing to the Catacomb.[1] As the burial-place of many early Bishops of Rome, it has always attracted a

[1] Rossi, R.S. ii. pp. 169, 281, 290.

great deal of attention.   But this seems to have had
one unsatisfactory result, that its frescoes have been
re-touched and restored, and sometimes, as it seems,
at great distance of time, and by very careless and
incompetent hands.   The publication of Mr. Parker's
photographs will now give everyone an opportunity
of inspecting the actual state of these paintings;
probably with greater certainty about them, as
has been said, than could be obtained without repeated opportunities and lengthened study on the
spot: and few things can be more disagreeably
surprising, or surprisingly disagreeable, than the
apparent rudeness, not to speak of the artistic
defects, of the painter or restorer.   The Agape of
seven persons is undoubtedly an ancient subject,
representing, as it really does, one of those points of
contact between Gentile and Christian observance
which may have greatly assisted many Heathen
in their studies of the Christian Faith.   There is
almost a parallel picture in the so-called Gnostic
Catacomb, where seven Priests of Mithras are represented holding a solemn feast.   But in both
pictures alike the workmanship is so grossly rude
and careless, that one is led to suspect that ancient
re-touchings have taken place, at some time in the
bathos of art; and the addition of the coarsest
outlines, both on the lighted and shaded side of
the objects, seems to show that the original painting
had nearly vanished from the wall when some well-
meaning and totally ignorant restorer made an
attempt at securing its meaning.[1]   Some account

---

[1] See Parker, Photog. 1614 : and the Callixtine Agapæ in De
Rossi and Bottari.

of the Agapæ will be found in the chapter on
Sacramental Decoration.   It need only be observed
here that the Feast of Bread and Fish, referring
as it does to St. John xxi. and the last Repast
by the Lake of Tiberias, falls naturally into the
Scriptural cycle of subjects, with which alone the
Primitive Christian Catacombs were ornamented.

When re-touchings and restorations are spoken of,
no more is meant, of course, than that the original
and nearly effaced subjects have been renewed; but
still the reader should, if possible, refer to some of the
newly-issued facsimiles of the present state of the
paintings, that he may form an idea of the difficulty
of framing anything more than general premisses of
argument from such data.   After some study of them,
and of the various standard works on the subject, the
present writer—who regrets not to have visited the
Roman Catacombs since 1859—feels convinced of what
is generally admitted—that the figures of Saints, as
of Abdon and Sennen, and SS. Marcellinus, Pollio
and Petrus, in the Catacomb of St. Pontianus, are all
of the New-Greek or Byzantine period.   As regards
such relics as the Good Shepherd, the Madonna and
Magi in St. Nereo, the Agape above mentioned, and
the same subjects in the Catacomb of SS. Saturninus
and St. Thrason, it is impossible that they can either
be or resemble originals of any early date, while the
least power of drawing remained in Rome.   The un-
naturally-sized heads of the figures ; the loss of all
clearness of outline and of sense of form in the
accessories—such as birds, flowers, &c., are decisive
on this point, and painful enough.   Yet the restorers
must have worked in good faith, and probably re-

peated the subjects they found below. In some ins'ances, as in the Orantes, from St. Saturninus,[1]— also that in St. Priscilla—a certain grandeur prevails over extraordinary disproportions of drawing; based, as it seems, on sincerity and power of feeling in the mind of the ill-taught artist. In others, as in the picture called the " Madonna and the Prophet of Bethlehem,"[2] some attempt at beauty has been made. The figure, apparently addressing the Virgin-Mother, was probably intended for a ministering angel.

The highly interesting picture of the Fish bearing Bread, and possibly Wine, is found in the Callixtine only; and given in De Rossi and by Dr. Northcote. Whether the wine-flask can be traced in the basket or not may be uncertain ; but it is immaterial, as the symbolic connection of the picture with St. John vi. is obvious.

Of the Seasons of SS. Nereus and Achilles, the Dolia, or Wine-casks of St. Priscilla, and other various birds—doves and peacocks for the most part —which are found in various cemeteries, some account is given in the Index of Subjects. The various figures of the Oranti in all parts of the Catacombs[3] lead us to make a few remarks on the subject of the representation and treatment of the Mother of Our Lord. That progress in her cultus which gradually converts her from Creature into Deity is partly traced in the chapter on Mosaics; and references are there given to photographs from

[1] 1470, Parker and Bottari.
[2] Parker, Catacomb of St. Priscilla, 1467, and in Dr. Northcote's and Mr. Marriott's works. · [3] See Index, s.v.

the originals. But it is not begun in the Catacombs. The Blessed Virgin is, to all appearance,
represented only as the Mother of Our Lord,
presenting the Holy Child to the Magi for their
adoration; nowise claiming it herself. In some
cases, female Oranti may possibly be taken to represent her in prayer. In one example only, a single
Orante is placed by the side of the Good Shepherd
as if in the position of a companion. That example
is simply pronounced by Bosio to be "una donna
orante;" and the picture of a scourge, originally
placed beside her, points to its being the portrait
of a martyr.[1] But the change in the Blessed
Virgin's position in Christian decoration, advances,
of course, in a parallel line with her actual cultus;
both having their rise together in the reaction
from Arianism, and exclusive contemplation of the
Divinity of Our Lord. "The more absolute deification, if it may be so said, of Christ; the forgetful
ness of His humanity induced by His investment
in more remote and awful God-head, created a want
of some more kindred and familiar object of adoration. The worship of the intermediate Saints
admitted that of the Virgin as its least dangerous,
most affecting, most consolatory part."[2]

The progressive signs of intensified devotion to
the worship of the Virgin are ably traced through
the art of the Early and Mediæval Church by Mr.
Marriott, and we are not concerned with them here.

[1] See Mr. Wharton Marriott, "Testimony of the Catacombs."
Male Oranti are frequent; as Leo (Aringhi, R.S. t. ii. p. 135) and
others given by Mr. Marriott, Vestiarium Christianum (pl. vi. pp.
109, 183, 247, 257).
Milman, "Hist. Latin Christianity," vol. i. p. 180.

The thesis of this work may be in great part expressed by De Rossi's expression of the Scriptural cycle of the Catacombs. We must proceed to consider certain additions of Baptismal and Eucharistic symbolism. They will be found necessary, perhaps, as concessions to that earnest æsthetic feeling and passionate desire for visible signs which characterizes modern devotion. But we cannot but feel that those limits of representation and of symbolism within which the Church of the first four centuries abode and prevailed ought to content us in our own day; and that artistic imagination of the highest flight, and creative skill of the mightiest vigour, may find scope and subject enough in the records of the History of Man's Creation and Redemption.

NOTE ON FRESCO-PAINTINGS AT NAPLES, IN THE CATACOMBS OF ST. JANUARIUS.

The Rev. C. F. Bellermann, late Chaplain to the Prussian Embassy, published, in 1839, some good coloured plates of these paintings, with text. The work was entitled " Ueber die ältesten Christlichen Begräbnisstätter und besonders die Katakomben zu Neapel mit ihren Wandgemälden" (4to. Hamburg, 1839). See, also, D'Agincourt, Hist. de l'Art., &c. pl. 11, No 9 : and several photographs taken with magnesium-light by J. H. Parker, Esq.

Their subjects include the usual peacocks, doves, and flowers. There is an Adam and Eve, beautifully drawn, and a curious picture of three female figures engaged in building a wall, illustrative of the Shepherd of Hermas. There are also anchors, dolphins, a jewelled cross, and another with the A and ω, and figures of St. Paul with St. Laurence, of Oranti, of St. Januarius, &c. A picture of Christ is on one of the vaulted ceilings, with the Nimbus. Bellermann observes that this picture has suffered much by being painted over, at a later date or dates ; and this remark applies more or less to all the subterranean frescoes.

THE ROMAN AND LOMBARD NOAH.
(CALLIXTINE CATACOMB.)   (GATES OF ST. ZENONE, VERONA.)

THE STATION CROSS AT MAYENCE.
(BACK VIEW.)

CHAPTER V

THE use of Mosaic, as applied to buildings dedicated to the service of God, may be said to be an especially Christian branch of fine art. It is connected in most minds with the Greek Church in particular; and almost all the great works of earlier centuries which will be referred to in this chapter are found near the shores of the Mediterranean and the Adriatic, or in countries where a Greek element yet remains, and in which the Greek influence can be distinctly traced even at the present day. The subject is, of course, a wide one, and the writer cannot undertake to speak from personal knowledge in every case; but he has inspected many mosaics in Rome and Ravenna, as well as those of St. Sophia at Constantinople, and the curious works to be found in the Convent of the Transfiguration at Mount Sinai; with a fair proportion, at least of the later pictures, found at Venice, Pisa, Florence, and throughout the north of Italy. A certain acquaintance with the original mosaics is of some importance to anyone who wishes to study them from the photograph. And here it seems necessary to make two remarks on copies of works in colour made by the camera; the first is, that for the purposes of theology or history, they are the only absolutely reliable documents which are accessible to the public at home. But in the second place it must be observed, that though their value is unmistakeable and their testimony conclusive, whenever their authenticity is fully ascertained; still, that photographic copies, in indifferent light and shade, can give no notion whatever of the beauty of their originals as art. Considered as a document, a photograph direct from a mosaic or fresco is a decisive evidence of its present state; and though many modern drawings, and photographs made from drawings, have been well and conscientiously done, still there is a difference between an original and a restoration. And it must be observed that the photographs circulated in Rome from the frescoes of St. Clemente, with a large proportion of drawings or photographs from the Catacombs, are restorations. Frequently, indeed, as regards the Catacombs, they are restorations of paintings already renewed by repainting, *in situ* on the wall, at early dates. The mosaics have considerable advantage over the Catacomb-frescoes as to their authenticity; but restorations have taken place in very many cases; often, as in the celebrated Church of St. Pudentiana at Rome, on an almost unlimited scale, and by artists of the greatest skill. Mosaic-paintings, however, are necessarily left in their original positions, with few exceptions, of which the above-named picture appears to be one. It may be taken as an example of admirable restoration, made in perfect good faith, and involving the assertion of no specially Roman doctrine. But it would be altogether wrong to speak of it as a work of the fourth or any earlier century, though it may contain fragments of the earliest date of Christian mosaic. There are grave reasons to believe that it is not now on the walls which originally bore it; and its archæological value is diminished in proportion.[1]

The same remark applies with still greater force to the Roman habit of collecting bas-reliefs, and especially inscriptions, in museums, under more or less conjectural dates and classification. It is obvious that such documents in their original place are evidence of twice the weight and interest which they bear in a museum, in a place assigned by

---

[1] Careful inspection of photographs in Mr. Parker's published collection (Nos. 1416—1419) inclines the writer to believe that Messrs. Crowe and Cavalcaselle are quite within the truth when they pronounce that no real or impartial judgment can be formed as to the real date of this mosaic from its present state. ("History of Paintings in Italy," vol. i. chap. i.) Restorations appear to have been made, in fact, during the sixteenth and seventeenth centuries, and with so high a degree of skill and sense of beauty as to amount to a re-creation of the original picture or pictures. The ox symbol of St. Luke appears not to be in mosaic at all—at least, a strong glass, which shows each separate tessera in the certainly restored Face of the Lord, does not enable the writer to distinguish any inlaying in the ox's head, which is more like distemper or oil-painting. Some mosaic is, however, left in the throat and wings. The noble Roman face of St. Peter is worthy of Raffaelle's Stanze in the Vatican, but the delicacy of the mosaic is unlike any early Christian work the writer is acquainted with ; and great part of the work seems to be too Christian for the Augustan age , and too skilful for any other period until the Raffaellesque. It is difficult to believe that the seventh-century Cross stood originally as it stands in this mosaic : the Nimbus round Our Lord's head is not round, but awkwardly flattened on one side : His right arm is too long, and has been restored with rather less care in the drapery of the arm, which ends in an abrupt, irregular edge without going over the limb. Speaking from the photograph, which gives very decisive testimony, under the magnifier, as to forms and interruptions in the work, one would say that this mosaic, in many respects the most beautiful in Rome, is little more than a number of fragments admirably pieced and renewed.

modern opinion.   It is, of course, a natural bias, or
tendency of mind, with what may be called the
Roman party in the archæology of Rome (with
which, of course, we are greatly concerned) to throw
back the chronology of inscriptions or paintings
which seem to be evidence in favour of distinctively
Roman usage or doctrine; and it appears to the
writer that an unnecessary haziness on the subject
may result in the popular mind.   It seems to him
an inaccuracy, as has been said, to circulate photographs (from correct and conscientious restoration-
drawings) of the newly-discovered frescoes in St.
Clemente, describing them as *vetustissimæ imagines*
—pictures of the *greatest* antiquity.   The work, or
gift, of Beno de Rapiza, in the eleventh century,
ought to be distinguished somehow, at least, from
the fifth-century mosaics of St. Constantia, or St.
Maria Maggiore.

Our second observation has reference to treatment, and artistic power over beauty, shown in these
ancient works.   As has been said, the photograph
gives an inadequate and unfavourable notion of all
works in colour; and the mosaics naturally suffer
more than the Catacomb-frescoes, because their
colour is extremely beautiful, and because they retain that brilliant effect of half-reflected light, which
is peculiar to tessellated-work, and in some degree
resembles the bold and skilful stippling of a consummate workman in water-colours.   It is to be feared
that these great works must be inspected in their
places before they can be understood to any purpose;
because photography only gives the student notions
of stiffness and ugliness which vanish altogether in

the glory of the actual hues—at least, to the eyes of a colourist. As accurate record of subject and meaning, the sun-picture may appeal with Virgil to the sun—"Who can gainsay the (sun's) light."[1] But it cannot give that sometimes quite unspeakable beauty of colour, which redeems the rigidity of ancient mosaics; and in fact justifies it, in decorative images subordinate to architectural form. There is a contrary extreme, which appears to the present writer infinitely worse than the ghastly figures of Sinai or Torcello. The frescoes of Sir James Thornhill in St. Paul's, London, or the ceiling of the Sheldonian Theatre at Oxford, are surely not more desirable models of architectural ornament than the roof of the Baptistery at Florence;[2] and the advocate of Italian Romanesque Gothic, or Byzantine ornament; may appeal to a certainly large number of travellers, who have looked with pleasure on the walls and cupolas of St. Mark's at Venice. The spectator must judge, if, after all, the quaint Old Testament histories of the Atrium, and the gaunt and solemn forms in the Baptistery, are not better ornament than the florid images of the sixteenth and seventeenth centuries which gesticulate and attitudinize on the central vaultings. There is a Law, or Rationale, or Reason for decorative stiffness and conventionality; and if it is exaggerated in Byzantine work of old days, it is certainly altogether lost sight of in the eighteenth century allegory, and in the naturalism of the nineteenth.

The art which is now called Mosaic consists in

---

[1] "Solem quis dicere falsum audeat."

[2] See the novel of "Romola," chap. iii. for a good sketch of the Renaissance or quasi-classical view of thirteenth-century Christian work.

forming pictures of small cubes in stone, or marble, or tile, or earthenware, or glass of different colours; and has been called by the various names, *opus musivum, musaicum, mosaicum,* or *museum;* also, *opus tessellatum, vermiculatum, reticulatum, albarium,* and *sectile.* The last means, in particular, that class of work which is not formed of small tesseræ, but of larger pieces of marble of different colours, cut out very carefully in larger sizes (and probably in irregular forms adapted to the work) and so carefully put together as to form a picture; or with incised lines filled up with colour. Of this kind is the celebrated group of the Tigress and Calf.[1] The original and some similar figures are now preserved in the Church of St. Antonio Abbate at Rome. This method evidently requires great sculptural skill, knowledge of form and colour, and wealth in materials. *Opus tessellatum* appears to be the ordinary term for what we still call tessellated pavements. *Vermiculatum* is probably similar work in small patterns, white predominating; and *albarium* seems to be much the same. All these varieties, except *sectile,* which is hardly mosaic at all in the modern sense, apply to floorings; and Pliny's general term for them is *lithostrotum,* or pavement; *Gabbatha* being no doubt the corresponding Hebrew term for a tessellated hall in the house of Pilate.[2] *Musivum* and its kindred words apply to the pictures re-

[1] Parker, "Photographs of Ancient Mosaics in Rome."

[2] St. John xix. 13, Gabbatha or λιθόστρωτον. See Mr. Grove's article in Smith's Dictionary of the Bible, where it is further suggested that the tessellated pavement may have been a portable one, such as we are told by Suetonius (Cæsar 46) Julius Cæsar used to carry with him on his expeditions, to give the Bema or Tribunal its conventional elevation. It is singular that the Gabbatha being

presented within a tessellated frame or border,[1] that frame being often very large and beautiful, and being called *lithostrotum*. Pliny[2] attributes the origin of mosaic pavement to the Greeks, though they probably derived its use from Syria and the East; and in fact the passage in Esther, i. 6[3] proves that mosaic was in use in Persia at a very early date. Its introduction into Rome is said to date from the time of Sylla; and at all times it seems to have been in the hands of Greek workmen. It is sufficient, for the present, to mention one or two of the best-known and most beautiful relics of mosaic of the earliest date, or at least of unknown antiquity; such as the great Pompeian mosaic called "The Battle of Issus," discovered in 1831.[4] The celebrated picture called Pliny's, or, the "Capitoline Doves," so well known by various copies, is supposed to be a copy of the "Cantharus of Pergamus," attributed to Sorus. Another curious Pergamene mosaic is mentioned by Pliny, which was called *asarotos œcos*, "The Unswept Hall," because it represented the unremoved relics of a banquet strewn on the tessellated floor of the rooms of a palace. With these works may be compared the beautiful inlaid picture of birds—the

evidently without the Prætorium, and the actual scene of M. Doré's enormous picture, so skilful an artist should have missed the only feature of the building mentioned in the Gospel narrative; and this, too, while he treats the public to range on range of imaginary architecture.

[1] See Smith's Dictionary, s.v. "House."
Ep. xxxvi. 60.
[3] Esther, i. 6 : "Upon a pavement of red, and blue, and white, and black marble." The evident use of colour here may remind us of the uniformly bright or rich colours of Byzantine mosaic, deriving from the East.
[4] Museo Borbonico, viii. 6, 36—45.

ducks in particular—-found in the Callixtine Catacomb, and probably of the second century.[1]

Two observations should be made here, which seem
of some importance. One of them relates to the great
difference (well understood, doubtless, but not generally enough insisted on) between works of the
Roman decadence, which follow Græco-Roman traditions of art, in drawing and composition; and
those of the Byzantine Renaissance, which dates
from the sixth century. Secondly, attention should
be paid to the change and treatment of subjects in
the earliest Mosaics, from the regular subjects of the
Catacomb-frescoes. Though there are many Byzantine paintings in those cemeteries, they are of comparatively later date; and the most ancient works
contain figures wearing old Roman secular dresses;
not the stiff and gorgeous vestments of Eastern
Greek art, but the tunic, with the single-striped
toga over it, which bears so marked a resemblance to
our own surplice and stole.[2]

The first of these distinctions will be frequently
repeated or appealed to in the following pages; but
the present seems to be the best place to go into the
second. One prominent and important subject disappears from Christian Art when it issues from the
Catacombs: that of the Agape, or Love-feast.[3] References may be made to SS. Augustine,[4] Ambrose,[5]

[1] Parker, Photographs, No. 1284.
[2] See Mr. Wharton Marriott's work on the Catacombs.
[3] The chapter on the Catacombs will contain an account of the
Agapæ there represented, and some remarks on their connection
with St. John vi., and xxi in particular.
[4] St. Augustine, De Moribus Ecclesiæ : Novi eos esse, qui calices in
sepulchra deferant, et epulas ostentautes cadaveribus super sepultos se ipsos sepeliantur.   [5] St. Ambrose, de Elia et Jejunio.

Paulinus of Nola,[1] &c., for the irregularities which in all probability caused the discontinuance of these celebrations, being found inseparable from them. Converts from heathenism must have had almost inveterate recollections of their habits of funeral or commemorative feasting, and have been too closely reminded of the ancient hearth-worship, and past banquets to the Lares of their families. So it is, in any case that no representation of an Agape occurs in the mosaics; though highly important symbolic reference is made, in the earliest of them, to the Sacrifice of the Death of Christ, and in instances of the sixth century to the actual celebration of the Eucharist. In SS. Cosmas and Damianus, at Rome, the Lamb is seen on an altar "as if slain;" in St. Vitale, at Ravenna, the sacrifice of Abel is placed in the same picture with that of Melchisedek, in the act of offering the memorial sacrifice before an altar. The latter work is of the time of Justinian. But there is a further change of subject in the mosaics, which consists principally in calling greater attention to the glorified condition of the saints, as engaged in continual worship of the Lord, though not presented as objects of worship themselves. It is true that the mosaics, like the frescoes, may be classed as either symbolical or historical; and also that the same leading subjects are repeated in both alike. The connection is established by the repetition of the Good Shepherd in the chapel of Galla Placidia

[1] He gives as a reason for painting the walls of a catacomb, that there are nightly meetings and feasts of country people there, whose devotion is sincere, but whose conduct is often disorderly. He hopes that the subjects on the walls, being properly explained to them, will give a more solemn tone to their thoughts and behaviour, or at least occupy their time in an orderly way.—Poema xxvii. de St. Felicis Natal, quoted *supra*, p. 3.

(Ravenna, A.D. 450—60); with 'the Vine, Lamb, and other subjects, as the Miracles represented in St. Apollinare Nuova, in the same city. The distinction is, that Our Lord begins to be more frequently represented as seated in Glory, or in the arms of the Virgin Mother, receiving the offerings of the Magi; less often as the Shepherd, though the faithful on earth are still constantly symbolized as His Sheep. But as early as the seventh century there are portraits or commemorative pictures of Saints in Heaven, presented to the Redeemer by Apostles in person, and the symbols of the Four Evangelists date as early as the fifth. The darkness and sufferings of the times on earth seem to have forced men to seek comfort in imaginations of the glories of the world to come. It is a difficult, and somewhat painful task, to trace how the pious remembrance of men and women who had lived saintly lives and died the martyr's death gradually changed to adoration, so that the Apostles' caution was reversed, and the love of brethren whom men had seen on earth took the place of personal devotion to their Lord, Whom they had not seen. But such progress did take place; and it is necessarily marked by changes in the mosaic-pictures of the Roman churches; since in Ravenna there are but few and unimportant signs of it. It would seem that a real and spiritual meaning attaches to the words of God concerning Himself, that He is jealous[1] of Man's devotion; that having Personally taken on Himself Manhood, He

---

[1] Jealous, *Kanna*, Gesenius. "Used of God, as not bearing any rival: the severe avenger of departure from Himself." Exod. xx. 5.

will not share with any created being the rule and possession of man's inner spirit; but will permit one misdirection of devotion or one misuse of art to lead to another. Men passed from loving commemoration of Saints to prayer for their intercession; and so the feeling gained on the people that these great brethren gone before were easier of access than the God Who is Man. Thus He was gradually deprived of His mediatorial position in the minds of the untaught or unthoughtful; and, as has been the case so often since, the madness or dulness of the people was gradually condoned and tampered with, and, in short, prevailed over the sounder doctrine of those who should have been their guides. Nor can there be any doubt that many early mosaics bear witness to tendencies of this kind. There is a marked change in their subjects, from the Scriptural teaching, symbolic or historic, which prevails in the Catacombs. The Lord Himself is no longer represented in symbols of His own dictation, as the Shepherd of souls; the idea of literal representation of Him seems gradually to have prevailed. Acute and spiritual minds, in that day also, may have felt that the grand and colossal Icons which filled the apses of their temples were no more, in intention, than symbols of His Presence in the midst of His gathered congregation. Nevertheless, prevailing ignorance, lapse of years, and the influx of simpler and more literal-minded worshippers, unprotected by those relics of the old Hebrew dread of graven images which were never lost in the Eastern Church, —seem to have had their full work in the West, by the second Council of Nice in 784. The distinction between historical pictures, or repetitions in picture of Scriptural symbolism and portrait-images as objects of worship, was felt and understood; it is visible from time to time, especially in the Libri Carolini, or answer of Charlemagne's bishops to the second Council of Nice.[1] Our own view of the subject must stand on it; and it may be maintained, if anywhere, in the Church of Christ in England. But it did not prevail with the mass of mankind; instead of a fundamental principle, it was treated as a compromise of principle between parties; and then, as always happened, the more numerous, dull, and powerful party interpreted it all its own way in the Western Church. It is not without thought and study of ancient works and records that the writer of this book is led to assert, as the main principles of Christian Church-art, that its subjects should be chosen entirely from the symbolisms or the histories to be found in Holy Scripture. As in the best days of Venice, let the walls of the Temple be as the illuminated pages of the Evangeliary or the missal. The artist whose genius leads him to other subjects may go to them freely, and his work may be as truly dedicated to his Lord as that of a church-painter: but no artist who holds any form of Christianity can complain that the Old and New Testament give him too narrow a range of subject.

The typical or representative mosaics of the Primitive Church, between the days of Constantine and that period of dissolution and desolation which is marked by the irruption of Attila in 450, may be said to be three in number. They are the decorations of St. Con-

---

[1] See Harold Browne, "Articles," p. 509.

stantia, at Rome; the Chapel of Galla Placidia, at Ravenna; and the Old Testament histories of the Church of St. Maria Maggiore. All these are old Roman, not Byzantine, and works of the Decadence rather than of the earliest Renaissance. Each has its special importance; the Ravennese chapel, because it contains a Good Shepherd, and other pictures which directly connect mosaic ornamentation, as to subject, with the primitive work of the Catacombs; the works of St. Maria Maggiore, as purely historical and instructive pictures (A.D. 432–440);—and the earliest church of the three, St. Constantia, at Rome, is of world-wide celebrity as containing tessellated work, in all probability little later than the reign of the first Christian Emperor. It is a round church, supposed by Ciampini and others to have been a temple of Bacchus, purified and consecrated by order of Con stantine; or it may have been built by him or his immediate successors, making free use of the materials of an ancient temple. The mosaics are in the vaults of the aisles,—that is to say, those of the fourth century, the later ones of the eighth century are not to be compared with them. One series represents the culture of the Vine, from ploughing with oxen,[1] and the treading in the vine-press. This is thought to be Gentile-Roman work invested with Christian meaning from St. John xv: "I am the vine, ye are the branches." The forms are not of high merit, but quite naturalistic in their style, with little reference to pattern or architectural form; the figures are quite Græco-Roman; naked, or clad in tunics, and in full action; without any of the stiffness or

[1] "Flectere luctantes inter vineta juvencos" (Georg. II., 318).

conventionalism of Byzantine works. The difference between old and new Roman art is well illustrated, by comparing with these the eighth-century mosaics of Hadrian I. over the doors. Roman art may be said to expire here; and except in St. Maria Maggiore, all Christian work henceforth, till the earliest Lombard churches of the seventh century, is due to Byzantine hands, or influenced by Byzantine instructions.

We have to notice, then, in the mosaics from the sixth century, a gradual advance of Iconodulism upon the ancient symbolic picture-teaching; as well as to give an account of its ordinary subjects and treatment. Many of these appear to us unobjectionable, and in fact desirable for use in our own churches, or at least in all round-arched ones, whether Byzantine, Romanesque, or Norman. The first and more painful part of our observations may be dealt with first. It is in the church of St. Agnese, without the walls of Rome, that the patron saint for the first time takes the central place in the apse, and the form of Our Lord is omitted. In this case the Hand, representing the First Person of the Trinity, is placed directly above the Saint, who is abstracted in prayer, with clasped hands, and does not as yet stand necessarily as an object of worship. This church was built by Constantine, rebuilt by Pope Symmachus, and adorned with mosaics by Pope Honorius, A.D. 626—638. One cannot but notice that true Iconodulism, the undue use of the Image of the Creature, begins with these works. Hitherto the portrait-symbol of the Lord has been presented as the dominant idea of every worshipper; here, and again in St. Maria, in Navicella, created beings take His place. The colossal image, without human beauty, intended only as a token to men that God became Man, is in this instance displaced; and a church, apparently for the first time, dedicated to the memory of created Saints and Popes. Pure symbolism has gone before, in the pictures of the Vine and the Pastor; pure historical painting has gone before, in those of the Miracles and the Hebrew history; pictorial interpretation of type and symbolic event has gone before, in the frescoes and bas-reliefs of Noah, Moses, Elias, Jonah, and Daniel. These are the first indications, in the ornaments of Christian temples, of man's yet unconquered tendency to make to himself a sign of Deity, and to have a visible image in the place of the Redeemer risen and gone.[1]

In St. Maria in Dominica, or Navicella, which dates from Paschal I., A.D. 820, the Blessed Virgin sits in the centre of the apse, holding the Lord on her knees. He is represented rather as a small man than an infant. The Church probably shrank as yet from open worship of her as mediatrix with her Son, or holder of authority or special influence with Him. At all events, she is not represented as an object of worship without Him. This figure, as painful in its technicalities as in its subject, is nevertheless the precursor of all the blue-veiled Madonnas of the Middle Ages down to the Borgo-Allegri picture of Cimabue. Many of them, as those of Torcello and Murano, are very impressive and beautiful, and the description [2] of them is hardly to be forgotten.

[1] The theoretic defence set up for portrait-images is briefly discussed in Chap. I.

[2] " Stones of Venice," vol. ii.

A further step remains, and it is made in St. Maria in Transtevere.[1] It is to place the Mother of the Lord by His side on His throne of Glory, as God made man. Her face is regular and beautiful, and of extremely delicate mosaic—as fine as that of the copies of pictures in St. Peter's. It may possibly be a restoration, and should be compared through a good glass with the bolder mosaic of the other faces (excepting our Lord's). As the Navicella Madonna is the type of the Venetian and Florentine tradition, so here we see the anticipation of Orgagna's fresco at Pisa, followed as it is, in this feature at least, by Michael Angelo in the Sistine. The consummation seems to be reached in the two last pictures. In the mosaic the Blessed Virgin sits as assessor and mediatrix for men, with her Son, Who has taken the place of His Father as Lord of all men. In the Late-Renaissance work, she is interceding in vain; the mediatorial office of the Lord is utterly lost sight of; He is represented as the Final Judge without pity, and His present function of Intercession is ignored altogether.

For the primitive and central teaching of the Roman Church in mosaic, we must turn backwards to the Churches of SS. Cosmas and Damianus, of St. Venantius, and especially of St. Prassede. All these display the higher qualities of the Græco-Oriental imagination, dwelling on the Future of the spiritual world; with all the Byzantine defects and excellences in form and colour. Whatever may have been the date of the regular establishment of a Greek School of Mosaicists in Rome (and it may probably be post-

[1] Parker's Photographs, No. 1915.

poned till late in the course of the Iconoclastic controversy), there can be no doubt of the type of Eastern asceticism which prevails in these ancient and awful figures. They may be taken as a type of the early decoration of the eastern end of a Romano-Byzantine church; glorious in colour, stern in form and expression. Their drapery is still Roman, without the overloaded splendour and jewellery of later work. The Apostles wear the toga with its stripes, which so greatly resembles the Anglican surplice and stole, as Mr. Wharton Marriott observes. The figure of Our Lord standing on the firmament, and coming with clouds, is indescribably grand. He is here, come to His sanctuary, specially present with the congregation, and He is in Heaven with the Church triumphant; therefore the Apse, and the upper part of the Arch of Triumph, represent Him in glory, with His own. But at their feet[1] flows the mystic Jordan, the river of Baptism into His death, the Lethe of life and death, pre-figured by Egyptian, Greek, and Roman; and it separates the glorified Church in Heaven from the sheep below, yet militant on earth. Six, or twelve, or a larger number of sheep, those of the Gentile Church issuing from the city of "Bethlehem," the Hebrew fold from "Hieru salem," are found in almost all these great symbolic pictures.[2] The River symbolizes the Sacrament of Baptism; and in St. Prassede the Lamb is placed on the altar before the Cross, "as it had been slain" (Rev. v. 6.), and shadows forth the commemorative

---

[1] In SS. Cosmas and Damianus, also in St. Prassede.
[2] Those at St. Apollinaris in Classe, at Ravenna, at the base of the great mosaic of the Transfiguration, will be remembered.

sacrifice of His Body and Blood. In SS. Cosmas and
Damianus, the Lamb, crowned with a nimbus, stands
on the earthly side of Jordan, on a rock from
whence spring the four rivers of Paradise. In the
later church, on the broad spandrils of the Arch of
Triumph, the Army of Martyrs is kneeling before the
Lord, all casting their crowns before Him with a
grandly-conceived unity of action, robed in glowing
white, and placed against a gold ground, like the great
Processions of St. Apollinare Nuova, at Ravenna.

The probable derivation of the Cross from the
Monogram of the Lord, and its development into
the modern crucifix, will be the subject of other
chapters of this book. It is sufficient for the present
one to say that the earliest crosses of the period of
Constantine, like that called the Lateran Cross at the
present day, seem to have been constantly associated
with the idea of Baptism, and primarily to have
represented the Person and whole Humanity of the
Lord, and His Death as a part of His Humanity.
The Cross is always richly jewelled and ornamented
in mosaic, and is frequently accompanied (especially
after the rise of Arianism) by the letters A ω : the
minuscular ω being invariably used. Sometimes the
form of the Lord bears the Triumphal Cross; but very
frequently, and especially at Ravenna, it represents
Him as if it were the Monogram.

The changes in Christian thought and doctrine,
between the earlier Catacomb-frescoes and the culminating period of the mosaics in the ninth century,
is both evident and striking, and might almost be
judged of from pictorial documents only. The choir
and apse of a church from the earlier sixth century

are made to represent heaven and earth in symbol:
the new Heaven of Glory, and the renewed Earth of
the Soul regenerated in Baptism. The Presence of
the Lord, and of witnesses who had seen Him on
earth, is no more a thing of memory, but of history:
the age of miracle has ceased, and affliction and
distress continue, so that the spirits of pious men
are more than ever longing for some sign of the
Lord's return, in belief that the great troubles
coming on the earth are indeed the troubles of the
earth's latter days. Accordingly the imagination of
the artist is directed greatly to the Apocalypse, and
he strives to realize for the Christian imagination,
amidst the trials that are, something of the glory
that shall be. The Miracles of the Gospel, and the
fulfilment of prophetic types, are less frequently
insisted on than in the Catacombs. The long ages of
error, of heresy, rebuke, and blasphemy have begun,
to continue to the end; and accordingly the theological symbols and definitions, conveying the Church's
interpretation of the doctrines committed to her,
appear in her graphic arts as well as in her literature.
There is no mistaking, either at Rome or Ravenna,
the pictorial assertions of the Eternal Trinity, the
Incarnation and Sacrifice of God for man, Baptism
unto His Death, Communion of Saints, the Resurrection and Glorification of the Body. The
Sacrifice is yet typified by the Lamb, crowned, or
bearing the Cross; the descent of the Holy Spirit by
the mystic Dove.[1] The Cross directs thought to the

[1] As has been observed in the chapter on the Catacombs, the Dove
represents the Holy Spirit in pictures of the Lord's Baptism, &c.,
and is more commonly used as a symbol of the soul of the believer.
When added to the figure of Noah, it appears, of course, in a third

fact of Christ's death, but men are not yet invited to dwell on the manner of it, or on the nature of His Bodily sufferings.

Enough has been said, perhaps, in all works which treat of the Byzantine period of Art, of its severity, morose asceticism, and generally monastic tone. It must be remembered, that at the time of the Schola Græca in Rome, it was hardly possible for any art to be practised except in convents, and that the monks, after all, kept alive some traditions of painting and sculpture; and, in fact, began a faint though beautiful Renaissance of their own in the centuries of desolation. It was not till the great Lombard race, half subdued by Charlemagne, had won back its stormy liberty from the House of Swabia, that its transcendent power of imagination and hand-work broke out in Pisa and Florence. The faults of Byzantine art are the necessary consequence of the sorrows of the time, which certainly should not be charged by implication on the only men who really made head against them. Nor has any modern writer, except the author of the "Stones of Venice," dwelt properly on that great Oriental gift of colour which the monastic workmen possessed and transmitted to their more brilliant successors. The cathedrals and

or simply natural sense. All birds are originally Gentile or secular symbols, and Roman painters seem to have had a rather simple and amiable pleasure in representing them with their utmost skill, and studying their forms, hues, and manners direct from Nature. The Callixtine mosaic and the Doves of Pliny have been mentioned; there are bird-frescoes of great beauty in the Catacomb of St. Prætextatus, which can hardly be later than the end of the second century. The ancient relics of the St. Paolo-fuori-le-Muri mosaics will be remembered, with the vaultings of St. Constantia. The best, perhaps, in execution will be found in the mosaics of St. Vitale, at Ravenna. (See chapters on the Catacombs and Index.)

baptisteries of Florence and Pisa, whether Tafi or Torrita be one person or many, or whether or not they be real persons at all, were executed under Eastern instruction and inspiration through Venice. Soon after, Mosaic is merged in fresco-painting; for with Cimabue and Giotto, Italian art breaks altogether from Byzantine rule and monastic subject, and for a while in the early Renaissance, in the hands of Sandro Botticelli beyond all other men, combines the fervour of the Faith with much of the renewed knowledge and innocent delight of Old Greek art.

Those who wish to understand what efforts the unarmed and helpless heads of the Italian Church made to protect her people, will do well to study the letters of intercession written by Gregory the Great to Agilulf and Theodolinda, the Lombard rulers of Italy in his time; and the results, immediate and consequent, of the conversion of the Lombard race to the Faith. If an example be required of the unspeakable relief, and calm approaching to happiness, afforded by the convent to a world-wearied soldier, courtier, and captive, the history and works of Paul Warnefrid, the Lombard deacon and historian, who closed his chequered life at Monte Casino about the end of the reign of Charlemagne, are to be found in Muratori, and are well worth studying by the historian, the poet, or the painter. But if the artist wishes to form an opinion of the religious vitality of graphic art, he should consider its life-in-death during the fifth and sixth centuries in particular. Twenty-two years after the sack of Rome by Alaric, the vast range of historical mosaics of St. Maria Maggiore must have been begun; and those of St. Sabina were eight years earlier. Even while the hoofs of Attila tread over the north of Italy, the lovely sepulchral chapel of Galla Placidia rises, to connect the art of the Catacombs with the later mosaics. In the rally of the Eastern Empire, under Belisarius and Narses, the great Church-works commanded by Justinian extended from Ravenna to Constantinople, and thence to Mount Sinai. In the agonies of the Lombard invasion in 568, the wrath of Alboin is half appeased by the entreaties of the clergy, and he spares Pavia for their works' sake,—for the Duomo of that city was, in all probability, begun before his time.[1]

Those who believe in a real use of Church-art for Christian instruction, and those also who desire to give the Christian artist an open career for dedicated work, will understand what great assistance his efforts may give to the oral teaching of the clergy. And many of us, who have had our share of the world and its ways, may sympathize with the Art-preachers of old, for whom the convent was the only refuge and the only field of progress; who, having their share of the painter's spirit, rose on it as on the wings of a dove, and got them away afar off, because of the stormy wind and tempest. To the wildernesses of Egypt, or the Apennine, and in spirit beyond the wilderness, to the desired Paradise, they fled away: they looked to that world where alone they had hope or comfort, and they came to look on mankind only in relation to that hope; whether they symbolized

---

[1] There is a passage in Paul the Deacon (De Gestis Longobardorum, book i. 27) which speaks of improvements made in work and design during Alboin's reign, though especial progress was of course made in the manufacture of arms.

them as the sheep of Jerusalem, their first Fold, or of Bethlehem, the "House of the Flesh" of God, Who took on Him our flesh—or if they represented the Gentile catechumen, or faithfully-hearing heathen, as the wild hart desiring the water-brooks of Baptism.

APPENDIX TO CHAPTER ON MOSAICS.

The yet remaining Churches in Rome and Ravenna, which contain the most important of these works, may be thus arranged chronologically. Those of St. Sophia and the Convent of the Transfiguration at Mount Sinai are of the period of Justinian (died 569). The great Norman-Saracenic works of Sicily, the alike-mingled work of Venice, and the probably contemporaneous art of Pisa and Florence, all belong to the middle, and not the primitive ages.

ROME.

Century IV.

a. St. Constantia.—Vine mosaics and ornaments of vaultings.

b. Apse, or tribune of the ancient church of the Vatican, preserved in record by Ciampini. (Vet. Monumenta.)

Century V.

St. Sabina, 424, restored 795 ; completion of mosaics, probably by Eugenius II., in 824.[1]

St. M. Maggiore, 432–440.

Oratory of St. John Evangelist, 461–467.

RAVENNA.

Century IV.

In St. Agatha.—The Lord in Glory, with two angels, A.D. 378. Lost ; supposed to have been carried to Russia.

Century V.

Baptistery of St. John.

Chapel of Galla Placidia.

Ancient mosaic in San Gioanni. Apparently Gothic : resembles Bayeux tapestry.

[1] See Parker, "Mosaics of Rome and Ravenna," p. 4.

ROME.

Century VI.

SS. Cosmas and Damianus.
St. Lorenzo, f. m., 577–590.

RAVENNA.

Century VI.

St. Apollinare in Classe, 567.
St. Apollinare Nuova nella Citta, 570.
Baptistery, afterwards St. Maria in Cosmedin.
St. Michael, 545. — Christ holding a jewelled cross.
St. Vitale, 547.—Historical, symbolic, and naturalistic subjects in mosaic.

Of this century is the Transfiguration at Mount Sinai.

Century VII.—Rome.

St. Agnes, built by Constantine, rebuilt by P. Symmachus. Mosaics by Honorius, 1628-38. Popes themselves in the mosaic.
St. Stephen.—Jewelled cross.
St. Venantius, 642.—Many saints, busts of our Lord and angels.
St. Peter ad Vincula.—St. Sebastian.

Century VIII.

St. Mary in Cosmedin.
St. Theodore.—The hand of God holding a crown over the head of Christ, Who is seated on a globe holding a jewelled cross. SS. Peter, Paul, and Theodore.
St. Pudentiana, 771–791.—Christ enthroned, cross, and saints.
SS. Nereus and Achilles, 796. Transfiguration, and Madonna addressed by angels.
St. Susanna, 797. Leo III.—Christ and Apostles : monogram of Leo.
Triclinium of St. John Lateran.—Saints and Charlemagne.

Century IX.

St. Maria in Navicella or Dominica.—The blessed Virgin enthroned with the Infant as a diminutive man. He is seated also over the arch.
St. Praxedes, or Prassede.—7th chapter of Apocalypse. The Holy City (818, by Paschal I., who also set up the great mosaic of SS. Cosmas and Damianus, Chapel of St. Zeno), Jordan, &c. &c.
Church of St. Cecilia, also by Pope Paschal.
Church of St. Mark (Pope Mark I. founded it, 337).—Mosaics added by Hadrian I., then (on entire rebuilding of church) renewed by Gregory IV., 828. Jordan, &c. Jerusalem and Bethlehem.
St. Maria Novæ Urbis, 858. Rebuilt by Leo IV.; mosaics by Nicholas I., 858-68. The Virgin enthroned, as in St. Maria in Dominica.

The first period of Roman, and also of Byzantine mosaic—with the first period of Christian art—may be said to close at the end of the ninth century. There is almost an entire blank here for two centuries, and the art seems to have taken refuge once more in Byzantium, where the compromise between Iconoclasm and Representative art had been by this time effected according to their present limits. The regular establishment and recognition of a Greek School in Rome seems to date from the Iconoclastic movement in the eighth century; but the Byzantine or Oriental influence as gradually prevailing over Roman art, dates, as has been said, from the sixth.

RAVENNA.

THE great historical mosaics of St. Maria Maggiore at Rome are connected with the earlier works of Ravenna, in the Chapel of Galla Placidia and the Baptisteries, by the fact of their being art of old Rome, perhaps rightly here called Romanesque, rather than Byzantine or Constantinopolitan. This distinction has been already noticed, perhaps more at length than it deserves. Still we think it may be of use in a rather popular work, as many well-educated persons, not interested in ancient art, seem to have difficulty in recognizing it and bearing it in mind. As might be expected, the Ravennese mosaics are superior to the Roman, alike in their state of preservation; in their originality of idea and treatment; in architectural arrangement as decorations of a building; in the technical skill of the mosaicist, and, above all, in their incomparable beauty of colour. As an almost inaccessible fortress—thanks to its morasses and lagunes—Ravenna was often and for long the safe residence of powerless Emperors, while Italy was overrun and Rome itself besieged.

The city was once a seaport, or rather possessed one. It is a stranded Venice, situated at the southern extremity of the great horse-shoe, or delta, which is formed by the Po and its tributaries from both Alps and Apennines. Venice is at the other extremity, and pretty continual labour on her system of canals is required to prevent her divorce from the Adriatic, to which she used to be solemnly wedded year by year. The conditions of her existence greatly resemble those of Ravenna, since the one is a fortress protected by the lagunes, the other a city of refuge, built on their islands. Romanesque and Byzantine art meet in both cities, though Old Greek and New Greek, Classical and Christian, work cannot be compared in either as in Rome. What was once the port in which rode the Adriatic fleet (classis) of Rome, from Augustus to Alaric, is now the pretty Maremma-looking village of St. Apollinaris in Classe; and the sea is only visible from the campanile of its church—the only campanile in Ravenna which was considered safe to ascend in July, 1871—so, at least, the writer was informed on making inquiries for a high point of view, which is generally a curious person's first care, in a flat country. The following sketches of mosaics found in this and the city churches are taken for the most part from notes made on the spot.

M. Vitet puts the distinction between Old-Roman

and Byzantine work very clearly and the same point is of course well understood and clearly brought out by Kügler, and by Messrs. Crowe and Cavalcaselle.[1] It is best, perhaps, to insert a brief description of these great historical mosaics in this place. They are represented in Ciampini's plates, which have been photographed by Mr. J. H. Parker, and form an admirable key to his parallel series of photographs from the actual state of the original mosaics. The two last ones have been broadly and skilfully restored in the sixteenth century, and appear to be very good models for mosaic work in large churches in our own time and country; combining severity of form with breadth and power of execution in large tessellation. The series is of forty Old Testament subjects, from the history of the Patriarchs down to the Exodus and the wars of Joshua. It is situated in the nave, over the arches and under the clerestory windows.

"The name of Pope Sixtus III." (432-440), says M. Vitet, "is in the mosaic at the top of the arch, and seems to apply to the whole series of pictures, not only those on the arch, but those on the side-walls also—of which twenty-seven original pictures are said to remain; some have been restored in the sixteenth century. The figures retain the antique Roman type and costume: the heads are much the same as those on the Column of Antoninus, and the toga preserves its cut and its ancient folds; but the heads are too large for the bodies. They are thick, short, and clumsy; the lines are undecided, the composition confused. Nevertheless, real art still

[1] Ch. i. vol. i "History of Early Italian Art."

appears here and there; thus, in the second picture, Abraham separating from Lot, the arrangement of the scene is not unskilful; the figures express well what they are about, and one feels that the two groups are separating. The fourth picture, Isaac blessing Jacob, has almost the same *pose* as Raffaelle has given to it in one of the compartments of the Loggia. The taking of Jericho and the battle with the Amalekites also have details which are not without a certain interest. Everything is not·lost, therefore, in works of this period: there remain some gleams of spirit and truth, some traces of the old traditions, mixed up with negligence, clumsiness, and ignorance almost incredible."[1]

As has been observed, the mosaics of Placidia's chapel in Ravenna correspond to these in date, and in their obedience to ancient traditions of art, costume, and composition. But they are so superior in colour, drawing, and workmanship, to the Roman pictures, that the somewhat severe words at the end of M. Vitet's criticism by no means apply to them. And though St. Vitale is one of Justinian's churches in the next century, its ornament certainly follows ancient Roman or Primitive tradition rather than the more severely ecclesiastical or Byzantine, representing birds and flowers with a charming naturalism. The Lamb is also repeated very frequently on capitals of columns and elsewhere, strangely conventionalized, and with muscular limbs and long neck, so as to have no slight resemblance to a small horse, for which the present writer at first mistook it.

[1] Index to Photographs, Centuries iv. and v.   Parker.

The historical mosaics in this church, and the highly important sacramental subject of Melchisedek, will be described elsewhere. The following sketch of some of the church pictures and decorations of Ravenna has been compared with and verified by Mr. Parker's valuable account of them. The leading difference in doctrinal import between these mosaics and those of Rome, seems to be that there is no instance here of either the Blessed Virgin or any created saint being made the chief person in a church, or occupying the vault or tribune of an apse, so as to take the place of the Lord as Head of the Church.

The justly celebrated church of St. Vitale is richly decorated with mosaics of the time of Justinian. On the vault of the tribune is the figure of Christ, seated on the globe, with an archangel on either side, introducing St. Vitalis, and Ecclesius, Bishop of Ravenna, 541—who carries a model of the church in his hand. He is the only figure without the nimbus. The Lamb is on a round medallion in the centre of the vault. There are four cherubim at the top of the walls of the vault, the surface of which is covered with a flowing pattern of foliage, very similar to that afterwards used in the thirteenth century. Round the edge of the arch in front of this vault are fifteen heads on round medallions—Christ and the Twelve Apostles; the two lowest heads bear the names of Gervasius and Protasius, saints of the fourth century. The apse is lighted by three windows, and on the jambs of the two side windows are the Evangelists, each with his symbol; under each of these windows is an altar in an arched recess or tribune, and over each altar the mosaics are thus arranged :—

NORTH SIDE.

St. Matthew, with Angel, desk or leggio, and basket of parchments.

St. Mark, with Lion on rock, desk, and open book in hand.

Angels supporting medallion bearing the monogram, with A ω.

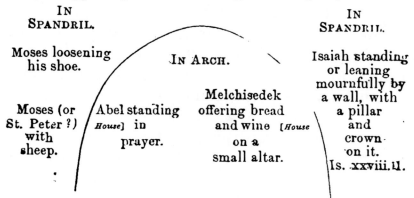

IN SPANDRIL.

IN SPANDRIL.

Moses loosening his shoe.

IN ARCH.

Isaiah standing or leaning mournfully by a wall, with a pillar and crown on it.
Is. xxviii. 11.

Melchisedek offering bread and wine [House on a small altar.

Moses (or St. Peter ?) with sheep.

Abel standing [House] in prayer.

'SOUTH SIDE.

Similarly arranged, except that the angels with the monogram are within the arch, not above.

SPANDRILS.

St. John, with Eagle.
Jeremiah, with crown of Jerusalem on pillar.
Jer. xiii. 18.

St. Luke, with Ox.
Moses in the Mount, with the Hand of God above him.
People below (doubtful ?).

Angels.

WITHIN THE ARCH.

Abraham attending on the Three, bearing a very small calf on a dish (Gen. xviii. 7). Sarah is at the tent door. Opposite is Abraham raising the knife to slay Isaac, the hand stretched from heaven to stay him, and the ram at his feet.

This last mosaic is highly remarkable for the skilful naturalism of the tree under which the three Holy visitors are seated ; and for a decided and successful attempt at afternoon or evening effect, by introducing a strong light against which the tree-branches are relieved; and also by small clouds with their lower edges brightly illuminated.

The walls on each side of the choir contain two large historical pictures with nearly life-size figures, of the greatest interest as records of costume. Justinian is the centre of one, Theodora of the other—both are richly dressed and crowned, and both bear the nimbus. Maximianus, Bishop of Ravenna in 547, precedes Justinian. He consecrated the church, and these pictures may be a memorial of the ceremony.

The tomb of Galla Placidia is contained in a small brick chapel in the form of a Greek cross. The whole surface of its vaults and upper part of its walls are covered with mosaic, chiefly in gold patterns on dark-blue ground; the gold being of specially rich tone of colour, alike from time and its nearness to the eye; and the blue being artfully varied with black, green, and purple, so as to have a kind of imperial or Tyrian effect, which the writer never observed in any mosaics except those of Ravenna. The central dome has a blue ground with gold stars, a cross in the centre, and the emblems of the Evangelists at the four corners. On the supporting walls are eight figures of prophets, and here, too, as on so many of the Ravennese sarcophagi, appear the two birds drinking from a vase or chalice, which recur in all good Byzantine work of the more decidedly Eastern type.[1]

---

[1] See "Stones of Venice," vol. ii. plate ii. "Byzantine Sculpture," for peacocks and other birds drinking. It is possible that a recollection of these symbolisms may have occasioned the ingenious but somewhat overstrained conjecture that the antique Gentile mosaic of Pliny's Doves was a Christian emblem of the universal participation in both kinds of the Holy Sacrament. The notion is not right, but it is highly excusable. There are endless authorities for Doves as

Few monuments of ancient art equal this in pure original authenticity of structure and ornament, and accordingly it has special value, as has been remarked, as a connecting link, in its subjects and in their treatment, between the Greco-Roman work of the Christian Church and the strictly new-Greek or Byzantine, between the fresco subjects of the Catacombs and the mosaics of Roman churches. Messrs. Crowe and Cavalcaselle point this out with their accustomed vigour and clearness. It may be added to their remarks, that the Good Shepherd in Placidia's chapel strongly resembles a Catacomb painting of Orpheus in its composition.[1]

"Christian art," says Mr. Crowe, "had not yet been illustrated by so noble a representation of the Good Shepherd, as that which now adorned the monument of Galla Placidia. Youthful, classic in form and attitude, full of repose, He sat on a rock in a broken hilly landscape, lighted from a blue sky, grasping with His left hand the cross, and His right stretching aslant the frame to caress the Lamb at his sandalled feet. His limbs rested across each other on the green sward. His nimbed head, covered with curled locks, reposing on a majestic neck, and turned towards the retreating forms of the lambs, was of the finest Greek type and contour. The face was oval, the eyes spirited, the brow vast, and the features regular. The frame was beautifully proportioned, classical and flexible. The emblems of the faithful : and the drinking Doves must be a sacramental emblem, at least, when they drink from, or are placed near a chalice, as in the church of St. Apollinare Nuova, in Ravenna. See Bottari, i. p. 118, where one of the mosaics of St. Clemente is represented. twelve doves on a cross.

[1] Bottari, tav. lxx.

blue mantle, shot with gold (lights beautifully put in with gold tesserae), was admirably draped about the form. A warm sunny colour glanced over the whole figure, which was modelled in perfect relief by broad masses of golden light, of ashen half-tones, and brown-red shadows. No more beautiful figure had been created during the Christian period of the Roman decline, nor had the subject of the Good Pastor been better conceived or treated than here.

" As in the rise of the Faith the symbolic type of the Saviour must necessarily be youthful, so in its triumph it was natural that the Redeemer should have the aspect of one mature in years. In the choir of this chapel He was represented in the fulness of manhood, majestic in attitude, bearded, with an eye of menace, His flying white draperies expressing energy of movement, His diadem, the cross on the right of His shoulder and the book on His left, being emblematic of the triumph of the Gospel and the Church. Right and left of Him, a case containing the Gospels (names on the books), and a grate, in which heretical works are burning (see also Acts xix. 19), indicated the end of the Redeemer's mission. His figure was as grand, as fine in conception and execution, as that of the Good Pastor ; nor were the prophets conversing in couples, round the arches of the cupola, less worthy of admiration. The ornaments of the chapel were completed by a cross in the centre of the dome, by the symbols of the Evangelists on red clouds, relieved on a blue ground, spotted with stars ; by rich foliated ornament on blue enlivened with figures in the thickness, and by the Greek initials of the Saviour in the keys of the arches. A mysterious and sombre light trickled into the edifice through four small windows in the (flat) dome."

An effect of colours, if possible more complicated, daring, and beautiful, is found in St. Apollinare Nuova; the following account is from the writer's notes on the spot :—

"The purple and white (?) marble columns of the central aisle of the basilica support on each side a processional frieze, in mosaic, of male and female saints on the opposite sides : ended on the male side, at the eastern end, with the Lord in Glory ; a head and face of great beauty at its distance from the eye, though with something of the sadness of later and fuller art : on the female side, by an Adoration of the Magi, exactly like some in the Roman Catacombs. All the figures are white-robed, and stand on emerald-green turf, separated from each other by palms bearing scarlet dates. The palm, it may be observed, is used in Rome as in Ravenna, but the Eastern workmen seem always to insist on the fruit, which is generally omitted in Rome. The white procession are all shod with scarlet, and bear small crowns in their hands lined with the same colour. The background is of gold, not bearing a large proportion to the size of the figures ; but there are white single figures above with ample golden spaces ; giving the effect of a lighter story or loggia over a more solid wall : and a third course of singular representations of New Testament subjects runs round just below the roof, with backgrounds of alternate gold and black ; black, or the darkest purple, also prevailing in the roof, fully relieved with gold. The splendid and jewelled effect of the whole is beyond praise, and its brilliant lightness makes it especially suitable to the dark aisles of a great city."

The two Baptisteries resemble each other in the decoration of their domical-vaulted roofs—the Baptism of the Lord in the centre, and the figures of the Apostles surrounding it on the vault, separated by palms. This subject will be more conveniently dealt with in the chapter on Sacramental Symbolism. The church now named St. Maria in Cosmedin is said to have been built for the Arians by Theodoric the Great, but purified by Archbishop Agnellus in 553. It is an ancient basilica rebuilt in the twelfth century, as Mr. Parker informs us ; having the old marble columns with Byzantine capitals used again. In the Chapel of St. Bartholomew, now a vestry, at the eastern end of this church, a very curious pavement of ancient mosaic has been preserved from the old church and built into the walls. There are Scriptural and historical subjects, figures of animals, conventional palm-trees, grotesque heads, a mermaid, &c., all of the quaintest and most barbaric character. Some of the historical compartments, however, are of the greatest interest, and their highly successful attempts at character make them amusing in the extreme. One in particular appears to represent the approach of Theodoric the Great to Constantinople in 487, when the Emperor Zeno induced him to divert his invasion to Italy and Odovakar. On one side Theodoric the Great advances in a long coat of mail and pointed helmet, which remind us of the Bayeux pictures. His straight and pointed sword is uplifted, and his countenance truculent in a degree which the modern spectator can hardly help contemplating in the most comic light; but which must certainly have been anything but a joke to the CONSTANTINOPOLITANI (so inscribed in Roman letters)—bishops, who are advancing to meet him with right hands outstretched, dalmatics and mitres. Their faces express a cheerful confidence by which the Gothic King appears for the present unconvinced, if not unmoved; and it is satisfactory to be informed by history that they and their Emperor came unharmed out of the transaction.

These mosaics, however, are scarcely equal in historical and doctrinal importance to the great works in the apse and choir of St. Apollinaris in Classe. Photographs of all of them may be obtained in London, excepting, we believe, those of the St. Giovanni pavement. But the picture in the church of Classe must be compared with the great seventh-century mosaics of SS. Prassede and Pudentiana in Rome, possessing as it does the great advantage of undisputed date, about A.D. 567. The wall of the Arch of Triumph above the apse is divided threefold down to the lower corners of the spandrils. In the first, clear of the top of the arch, is a medallion of Our Lord, with the four symbols of the Evangelists, bearing their gospels. Next comes the well-known picture of the Hebrew and Gentile Church, represented by six sheep on a side issuing from the two Houses of the Old and New Dispensation, named HIERUSALEM and BETHLEEM. The corners of the spandrils are occupied by two palm-trees, skilfully inlaid from nature, as it would seem. Within the vault is a representation of the Transfiguration, not unlike that of nearly the same date at the Convent of Mount

Sinai. The Presence of God the Father is represented by the Divine Hand, the sky indicated by streaks of light. Half-length figures of Moses and Elias are on either side, and in the centre of the half vault a large Cross, jewelled and ornamented to the full power of the mosaicist, stands for the Person of the Lord. The three Disciples present at the Transfiguration are represented by three sheep of larger size, contemplating the Cross. The mystic Jordan is not given, but below the Cross round the dome are twelve more sheep among lilies and other vegetation, St. Apollinaris standing in prayer in the midst,—the whole evidently symbolizing the condition of the Church or Fold on earth.

Such are the great mosaics of Ravenna; and they give decisive evidence of what the richest and most gorgeous decoration of the Church was, to the end of the sixth century, in the protected stronghold of Italy; in a city midway as it were between the influence of the Eastern and Western Empire; unhaunted by the traditions of temporal power—untempted by the ignorant devotion of barbaric pilgrims; free as yet from the antagonism of East and West, which forced on Iconodulism in Rome, chiefly because it was condemned in Constantinople. Throughout the mosaic-works of Ravenna there is no image which could ever invite, or indeed permit, the worship of any creature in any degree. Their symbolism is as mystic and severe in its avoidance of idolatry, as it is grand and lovely in form and colour. Of all existing works of religious art, these appeal most strongly, with the solemnity of fourteen centuries, to the great instinct of colour. All that is noble, spiritual, and purify-

ing in that sixth sense of hue, which is to the eye as
music to the ear, is brought into religious service in
these temples.   No idea of them can be conveyed by
description, none has been attempted yet by painting,
and the best would be inadequate ; but few who have
seen them are likely either to forget or under-rate
them.

STATUE OF THE GOOD SHEPHERD.

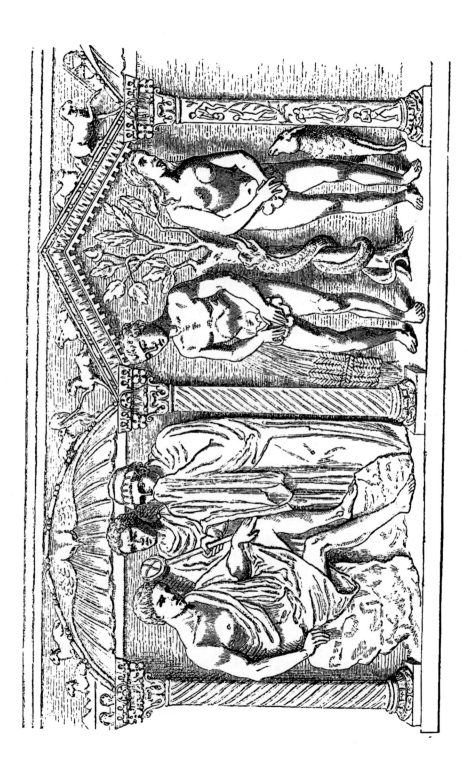

CHAPTER VI.

CHRISTIAN SCULPTURE.

THE distinction already quoted from Dean Milman [1] as a basis of tacit compromise at the end of the Iconoclastic controversy, appears to have been in some degree felt in the earlier days of the Church; that is to say, with regard to solid and separate figures or images. At the end of the long and lamentable divisions which had begun with Leo's intended reform, pictures were restored, but not images; and this gradually became a fixed and unbending rule in the Eastern Church; the statue or separate figure asserting more of a personality, and approaching nearer to the graven idol, than a picture or even a bas-relief. For, whatever the feeling of the Eastern Church may have been in later days, the eyes of early Christianity seem to have looked on a bas-relief simply as a picture in light and shade. Doubtless, also, the further difference made itself felt, that a bas-relief, representing an event or events, with groups of figures, gives no opportunity or temptation for idolatrous emotion, or adoration of any of its characters. At any rate, the bas-reliefs are almost universal in Christian art, and statues so very rare, that we may suppose that but few of them ever were

[1] "Latin Christianity," ch. ix. book xiv.

made. The Good Shepherd of the Lateran, and the now lost St. Peter, taken from Berlin by the French, and never returned or discovered, are in fact almost the only known specimens.

This abstinence may not have been maintained from any special scruple. Primitive Church-art arose, like any other healthy and natural form of art, suitably to the spiritual or domestic needs of its producers ; and as the object of all Christian sculpture was to decorate sepulchres, and all its works were intended to be seen only by faint torchlight, or perhaps by feeble gleams from the luminaria, statues were scarcely more effective than reliefs. The decaying power of the artists is certainly to be taken into consideration; but still we must suppose that the carvers of such sarcophagi as that of Junius Bassus, or Probus and Proba, were able to produce at least fairly good isolated figures, if they had been desired. The Hebrew feeling of the Early Church would be strongly moved against such works in the earliest times; and the gathering uneasiness and uncertainty about image-representation of any kind, to which Epiphanius's proceedings with the embroidered curtain bear witness, would be awakened irresistibly by a statue in solid form.

At all events, with the few following exceptions, early Christian sculpture is entirely sepulchral. An excellent small statue of the Good Shepherd is preserved in the Lateran Museum ; which can hardly be later than the early part of the fourth century.[1]

The statue of St. Hippolytus, probably of the fifth

---

[1] See wood-cut, p. 174, with reference to Martigny's Dictionary ; s. v. Pasteur. Two other statues of the same subject exist, in Rome ; one of them represented in Perret, vol. iv. pl. 4.

century, will be found in D'Agincourt.[1] The inscription on the chair is not later than the sixth century.

The statue of St. Peter, in St. Peter's at Rome, is attributed to the fifth century, and said to have been recast by Leo I. (about 440) from a bronze Jupiter in the Capitol.[2] The Berlin statuette of St. Peter is engraved by Bartoli, and Martigny gives it in a wood-cut.

The simplest form of the early Christian grave was the narrow loculus, or stone cell, like a bed-place in a cabin, cut in the cemetery-wall. This would be, for the most part, ornamented with little more than a hastily-cut inscription, the Monogram, Fish, Anchor, and Palm, or one or more of the birds in which Roman Christians, and indeed Gentiles also, seem to have taken a natural and amiable delight. But in the days of martyrdom, the custom naturally arose of celebrating the Eucharist on the graves of martyrs; and the constructive modification followed, of hollowing out a space above the loculus or actual grave, leaving a slab above the corpse. This formed the arcosolium, half-dome or apse; and the sarcophagus or massive chest of stone, originally cut in the living rock, faced with sculpture and with the arcosolium above, variously filled with ornament, is the ideal of the early Christian tomb. As has been mentioned in the case of the tombs in the Vault of Domitilla, the ornamental sarcophagus had been of old the accustomed resting-place of

[1] "Histoire de l'Art-Sculpture," pl. 3, No. 1. It is represented in Bunsen's "Life." See also Munter's "Sinnbilder," part ii. pl. 13, No. 92.
[2] Lübke " Geschichte der Plastik," ed. 2, v. 1, p. 325.

Romans of the higher orders. And the Christian custom of celebration on the altar-tomb, giving occasion, of course, for ornamenting it in every possible way, seems to have been connected in later times with an increasing tendency to Saint-worship. The martyr lay below ; his sarcophagus was carved with symbols of the faith for which he had died ; his own figure, or a memorial portrait of him, would in process of time appear in the apse above. It happens, accordingly, that we are best able to trace the progress of polytheistic tendencies in the Church by the mosaics, since that kind of ornament is peculiarly suited to vaultings. The founders, or persons specially commemorated, are presented to the Redeemer, Who occupies the centre of the apse ; as in SS. Cosmas and Damianus, St. Lawrence, and elsewhere ; and the inferiority of the minor saints is shown by their effigies being of small stature : a founder of a church bears the model of his building in his hand, as early as Pope Felix IV. in SS. Cosmas and Damianus, 526-53).[1]

It may be said, then, with certain limitations, that Christian Church-art begins at the east end of every church, with its altar and apse ; and that, like everything else in the Faith, it directs the attention to Death as the desired and hopeful end of all believers. It is no wonder that none of the sarcophagi contain melancholy emblems of death or corruption, or give any sign of the fear of dissolution. In the declining days of Rome it was, perhaps, easy for poor men to think death better than life : but there

---

[1] See, however, Chapter on Mosaics as to the date of these works, and Parker, "Antiquities of Rome."

can be no doubt, from the actual documents of their sepulchral ornaments, that the Christian had also a positive and personal hope and desire to depart and be with Christ. It is no doubt incident to a period of decay and hopelessness that good men should direct their hopes too exclusively to the spiritual world. To be active and laborious in improving the state of the living world around us, is rightly our own leading idea; for that, too, is specially enjoined by the Author of our Faith. But the far greater sufferings, and utter powerlessness, which so many men must have felt in the earlier ages, gave them far greater reason for withdrawing in thought, and sometimes altogether in the body, from intercourse with a world which they could not mend: and this, and the general expectation of the Lord's speedy return to judgment, is doubtless, as has been so often observed, the secret of the anchoritism of the second and third centuries, and the monastic or cœnobitic life which has prevailed up to the present time.

The subjects of the sarcophagi, then, continue the lessons of the Catacombs—that to die is gain, because of the gospel of Christ, Who has overcome death. A larger number of decorative subjects come before us; but they are most of them repeated with a constancy which makes them no less than a body of doctrine expressed in bas-relief. And we find the prophets and typical persons of the ancient dispensation continually referred to in connection with the Gospel. The ancient Law confirms the New, the New fulfils the Old.[1] We must once more quote St. Paulinus of Nola's rough hexameter; since it contains the

---

[1] "Lex antiqua novam firmat, veterem nova complet."

principle of all sound Church ornament from the
beginning. But it is quite clear that the pupil of
St. Ambrose expressed a principle of popular teaching which has lasted from his time [1] to ours, and
must endure while the faith has to be taught. Nine
generations of Gospel teaching had passed by his
time, and able and thoughtful men felt that they
must tread the old paths in teaching the Gospel, and
begin, as their Lord had begun, with Moses and the
Prophets. And now, that is to say from the fourth
century, there would seem, by all this decoration, to
have been a more general study of the Old Testament, almost from end to end, in the light of the
New. The Fall of Man, with the Serpent, and the
tokens of the curse of Toil on the earth, is one of
the most frequent subjects, only excelled in number
of repetitions by Daniel between the disarmed lions
and the three Children unhurt amidst the flames ·
Abraham, Noah, and Jonah are as common as in the
frescoes. But it may be better to describe, or at
least enumerate, a few of the chief relics of the kind
which are now accessible.

The earliest sarcophagus given in Bottari (the
earliest known by its consular date) is the far-famed
one of Junius Bassus, A.D. 359. It shows that the
habit of emblematic expression, which Paulinus and
others developed into a system of teaching, had made
progress since the earliest work of the Catacombs;
still adhering to Scriptural subject, with the exception of the various portraits or commemorative figures
now introduced, which indeed appear as Oranti, as
in the frescoes. Sometimes the front only of the

[1] A.D. 353—431.

sarcophagus is ornamented with figure-subjects, sometimes the front and back, in some cases the ends
also. Frequently the ends, or the ends and back
are strigillated; that is to say, covered with spiral
channels or lines cut in the stone. The stone chest
itself may be made to contain one body also, or two,
three, or even four (bisomus, &c.). When no other
ornament is given, the Monogram of Christ is seldom
omitted. Sometimes one range of figures occupies
the front or back; more often there are two,
one above another. As works of art the earlier bas-
reliefs are often of great merit in balance of compo-
sitiou, and choice of the right size and number of
subjects in a row, and of figures in a subject. The
tomb of Junius Bassus [1] displays this in a special
degree. There is uniformity enough in the subjects,
and indeed in their treatment, to make us suppose
that a traditional school of Christian art existed, retaining much of the skill of its Gentile predecessors
in sculpture, and having a well-defined body of
doctrine to enforce by means of art. We do not
observe either the crowding and imperfect composition, or the energy, the character of feature, and
indescribable originality, of the early mediæval work
of Northern Italy from the eighth to the thirteenth
century; but considerable grace of arrangement is
shown, and there is no want of fulness in, or
devotion to, the work. On the front of the sarcophagus of Junius Bassus, for example, besides ten
figure-subjects divided by beautifully-cut columns,
with varied and elaborate borders, the spandrils
between the columns and low arches of the recesses

---

[1] Bottari, tav. xv., and see wood-cut, *supra*, p. 176.

are filled with symbolic Lambs variously employed in acts of ministry or of miracle. In the great sarcophagus from the Vatican,[1] the Lambs appear at the base, below the feet of the figures, headed by one greater Lamb. The introduction of this emblem of our Lord with His Church probably synchronizes with the insistence on the Apocalyptic Lamb in the mosaics, and also with the increasing tendency to dwell on the Sacrifice of the Lord's death, by joining the Lamb to the Cross. The Rock, the Vine, the Phœnix in a highly conventionalized Palm, and two small portrait-figures, occur in this elaborate and beautiful work. The mosaics, and such bas-reliefs as these, at all events prove that Church-art died harder, as it revived earlier, than any other form of art in the Dark Ages.

The subjects of the tomb of Bassus are arranged in two rows or tiers of five, separated by columns of the height of the whole sarcophagus. Beginning at the spectator's left in the upper row, we have the interrupted sacrifice of Isaac; at a small classical altar, with the Hand of God withholding Abraham's arm, and a hornless Ram behind Abraham. Next comes a dubious subject, conjectured by Bottari, somewhat vaguely, to be either the Denial of St. Peter, or Joseph and his Brethren. Next to this is the central group, the Dispute with the Doctors; a singular figure, always said to represent Uranus or the Firmament, being placed below Our Lord's Feet. The fourth subject is again uncertain, and may represent Our Lord led before Herod. The last is certainly Pilate washing his hands. All these,

---

[1] Bottari, tav. xxxviii.

except the first, consist each of three full-length figures. The lower range begins with Job, his wife, and one of his friends; Adam and Eve and the Serpent, with the Lamb on Eve's side, probably in the emblematic sense of the Woman's portion of toil on the earth, as Adam receives the sheaf of corn.[1] In the centre is the Entry into Jerusalem, adding also Zacchæus in the sycamore, and thus combining the beginning with the end of Our Lord's last journey. Daniel follows between two lions, with two other figures; and the last may be either St. Peter led to prison, or possibly St. James, as the soldier who precedes him is drawing his sword.

This bas-relief, with that which follows in Bottari, from the tomb of Probus and Proba (A.D. 395), may be taken as representative specimens of Christian sculpture in the fourth century. The latter has saints and Apostles arranged in pairs on its front and ends, full-length figures of the whole height of the sarcophagus. Between the central pair on its front is the Lord, bearing a Cross of triumph of the Western form, and standing above the others on the Rock of the Four Rivers. Round arches cover these groups, and their shallow spandrils are filled with doves feeding from the same baskets of small loaves which occur so frequently in the Catacomb paintings. The back is partly strigillated, with two portrait-figures of wife and husband, weeping and bidding farewell.

The period of these sarcophagi is fixed exactly by their consular date. But others exist of undoubtedly greater antiquity, and one in particular

---

[1] See Index, s. vv. Adam and Eve, Corn, &c.

deserves careful notice in this place, as it is in every respect a parallel to the especially-important Vintage-Mosaics of St. Constantia.[1] It is the porphyry coffin of Constantia, daughter of Constantine and Helena, and is somewhat rudely carved with huge triumphal wreaths or scrolls : the hardness of the material must have greatly hampered the workman. With these are vines, and boys engaged in grape-gathering, and at the wine-press : three in particular are treading it at one of the ends. Peacocks are also introduced, and finally the Lamb. There is scarcely anything to be called composition in the work, but the Lamb cannot have been added to the rest of the decoration without decisively Christian meaning. This most interesting work, doubly important as a point of junction between the mosaics and the sculptures, still remains in the Hall of the Greek Cross in the Vatican, with those before-mentioned; and was the temporary resting-place of Pope Zosimus (d. 417), and afterwards occupied by Damasus II., 1048. Bottari gives another,[2] which contains the miracles of Cana, the Blind and the Issue, the Loaves and Fishes, (perhaps) Lazarus, and the curious Apocryphal subject of Daniel with the Serpent or Dragon.

There are ancient fluted sarcophagi in the church of St. Prassede ; but the new Lateran Museum contains some of the most important examples yet remaining. The largest is given by Martigny in woodcut, and described by Dr. Northcote. It is assigned to the fourth century, and contains two rows of closely-arranged figures, beginning with (as it ap

---

[1] Bottari, tav. cxxxii.　　　[2] See tav. xix.

pears) the Holy Trinity engaged in the Creation of Eve (the human pair, of minute proportions); then the Fall, and the delivery of the Corn-ears and the Lamb to the First Parents ; next the Miracles of Mercy, which complete the upper range of carvings. Below are the Adoration of the Magi, the Cure of the Blind, Daniel with the lions and Habbacuc, the Denial of St. Peter foretold and accomplished, and (as Martigny says) Moses striking the Rock. This most important work of Christian sculpture was found among the foundations of the ciborium of the altar of the church of St. Paul-without-the-walls. Another in the same Museum, one of the oldest known examples, was found before the gate of St. Sebastiano, and represents grape and olive gathering. There is a photograph of it in the Art Library at South Kensington, A third of great antiquity is represented in Aringhi[1] and Bottari,[2] and will be distinguished at once by the clever composition of the double Whale of Jonah, by its quaint natural history of snails, cranes, fishes, and lizards— by its angler and Good Shepherd. Dr. Labus, as Martigny informs us, thinks so highly of the composition of this relief, that he cannot place it later than the end of the third, or first years of the fourth century. The ingenuity of the doubled and reversed dragon-monster, which receives Jonah to the left and returns him to the right, is certainly very great, and seems to have a dash of the comic grotesque. The angler of course represents St. Peter, and all fishers for souls. Many will remember how constantly that pursuit is represented in ordinary

[1] II. 620.　　　　[2] Vol. I. tav. xlii.

Roman wall-frescoes.[1]   It is only one instance of
the easy-gliding adaptations, by which common
objects of life and their symbols were invested with
Christian meaning, mainly on Scriptural authority.
If our Lord told Peter he should become a Fisher
of men, this way of adopting Gentile ornament is
as strictly Christian as the use of human grammar
and rhetoric, or of Gentile paint, brushes, or chisels,
for the operations of fresco and sculpture.

A fourth or fifth century relief in this Museum is
very rare and remarkable, as containing undoubted
subjects from the Passion of our Lord.   In one group
He is before Pilate bearing the Cross ; in another He
is crowned—but with something like *flowers*.   This
is of great interest, and in particular to the author of
these pages, who thinks it possible that the same
idea may have struck the workman which he remembers to have occurred to him in many walks
about Jerusalem ; that the Crowning with Thorns
was not an additional torture, but only a wreath
made in mockery from the wild hyssop which springs
from the ruined walls of Solomon at this day, and
may have grown there as freely, except among
Herod's restorations, on the central dav of the
History of the world.

A celebrated group, Elijah in the Chariot, almost
certainly copied from a relief of Helios, is in this
Museum.[2]   And this, with a sarcophagus in the Capi
toline Museum, and the marble bas-relief in the
Apollinare College of the Good Shepherd, bearing
the pedum or crook in his left hand, from the Cata-

---

[1] See Parker, s. v. " Fisherman " in Index of Subjects.
[2] See Aringhi, vol. ii. pp. 305, 309.

comb of St. Agnes, must complete our slight account of the remains of early Church sculpture in Rome. A classic portrait-figure of the youthful Christ occurs on an ancient tomb in Perugia.[1] The usual subjects occur upon works at Fermo, Ancona, Florence, and Pisa; and the less common one of the Deliverance of St. Peter at the first-named place.

As the Catholic stronghold of the falling Empire, with no history of persecution and concealment, Ravenna may be expected to equal or excel Rome in the beauty of her mosaics; as is indeed the case. But it is by no means so with sarcophagi and sepulchral relics. The five marble tombs of the fifth century, in Galla Placidia's chapel, include her own and those of Honorius, her half-brother (d. 423 at Ravenna), and Constantius III. (d. 421). Her own is of the date of the building, about 450. It is without sculpture; but the holes which remain prove that it was covered with golden or other metallic imagery. The subjects on the other tombs are, as usual, the Lamb of God; the two doves resting on the Cross; the drinking doves; palms; and the Lamb on the Rock of Four Rivers. The Monogram and Cross, with lambs and peacocks, are on the alabaster altar. The Magi adorn the Exarch Isaac's tomb in St. Vitale; and St. Apollinaris in Classe, besides other works, possesses a bas-relief of the youthful Redeemer between St. Paul (with the Volumes of the Gospel) and St. Peter with Cross and Key. On one of these sarcophagi there is a singular combination of acanthus and vine.

The Christian sepulchral remains in France are

[1] Rumohr, Ital. Forsch., vol. i. p. 168.

very numerous and important—especially, of course, in the South. One sarcophagus of the fourth or fifth century, now to be seen in the Louvre, was brought from the Villa Borghese. It has a bearded figure of Our Lord on the Rock of Four Rivers, bearing the volumen or roll of the Gospel. Elijah is at one end, leaving his mantle for Elisha; the four Evangelists are at the other.

An excellent sketch of the sculpture of Southern Gaul will be found in Martigny.[1] A few examples occur, he says, more frequently in Southern France than in Italy—as the History of Susanna, and one or two subjects from the Passion of our Lord. This may be specially commemorative of, or allusive to, Arian persecutions; at all events, there is reason to believe that Susanna is the emblem of the persecuted Church.[2] The Passion carvings seem of later date, probably not earlier than the sixth century. They do not go farther than the representation of Our Lord before Pilate. The Betrayal by Judas is on a great sarcophagus in the Museum at Arles. Adam and Eve, Cain and Abel, the Miracles of Cana, the Loaves, and Bartimæus, Job, Jonah, Susanna and the Elders, Moses, Abraham, and Daniel are also represented. Aix contains a sarcophagus with carvings of Israel leaving Egypt, the overthrow of Pharaoh, Moses and the Rock, and the Quails. In the crypt of St. Maximin there are carvings of these usual subjects, with St. Peter raising Tabitha, and the rare one of the Massacre

[1] His chief book of reference for this part of the [service is Millin's " Voyage dans les Départements du Midi."
[2] See s. v. in Index.

of the Innocents. At Avignon, the still more un-common Delivery of the Keys to St. Peter occurs on an early tomb ; and the Marseilles Museum contains a sarcophagus ornamented with figures of Apostles, with serpents and doves, and with stags drinking at the waters of the Rock.[1]

There is a tomb of the fourth or fifth century with the usual Old and New Testament subjects as types and antitypes, at Toledo ; and one nearly similar at Astorga, in the Cathedral. Others are scattered over Spain—as at Barcelona, Zaragoza, and probably elsewhere.

It would be a subject of great interest for the student of modern or mediæval history to trace the development of later tombs, in Venice and Florence in particular, from the typical or original sepulchres of the Catacombs. This has been partly done, in a rapid and masterly sketch by Professor Ruskin.[2]

[1] Millin, Atlas, pl. 584.
[2] "Stones of Venice," vol. iii. See also Aratra Pentelici, p. 76, sec. 80.

THE LATERAN CROSS

CHAPTER VII.

THE CROSS.

In giving such an account of the chief of all Christian symbols as shall amount to an endeavour to trace it with certainty from its earliest use in the Christian Church, we have nothing to do with the earlier uses of the decussated figure, or of various symbols, which are more or less reasonably supposed to have represented the Cross, or to have been mysteriously connected with it, before the æra of the Lord's Visible Presence on earth. The subject possesses considerable interest, of a somewhat vague character. There can be no doubt that the Egyptian, or Tau-Cross, without the upper limb, is a pre-Christian emblem; and as such, connected with pre-Christian meanings. We ourselves have to do with the Cross as the Symbol of God's having become Man for man, submitting finally to death as Man. The earlier meanings, either of the Tau or the decussated or intersecting symbol, may be arranged, perhaps, in two classes, as far as we are concerned, and so dismissed. They will be: 1. Such interpretations of speculative minds in all ages as connect the Tau-Cross with Egyptian nature-worship, through the Crux Ansata: which will probably include all the Ophite and Gnostic uses of the symbol, and account for its connection with the Serpent, as a sign of strength, wisdom, &c. 2. Interpretations of Hebrew origin, or coming to us through the Old Testament; found therein in typical senses, and thus connected with the Christian Faith ; as the wood borne by Isaac, and the Tau or Cross on which the Brazen Serpent was suspended. Our Lord's own allusion to this event justifies a remark, made we believe by Didron, that the Tau is the anticipatory Cross of the Old Testament.[1]

We have to do with the Christian Cross. And the first question which arises as to its decorative use, as a symbol to be painted, carven, engraved, inlaid— to be set up in public or worn on the person, as a subject of constant contemplation—is : In what sense does it belong to that cycle of Scriptural symbol and history, to whose limits we wish that Church Scriptural art may ultimately confine itself ? Was it used originally as a Sign of the Lord's Death, or simply of His Person and Human Life on Earth ? or did it from the first convey both these meanings? The answer to these questions must, of course, depend on what we know of the earliest uses of the Cross; and though it may doubtless have been commonly employed in private life as a sign of fellowship, made by gesture or motion, or expressly named among brethren, its official, public, or avowed use seems to begin with Constantine, however familiar it may have been to Christian thought before. In the Catacombs and their inscriptions, and in all the earliest

---

[1] Much interesting and erudite speculation on the pre-Christian cross, or decussated figure, will be found in the text and references of an article in the *Edinburgh Review* of April 1870.

records, it is constantly used in combination with the Monogram of Christ, and can hardly be said to have a separate existence from that. This seems to point to the double meaning in the use of the symbol from the earliest times. As derived from or joined with the Monogram, which is certainly one of the earliest of Christian symbols, especially in its first or decussated form, ☧, the Cross, denotes the name and person of Jesus Christ simply. As used with the somewhat later or transverse Monogram, ⳨, or when separated from the Monogram and used by itself, it directs special attention to the sacrifice and death of the Lord, and, as it were, avows and glories in the manner of His death. "The triumph of Christianity," says Martigny, "was announced on this ensign more openly, by means of the Monogram, as expressive of the name of Christ, than by the idea of the Cross."[1] This use of it as the symbol of His Person is certainly of the greatest antiquity,[2] though it may have been in some measure discredited by the quasi-personification of the symbol in later days, after the publication of the Legends of the Cross; when churches were dedicated to it as St. Cross, and it became an object of prayer. This has to do with the distinct subject of the Sign of the Cross. What may be the date of the earliest concealed Crosses, worn on rings or seals, is impossible to say; more particularly as the Cross first appears in combination with the

[1] "Le triomphe de la Christianisme s'affichait bien plus ouvertement sur cet insigne (the Labarum) au moyen du Monogramme, comme exprimant le Nom du Christ, que par l'idée de la Croix."
[2] See Ciampini, "Vet. Mon." t. ii. pp. 81, 2. tab. xxiv. and c. viii. tab. xvii. D.

Monogram. But there certainly were Christian adaptations of pre-Christian Crosses at a very early date. The annexed forms are called by Martigny "disguised Crosses," or ancient symbols adopted by Christians, as sufficiently like the Cross or Tree of punishment to convey to their minds the associations of the Lord's Sufferings, without proclaiming it in a manner which would shock heathen prejudice unnecessarily.

Constantine appears to have felt that a time was come when his authority could enforce a different feeling with regard to the death of the Lord for men. It must have been more fully understood, after the Council of Nice, that the perfection of His Humanity involved human submission to death; and after crucifixion had ceased to exist as a disgraceful punishment, it was at once sanctified as the manner of the completion of the Sacrifice of the Humanity. Constantine, at all events, seems to have set the example of public as well as private use of the Cross. He impressed it on the arms of his soldiers, and erected large Crosses on the Hippodrome and elsewhere in Constantinople. The form of his standard or Labarum is well known.[1] "It was a long lance, plated with gold, and having a transverse piece like the Cross. Above this, at the end of the lance, and pendent from it, was fixed a crown of gold and jewels. In the centre of the crown was the sign of the Saving Name, that is to say, a monogram designating this sacred name by its two first letters, combined as above, the P in the centre of the X. The Emperor assumed the habit

[1] Eusebius, Vita Const. L i. p. 39.

of wearing these same letters on the front of his helmet from that time ; and on the transverse piece of the Labarum, which was obliquely crossed by the lance, a kind of veil was hung, a purple web enriched with precious stones, arranged in artistic patterns and dazzling the eye with their splendour, and with magnificent gold embroidery. This veil was as long as it was broad, and had at its upper end, in golden threads, the bust of the Emperor, beloved of God, and those of his children. The Emperor always made use of this preserving standard as a protecting sign of Divine power against his enemies, and he had ensigns of the same kind borne in all his armies." [1]

Eusebius also refers [2] to the triumphal Cross made and set above the Dragon by Constantine [3] Whatever degree of Christian knowledge, or of purity of religious motive, may be allowed to the Christian Emperor, it seems to have required at least a sincere belief in Christ, founded on just ideas of His mission and nature, to induce the Roman lord

---

[1] Prudentius describes the Labarum thus, Contra Symmach. 1 :

    " Christus purpureum, gemmanti textus in auro,
      Signabat labarum : clypeorum insignia Christus
      Scripserat : ardebat summis crux addita cristis."

Medals, generally speaking, place the Monogram on the veil, sometimes with the words of Constantine's supposed vision, Ἐν τούτῳ νίκα ; the Monogram took the place, on the banner-spear, of the dragon or serpent, which had become an usual ornament of the Roman ensigns, having been adopted from Greek or rather Syrian standards. Hence Draconarius was the title of a standard-bearer; "vexillifer, qui fert vexillum ubi est draco depictus" (Du Cange, ad verbum). The term passed into Christian usage, and was applied to the bearer of the Labarum in battle, and also to Cross-bearers in Church-processions. The Italian gonfalon, gonfaloniere, &c., are said to be derived from the custom of bearing the Labarum.

[2] Vit. C. iii. 3.

[3] See also Bingham, Antiq. s. v. Crucifix.

of the world with one hand to suppress the punishment of the Cross, owning its infamy; and with the
other to adopt the symbol of Christ's death, and as
far as he could, to share the infamy of the Cross.
His mind was probably encumbered with the wrecks
of Pagan mythology and unsatisfying philosophies.
It seems hardly to follow that he meant to adore the
Sun because it appears on his coins with the title of
Invictus; and his refusing to persecute the Pagans
of his time seems to be the principal reason for his
being claimed by their successors in our own day.
In any case, it seems to have been the idea of a
believer, as well as of a successful soldier, to make
a despised and dreaded symbol the token of union
for his vast empire.

The words of Tertullian may suffice to show the
general use of the Cross in private, in his time.[1]
" Wherever we go, or whatever we attempt, in all
coming in or going out, at putting on our shoes, at
the baths, at table, at candle-lighting, at bed-time,
in sitting down to rest; whatever converse we are
employed in, we impress our foreheads with the sign
of the Cross." This is paralleled by the words of
St. Chrysostom : " The cross is found everywhere
with rulers and people, with women and men; in
the camp and in private chambers, on silver plate
and in wall-paintings."[2] The Pagan feeling against
the Cross after Constantine's time is shown by

---

[1] " Ad omnem progressum atque promotum ; ad omnem aditum
atque exitum ; ad calceatum, ad lavacra, ad mensas, ad lumina, ad
cubilia, ad sedilia—quæcunque nos conversatio exerceat, frontem
crucis signaculo terimus." (De Cor. Mil. c. iii.)

[2] πανταχοῦ εὑρίσκεσθαι (τ. σταυρὸν) παρὰ ἄρχουσι, παρὰ ἀρχομένοις,
παρὰ γυναιξί, παρὰ ἄνδρασι . . . . ἐν ὅπλοις καὶ ἐν παστάσιν, ἐν
σκεύεσιν ἀργυροῖς, ἐν τοίχων γραφαῖς.

Julian reproaching the Christians for making gestures in the air of the sign of the Cross on their foreheads—σκιαγραφοῦντες ἐν τῷ μετώπῳ—and by the accusation of worshipping it as a fetiche. See the words of the Pagan Cæcilius: "They also tell us wondrous tales of a man who suffered capital punishment for his crimes, and (that they adore) the doleful tree of his Cross with solemn rites—a tree befitting such wretches and villains . so that they worship that which they deserve."[1] He is answered simply :·" We neither worship nor desire the Cross."[2] This is referred to also by Molanus,[3] which, with many other passages, is enough to show that Constantine, in accepting the Cross as his symbol and personal cognizance, was assuming a despised and unpopular emblem to which he need not have given prominence, and which he would hardly have felt compelled to retain, but by understanding the importance of the Death of the Lord in Whom he imperfectly believed. He avowed to the Pagans, and therefore more vigorously enforced on Christendom, the sacrificial act of death for man. The office of Christ, marked by the Cross, was now distinguished from His Person, marked by the Monogram. And though the further advance from the purely symbolic cross which indicates the Lord's Death, to the Crucifixion-picture which attempted to represent it, and still further to the portrait Crucifix, may have taken nearly 300 years, as it did, that advance seems highly

[1] "Et qui hominem summo supplicio pro facinore punitum, et crucis ligna feralia corum cæremoniis fabulantur, congruentia perditis sceleratisque . . . ut id colant quod merentur." (Minucius Felix Octav. cc. ix. and xxix.)
[2] "Crucem nec colimus nec optamus."   [3] "De Picturis," c. v.

natural. With whatever reverence the Lord's corporeal sufferings may have been veiled in symbolism —though reticence and distant contemplation of that awful subject may have been as desirable then as it is now—the progress of large sections of the Church to actual representation of Him in the act of death seems to have been logically and practically certain, from the time when His execution as a malefactor was avowed and proclaimed to the heathen. The transition from the symbol to the representation will be traced out, in the several steps of which we have evidence, when we come to speak of the Crucifix. What is principally to be said here is, that as the words Cross and Crucifix are in great measure confounded in their popular use in most European languages, the following distinction may be taken between them, generally speaking ; — that a Cross with any symbol or other representation of a Victim attached to it or placed on it, passes into the crucificial or sacrificial category.

The usual threefold division of the form of the Cross into the Crux Decussata, or St. Andrew's Cross ; the Crux Commissa, Tau, Egyptian or patibulary, Cross; and the Immissa, or upright four-armed Cross (Greek or Latin), seems most convenient. It is probable that the distinction between the Greek or Latin, Eastern or Western symbol, belongs to the time succeeding the Iconoclastic controversy. The Latin Cross, as all know, has the upright of greater length than the transverse limb : the Greek is equal in all four limbs. The Latin mind continued to insist specially on the Cross as the actual instrument of the Lord's Death, and carefully selected that particular form of it on which in all probability He suffered. The symbol of intersecting bars was enough for the Greek, who stood at more reverent and mystic distance from the manner and details of the Event, and viewed the Cross as a symbol of Redemption, or of the Person of the Lord in full Humanity. Perhaps the chief examples of this wide, and in fact truly Catholic meaning are to be found in the sixth and seventh centuries. At that time, speaking generally, the symbolism of the Cross seems to have been nearly as follows:—The Cross itself represented the Second Person of the Trinity in His Divinity and Humanity, as God made Flesh, even to the death appointed for all flesh, for the salvation of all men. We find it accordingly, as in some examples given below, ornamented to the utmost power of the mosaicist or painter; and if it occur in sculpture, it begins to be varied in form, or is borne in triumph by the Lord Himself, or an Apostle, affording the earliest examples of what is called the Triumphal Cross, the Sign of His accomplished work, which is often placed in the hand of figures of Christ at the present day. It seems to have been to every believer the sign of the whole New Covenant, and of his own personal share in it. It had also been associated (as will be seen almost immediately) with Baptism since the time of Constantine, so that the leading idea of Death, with which it was still connected, was that of Christian baptism into Christ's death. Consequently, though now long separated from the Monogram, and confessed as the penal Cross, it only developed the idea of the Monogram; and was expressive of the Lord's Work, as that

K 3

expressed His Name. Meanwhile pictures of the Crucifixion, and Crosses bearing the Apocalyptic Lamb, were coming into use, and formed another class of symbols with further import, leading to developments of meditation, if not of doctrine, on the Manner and Nature of the Death of the Sacrifice for Man. Still the Cross itself meant that and more ; for it stood for Christ and all His work. The best example of this is the great mosaic of St. Apollinaris in Classe, near Ravenna, A.D. 545, so often referred to in these pages. Its subject is the Transfiguration, and photographs of it are to be had in this country ; but it is sufficiently represented in Ciampini's " Vetera Monumenta." It covers the vault of an apse, and is described in the chapter on Mosaics. Its Cross is of the Western form, lightly widened (pattée) at the extremities, and so tending towards what is called the Maltese form. It is ornamented in colour as brilliantly as possible, and at its intersection appears (for perhaps the first time) a Face of our Lord. It is scarcely discernible in Ciampini's small engraving, but it is clearer in the photograph, and the author has personally verified it. It seems to import no more than the name or Monogram ; but it is found again on the oil-vessels of Monza.[1]

The figure of St. Apollinaris in this mosaic con neets the upper and lower divisions of the composi tion in the beautiful and time-honoured arrangement which may be observed in Orgagna's Last Judgment, in Michael Angelo's (in tripled form), and (in its frankest and most beautiful shape), in Titian's Assumption of the Virgin. The ascent of the mountain

---

[1] See Martigny, s. v. Crucifix et infra.

is indicated by trees and birds, accompanied by the sheep of the Gospel. The Holy Dove is not represented, the mosaic having reference to the Transfiguration only, as described in the three first Gospels. Above the Cross are the letters IMDUC, which Ciampini interprets as "Immolatio Domini Jesu Christi." Below it is "Salus Mundi." Didron however asserts, in "Christian Iconography,"[1] that the upper inscription is really the usual IXΘΥΣ, on the authority of M. Lacroix, who has given particular attention to the Church of St. Apollinaris in Classe. A very curious silver cross in the Duomo of Ravenna, composed of medallions, is referred to the sixth century, and called the Cross of St. Agnello. The central medallion is larger than the others, and represents Christ seated in Glory in the act of blessing. He is standing with the same gesture on the back of the same piece of metal.

In the Pontifical, or Bishop's Office-book, of Ecbert, brother of Eadbert, King of Northumbria (consecrated Archbishop of York in 732), there

---

[1] Diction. Icon. Christ. vol i. 367. Bohn. "Christ is embodied in the Cross as He is in the Lamb, or as the Holy Spirit in the Dove * * * In Christian iconography, He is actually present under the form and semblance of the Cross. The Cross is our crucified Lord in person, &c. &c." In the ninth century the praises of the Cross were sung as of a god or hero, and expressions of this kind descend into modern hymns. Hrabanus Maurus, the pupil of Alcuin and Abbot of Fulda, wrote a poem in honour of the Cross, de Laudibus Sanctæ Crucis. See his complete works, fol. Col. Agrippinæ (Cologne), 1626, vol. i. pp. 273—337. He quotes St. Jerome's comparison (Comment. in Marcum) of "species crucis forma quadrata mundi,"—embracing the four quarters of the universe ; and of the birds, who, when they fly, take the form of the Cross in mid-air—of the swimmer, of a person in prayer, of the ship with squared yards. "The letter T," he continues, "may be called the sign of the Cross and of our salvation."

is an office for the dedication of a Cross, which
makes no direct mention of any human form thereon.[1]
" We pray Thee to sanctify to Thyself this token of
the Cross, which the religious faith of thy servant
hath set up, with all devotion of his spirit as for
a trophy of Thy victory and our redemption. Here
let the splendour of the Divinity of Thy only-
begotten Son be bright in the gold ; may the glory
of His Passion shine forth from the Tree, may our
redemption from death burst forth in the Blood, and
in the brightness of the jewel-work ; may (He or It)
be the protection of His own, their certain confidence of hope ; may it confirm them (*suorum* appears
to be restricted to clergy) in the faith, along with
nobles and commons ; may it strengthen in hope, and
make fast in peace; may it increase their victories,
enlarge them with prosperity, avail them for ever in
time, and unto the life of Eternity."

This passage indicates a curiously mingled state of
thought or feeling. The Cross is a symbol of Christ
and a token of His victory : it is of material wood,
gold, jewels, &c. ; but a sacramental power seems to
be considered as adherent to the symbol ; its couse-
cration gives it personality ; and it is to be addressed
in prayer as if possessed of actual powers. For a
time this state of ideas might do but little harm, at

---

[1] (V. Surtees Society, 1853, pp. 111—113.) "Quæsumus ut
consecres Tibi hoc signum Crucis, quod tota mentis devotione
famuli tui religiosa fides construxit trophæum scilicet victoriæ
tuæ et redemptionis nostræ. Radiet hic Unigeniti Filii Tui
splendor divinitatis in auro, emicet gloria passionis in ligno, in
cruore rutilet nostræ mortis redemptio, in splendore cristalli
nostræ mortis redemptio, ut suorum protectio, spei certa fiducia,
eos simul cum gente et plebe fide confirmet, spe solidet, pace con-
societ ; augeat triumphis, amplificet secundis, proficiat eis ad
perpetuitatem temporis et ad vitam æternitatis," &c. &c.

least among the educated clergy ; but **one** cannot help seeing in it the germs, not only of idolatrous **representation** of a person, but of gross fetichism, in **supposing** virtue inherent in the wood and metal. If the Cross were once allowed to be sacred for any reason except its meaning, the worship of Christ would be obstructed, as it were, and directed to the material image. And this is tested, as in the case of different statues of the Blessed Virgin, by the fact of one statue being popularly preferred to another, as more blessed, or sacred, or powerful **for** good.

THE CROSS OF BAPTISM.

The Cross, of course, conveyed, to the earliest Christians as to ourselves, the personal lesson of sacrifice, or self-dedication to Christ, and the thought of His command to " take up the Cross." Hence doubtless its constant use in times of actual **or** remembered persecution, when the idea of Death in Christ was a terribly practical and familiar one, and when baptism into His death had a literal meaning of personal danger, and of sharing His sufferings. Accordingly we find the earliest Crosses associated with all ideas involved in the rite of Baptism. 'As the sign of the Lord's life and humanity, the Cross is connected with both the Sacraments; but the continual and exclusive contemplation of it as a sign of sacrifice, which is involved in the use of the Crucifix, tends to forgetfulness of its close connection with Baptism. This, however, is observable, in particular, in the ancient and celebrated Lateran Cross, so called; which is referred to the time of Constantine, **and** apparently accepted as of that date by Archbishop Binterim.[1] A reproduction of the frontispiece of this volume, representing the Cross in question, is given at p. 192. The original was in mosaic, and though restored by Nicolas IV., was not probably modified as to subject. It is a plain cross, with flattened and widening extremities, having a medallion of the Lord's Baptism at its intersection. The Holy Spirit, in form of a Dove with the Nimbus, hovers above; and from Him seems to proceed the baptismal fountain, which at the Cross-foot becomes the source of the Four Rivers, Gihon, Pison, Tigris, Euphrates. Between the rivers is the Holy City of God, guarded by the archangel Michael, behind whom springs up a palm-tree, on which sits the Phœnix (with the Nimbus) as a symbol of Christ. Two stags below, near the waters, represent the heathen, seeking baptism; and three sheep on each side stand, as usual, for the Hebrew and Gentile Churches. This relic should be compared with a similar one given by De Rossi,[2] where the Cross stands on a hill, and the four rivers and spring form its foot, with stags, &c., and also with the Baptism-painting in the Cemetery of St. Pontianus (eighth century), and the similar collec-tion of emblems on a seal or medallion, given by Dr. Northcote.[3] All have special reference to Bap-tism, and connect the Cross with the Baptism of the Lord, rather than with His death. In later times, Crosses were made like that of Mainz, orna-mented with elaborate metal-work, and containing

[1] "Denkwürdigkeiten," vol. iv. part i.
[2] "De Titulis Carthageniensibus."
[3] In "Roma Sotteranea."

almost the whole Biblical cycle of Old and New Testament images, type and antitype answering to each other.[1]

The familiar image of the River or Rivers of Baptism of course reminds us of the actual stream of Jordan. It is well worth the consideration of any thoughtful person of our own day, how Hebrew eyes have looked on that strange river. since the feet of the priests touched it in the days of Joshua; and then how, since the Priest and Sacrifice of Humanity entered it for Baptism, it has drawn to it the thoughts of all His followers; so as to continue to this day the symbol of Death and the new birth; even to the Puritan mind, in its peevish rejection of all the historical Past of the human Church and the human race. Overwork and idleness, mutiny and oppression, vice and monotony, and the unspeakable and unavoidable dulness of their lives and thoughts, have not taken away entirely, either from the British artizan and ploughman, or the transatlantic negro, some glimmering of strange hope in the name of the mystic Jordan. It represents to them the greatness of Death without his terrors. It is the river they yet hope to pass in the Spirit, when they shall be gone forth to the presence of Christ, from the dull and terrible world in which they have to look for Him unseeing. In their imaginations Jordan is the boundary stream between penal labour and the rest of reward,—between the promised land and the outer Edom. Associations of this sort have at all times directed the thoughts of Christians in all places towards that separated and

---

[1] See account below of the Station-Cross of Mainz.

unknown river, so far away from and so unlike any
other stream : not charged, like any other stream, to
fulfil the common wants of man and bless him with
ordinary blessings, but having its source and its
outflow, and all the line of its tortuous and violent
wanderings in desert places where no man dwells.
It may be said with but little exception, that no
permanent habitation of man ever stood beside
Jordan, no home except the tent of the shepherd
and the robber; that scarcely any boat ever floated
on its waters; that none except wild men who have
never seen the world, or hermits who have quitted
it for ever, or travellers and pilgrims for a season,
ever drank of them or bathed in them. Yet to this
day it is the special Water of solemn Baptism; and
the whole Greek Church desires immersion in its
waters, without which pilgrimage to Jerusalem is
incomplete. The traveller observes the curious
analogies of its appearance, which remind him of
the life and death of man; how it flows through
desert lands and falls into a desolate sea, ending to
all appearance all in vain and in bitterness, as life
so often does. He notices that feature which the
ancient illuminators dwell on with special energy
of drawing, the strange tortuousness of its course ;
and in particular, how the many turns of its whirling
and vehement stream appear from time to time sud-
denly at his horse's feet, like the coils of a snake
gliding through cover, so that the River of death
opens before him as a pitfall; how the cliffs of its
steep banks allow no passage or landing for the
strongest swimmer. Thus it always has impressed
those who have seen it: it is one of the most

striking and important natural objects in the world, because, perhaps more than all other objects, it bears witness to the visible Presence of God of old, and to His interference in the world. It is like no other river; no other place or thing is to this day in the same sense and degree a Sign to men.

The use of the ribbon-like stream of Jordan in the ancient mosaics has been fully described in the chapter on that subject, as the death-stream separating the Church militant from the Church Triumphant. In these, too, the Cross represents the person of our Lord; as in the great picture of the church of St. Puden tiana at Rome. Another baptismal Cross worthy of special notice is that of the catacomb of St. Pontianus, where it is found as one of the chief ornaments of a regular baptistery, with the A and ω hung from its arms, and flower-work on each side. Near it is a Baptism of the Lord in Jordan, which appears to have been restored in the eighth century, but, to judge by the photograph, gives signs of a more ancient and able picture below.

It is now an unanswerable question whether the Christians of the primitive or martyr ages made use of the Cross in private; that is to say, on rings or gems, or by wearing actual Crosses for ornaments. Martigny refers to Perret[1] for certain stones apparently belonging to rings, on which the Cross is engraved, and which appear to be of date prior to Constantine. At that time, perhaps, the principal distinction between the Cross and the complete Monogram, was that the Cross was felt to remind the believer of the prospect of suffering for

---

[1] "Catacombes de Rome," iv. pl. xvi. 74.

Him Whose name the Monogram expressed. The
Tau-Cross is combined with the Monogram, in an
engraved stone of the earliest epoch, given by Didron.[1]
The serpent is coiled round the cross foot, the
A and ω are on each side above, and two doves
below with the word SALVS. The general use of
the Cross in all times of public and private suffering
is well described by Tertullian (above) and by St.
Paulinus of Nola, who placed the following inscription under a cross at the entrance of the church
of St. Felix :—" Behold how the crowned Cross stands
above the vestibule of the house of Christ the Lord,
promising high wage for hard toil. Take thou the
Cross, who wouldest fain bear the Crown."[2]

Perhaps the most interesting small Cross for personal wearing now in existence is the pectoral or
ἐγκόλπιον in gold and niello, last described by M. St.
Laurent.[3] It is said to contain a fragment of the wood
of the true Cross, and bears on its front EMANOYHΛ
NOBISCVM DEVS; on the back, " Crux est vita
mihi; mors, inimice tibi ;" in the same characters.
It must date from near the time of the Empress
Helena, when many like Crosses began to be worn.

There is a passage from Severus Sanctus Endel
echius or Entelechius, a Christian poet,[4] probably of

[1] " Iconographie Chrétienne," vol. i. p. 396.

[2] " Cerne coronatam Domini super atria Christi
　　Stare crucem, duro spondentem celsa labore
　　Præmia.　Tolle crucem, qui vis auferre coronam."

' - (See Binterim, vol. iv. part i. and Molanus De Imaginibus, s. v.
De Picturis.)
[3] Didron's " Annales Archéologiques," vol. xxvi. p. 7.
[4] Severus Sanctus Endelechius.　Poema de Mortibus Boum, an
eclogue in choriambic metre.　Gottingen, 8vo. The editor appears
to consider the authenticity of the poem and the personality of its

Aquitaine, in the latter part of the fourth century, where a Christian shepherd has secured his flock from disease, by planting or marking between their horns or on their foreheads (signum mediis frontibus additum) the Cross of "the God whom men worship in the great cities." "The sign which they tell us is that of the Cross of the One God Who is worshipped in the great cities, Christ, the glory of Eternal Deity."[1]

This is interesting in more than one particular, as it confirms, accidentally to all appearance, what we know of the prevalence of the faith in the cities of the empire rather than in the country, so that *Paganus* came to mean an untaught believer in the old gods; and also, supposing the works of Entelechius to be genuine, the passage illustrates the tendency of the first disciples to seek for a sign, or expect miraculous tokens of God's presence with them; and further, that lingering heathen propensity to call for special interference in everyday matters, which arose from the ancient belief in the local deity of Nymphs, Sylvans, Penates, and the like, and which re-appeared in after-time in the universal appeal to patron-saints.

Count Melchior de Vogué[2] gives a highly interesting account of the ruins, or rather the scarcely injured remains, of four ancient Christian towns, on the left bank of the Orontes, between Antioch and Aleppo. They contain many ancient crosses, and were pro-

author sufficiently well ascertained. St. Paulinus of Nola mentions him (Ep. ix. or xxviii. Ad Sulp. Severum) as "benedictum, *i.e.* Christianum virum, amicum meum Entelechium."

"Signum, quod perhibent esse crucis Dei
Magnis qui colitur solus in urbibus
Christus, perpetui gloria numinis," &c.

[2] "Revue Archéologique," vol. vii. p. 201.

bably deserted at the same time, on the first Mussulman invasion. "We are transferred," he says, "to the centre of a Christian society: it is no more the hidden life of the Catacombs, nor an existence of humiliation and fear, yet in its infancy: the tone of these sculptures is that of a period not far removed from the triumph of the Church. . . The 'graffito' of an obscure painter, who, in decorating a tomb, has traced on the inner surface of the rock, Monograms of Christ, to try his brush and in the enthusiasm of a Christian freeman writes, altering the motto of the Labarum, 'This conquers.'"

We have already glanced at the feeling of subdued triumph with which the Cross was regarded in the earliest times, as a symbol, first of the Lord's life and death, and then of man's life and death, of hope in Him. It is evidenced by the constant addition of flowers and leaves to the emblem. As late as the oil vessels preserved at Monza, it is represented as a twining and budding tree; and the cross of the baptistery of St. Pontianus, which is probably at no great distance of time from them, breaks out in golden or silver flowers half way up its stem.

It is very difficult to assign a date for the public display of the Cross, out of Constantinople; at least for the time when its display became an ordinary

---

[1] "On est transporté au milieu de la société Chrétienne, non plus la vie cachée des catacombes, ni l'existence humiliée, timide, *infante*; mais une vie large, opulente, artistique..... Des croix, des monogrammes du Christ sont sculptés en relief sur le plupart des portes; le ton de ces inscriptions indique une époque voisine du triomphe de l'Église. . . . Le *graffito* d'un peintre obscur, qui décorant un tombeau, a, pour essayer son pinceau, tracé sur le paroi du rocher des monogrammes du Christ, et dans son enthousiasme de Chrétien émancipé écrit, en paraphrasant le labarum, τοῦτο νικᾶ, Ceci triomphe."

matter. Boldetti gives an instance of a Tau-Cross, dating A.D. 370, according to the Consuls; but this is after the earlier sarcophagi. This question cannot be decided in the Catacombs, from the unfortunate removal of the sarcophagi for arbitrary arrangement in museums, and from the fact that pilgrims of all ages and nations, have habitually inscribed Crosses on the walls of the subterranean cemeteries. The Tau appears in the Callixtine Catacomb, in a sepulchral inscription referred to the third century, thus: IRE**T**NE. This is frequent.[1] It occurs in black marble mosaic of early date.[2] The Tau is certainly earlier than the Eastern or Western Cross, and may have been used even by Christians, in its pre-Christian sense as the emblem of the future life. In many ancient crucifixions, it is appropriated to the robbers. St. Paulinus of Nola, whose life closes the fourth and extends far into the fifth century, speaks of the Cross as displayed or set up on the ship which was to convey Nicetas, bishop of Daria, on his return voyage from Italy.[3] But from the passage it seems a little doubtful whether Paulinus may not have been thinking, with Jerome, that the squared yard of a Roman vessel under sail was a vivid representation of the Cross:—"And thou shalt go forth victorious, safe from waves and winds, in thy ship, furnished (in or on) its yard-arm with the Token of Salvation."[4]

The idea of the Cross as Anchor of the Christian

---

[1] De Rossi, Bullet. 1863, p. 35.
[2] Boldetti, lib. ii. c. iii. p. 353.
[3] See Gretzer de Cruce, c. xxiv.
[4]   " Et rate armata Titulo salutis
       Victor antennâ Crucis ibis undis
       Tutus et Austris."

soul is found very early, and carried out in numerous inscriptions, gems, &c.[1] Its earlier and freer use in Africa is spoken of by M. Laurent, who quotes De Rossi,[2] where fourth-century marbles are mentioned as bearing the Cross. That of Probus and Proba, we believe, is the only sarcophagus within that age on which the Western Cross appears.

The Monogram in its older form, with the decussated Cross, appears on the reverse of a medal bearing the name and laurelled bust of the younger Licinius, which must therefore be earlier than 323, the date of the victories near Byzantium which terminated his father's reign.[3] The Cross alone appears, probably for the first time, in the hand of a Victory on the reverse of a coin of Valentinian I :—the upright Monogram ☧ on that emperor's sceptre about 364.

Both Greek and Roman Crosses, and in particular cruciform Churches,[4] sometimes possess one or two additional cross-limbs, shorter than the main or central one. The upper additional bar is supposed by Didron to stand for the title over the head of the Crucified One. If this be so, the lower one may be taken to represent the suppedaneum, or support for His feet. In cases where the shorter limbs are both placed above the main cross-bar, as in Boldetti,[5] they certainly represent the crosses of the male

---

[1] See "Annales Archéologiques" (Didron aîné), vol. xxvi., frontispiece.

[2] " De Titulis Christianis Carthageniensibus."

[3] See Father Garrucci, Appendix to his works on gilt glasses of the Primitive age—" Numismatica Constantiniana, portante segni di Christianismo."

[4] Constantine's ancient Churches of St. Peter, St. Paolo fuori della Mura, and Sta. Maria Maggiore, were all built in the form of the Cross : in the last, the apse alone projects from the upright bar.

[5] Lib. 1. cii. p. 271.

factors. There are two coins of Valens and Anthemius[1] one of which, a *nummus œreus*, has three crosses, the other has one with two smaller cross-beams under the larger one.

The term Station-Cross is derived from the Roman military term Statio, and is applied to a large Cross on the chief altar, or in some principal place in a Church, which may be removed or carried in procession to another place, which it then constitutes a special place of prayer.[2] The distinction between the Triumphal and the Passion Cross is connected with this; the former of course symbolizing the victory gained by the sufferings which the other commemorates.

The statement of Bede[3] relating to the four kinds of wood of which the Cross of our Lord was made—the upright of cypress, the cross-piece of cedar, the head-piece of fir, and the suppedaneum of box—departs from the tradition that the smaller parts were respectively of olive and of palm. For this, Curzon[4] refers to the apocryphal Gospel of Nicodemus. It is part of the Legend of the Cross; beginning with Adam's prayer at the gates of Paradise for a branch of the tree of life in his last sickness, which was planted on his grave, and from whose wood, in the fulness of time, the Cross was made. With this, or the mediæval history of the Cross, when the sign became more to men than the event it represented, we are not now concerned.

The only remarks to be made by way of conclusion or summary of this chapter are much as follows. Whatever the various meanings of the decussated

[1] Angelo Rocca, Bibl. Vaticana, vol. ii. p. 253.
[2] See above on the subject of the Labarum.
[3] Binterim, vol. iv. i. p. 501.
[4] "Visits to Monasteries," &c., p. 163.

symbol may have been in Egypt and elsewhere, before
the Lord's coming, the cross letter **X** was the initial of
His Name or Title.   As such, it came to mean, as we
say, or recall to the Christian mind, all the thoughts
and associations which that Name can awaken—and
stood in the place of a portrait-figure, as a symbol
of the God-Man.   For a time it was, as it were, all
things to all men.   To the first members of the
Church it represented their Master, Who was all in all
to them : and in that view, a somewhat wider and
happier one than any of later days, it represented all
the Faith; the Person of Christ; His death for Man;
and the life and death of man in Christ.   The
Lateran and other Crosses point to Baptism and all
its train of Christian thought, without immediate
reference to the manner of the Lord's Death.   Constantine indeed [1] seems to have attached the symbolic
Lamb to the Baptist, and the Sacrament he adminis-
tered; as well as to the Lord's Supper and the shewing
forth of Christ's Death.   The tendency of Christian
feeling towards special or exclusive contemplation of
the Lord's suffering and death is matter of ecclesiastical history:—and its effect on Christian emotion,
and therefore on Christian art, is the transition
from the Cross into the Crucifix   That transition seems to have been a certainty, from the
substitution of the penal Cross in the Monogram ;
and from that earnest meditation on the sacrifice of
the Apocalyptic Lamb, to which the great mosaics
bear special witness.

The use of the Crucifix, or representations of the
Crucifixion, in the Early Church, is matter for a
subsequent chapter.

[1] See Anastasius, Vita Pontificum, Sylvester.

CHAPTER VIII.

EUCHARISTIC SYMBOLISM AND REPRESENTATION.

THE Cross has been connected in the last chapter, as it undoubtedly was in the earliest art of the primitive church, with the Sacrament of Baptism. Being the symbol of our Lord's Person, and of His death it stood also for our Baptism unto Death in Him. Before we enter on the history of the Crucifix, or the various crucifixion-scenes in painting or sculpture which remain from the earliest date of such works, it seems best to answer, as well as we can, the question ;—what examples are left us of attempts at representing Eucharistic rites, or the earliest Breaking of Bread, the repetition of the Lord's Supper, according to His command, and the commemorative sacrifice of His Body and Blood ? It may be repeated here, though it has been repeatedly observed before, that the key-note and connecting principle of Primitive Church Art is the interpretation of the Old Testament by the New, and the confirmation of the New by the Old. Accordingly, the promise to Adam at the fall, the sacrifice of Isaac, the deliverance of Joseph from Egypt, the Rock stricken in the Wilderness, the Brazen Serpent, the history of Jonah, and the deliverance of Daniel, with many other subjects, are again and again insisted on as directly

prophetic of the coming and the sacrifice of Jesus'
Christ of Nazareth. These pictures were indisputably
drawn among the graves of martyrs, or witnesses to
death, by other men of like creed and temper; who
were prepared to die in attestation of their belief that
these episodes of Hebrew history were meant, as God
would have it, to shadow forth the Life and Death of
His Only Begotten Son.   That is their witness to us.
We have now to consider what symbolical images or
adumbrations of the Paschal Supper are left to us. For
if anything in the ancient covenant is symbolical of
the new, it is that.   And though the Death of the
Lord closed and sealed the testimony of anticipatory
Sacrifice, it becomes, for that reason, of the greatest
interest for us to know in what form the Church took
up and obeyed His plain and unmistakeable command
to repeat the breaking of the Bread and outpouring
of the Cup in remembrance of Him.

The Agape, so frequently represented in the Catacombs, is of course the first thing in early art which
appeals to our notice on this subject. These meet-
tings undoubtedly took place in apostolic times
(1 Cor. xi. 20) and may be for the present, described
as suppers which preceded the actual Eucharistic
breaking of bread at that early date.   For it is at
least to be presumed that at solemn assemblies to
obey the Lord's commemorative injunction, the order
of His Last Supper would be followed; and that the
celebration, the breaking and pouring forth, took place
after the meal, and towards its end.[1]   The two latter
passages seem only to prove that when the Church
was assembled in private houses, the Eucharist was

[1] See St. John xii. 2. 4 ; Acts ii. 46 ; xx. 11.

celebrated in them. The real question, of course only to be answered with grave limitations, is what constituted such a congregation or assemblage of the Church as had a right to hold the Agape; supposing that it was always a prelude to the Eucharist, which in all times of Apostolic purity and discipline it must have been. No doubt the presence of an Apostle, or of the bishop, or chief person in a given church would be required. St. Ignatius's letter to the Smyrnean Church says, "It is forbidden either to baptize or to hold Agape without your bishop"[1] Doubtless, in all their churches there would be a tendency to irregular feastings of this description, chiefly from old heathen habit. For though Martigny justly calls attention to Hebrew customs of funeral festivity, and argues that the Christian assemblies were derived entirely from them, there can be no doubt of the close resemblance of Hebrew, Christian, and heathen funeral feasts alike. This is M. Raoul Rochette's view, and it is fully confirmed by Prof. Mommsen's essay.[2] It is possible that in the days of persecution this resemblance may have been welcome to the Christian congregations, as avoiding dangerous observation. And, from among the various representations we possess, there is no disputing the close resemblance between the Agapæ of the St. Domitilla catacomb, or those of St. Callixtus, and the certainly heathen or gentile banquet of the seven priests in the Gnostic catacomb.

In the earliest times the Agapæ naturally began to

---

[1] "Non licet sine episcopo, neque baptizare, neque agapen celebrare, ποιεῖν." Cap. viii.
[2] "Contemp. Review," May 1871.

be celebrated in the Catacombs, the tombs of martyrs being used as altars, having arcosolia hollowed out above them. Consequently, as might be expected, the Agape is freely represented in the catacomb of St. Domitilla, as has been said; and repeatedly in that of St. Callixtus. Nor can there be much doubt that Eucharistic celebration is implied. Yet it seems that the last repast of the Lord with the six disciples (St. John xxi. 2) was present in the mind of the designer; as well as the last paschal supper of the first Eucharist; since bread and fish are invariably placed on the table (seven or more baskets of the former). In one instance in the Callixtine, a man is in the act of blessing the bread. Again, it is probable that the Vine, so early and so often represented, was connected in Christian thought not only with St. John xv., where the Lord speaks of Himself as the True Vine, but with the Eucharistic blessing, where He speaks of the fruit of the Vine as His Blood. If, as we cannot well avoid doing, we connect the institution of the Lord's Supper with the equally mysterious language of St. John vi.—it is difficult not to connect the similitude of the Vine with both of them. In St. John vi. 5, 6, 8, He speaks of His followers eating His Flesh and drinking His Blood; in the words of consecration, He says the bread is His Flesh, and the fruit of the vine His Blood. We cannot suppose that His earliest followers failed to notice this; and if so, it follows of course, that their symbolical vines and grapes had Eucharistic meaning. But so it is, that until the sixth century and the Melchisedech picture of St. Vitale at Ravenna, all representations of the memorial banquets seem to point rather to the Agape or commemorative love-feast, than to the memorial sacrifice of bread and wine. It may have been possible that the feast of bread and fish was allowed to be eaten in more private meetings, without the presence of a bishop or a priest, for whom the sacrificial act was, of course, reserved. This would imply a separation of the Agape from the Eucharist; but there can be no doubt that such separation took place when the Agapæ were discontinued; and, in all human probability, it had taken place long before, wherever the Agapæ had become hopelessly ill-regulated and disorderly, as we shall find below they did become. Moreover, it is forcibly argued by the Rev. M. F. Sadler,[1] that a tradition existed (orally preserved, we must suppose, as a mystery of Christian mysteries) of some directing words of our Lord's, concerning the rites of the principal act of His worship. For this he relies on the annexed quotation from St. Clement of Rome,[2] and it certainly seems to prove well-known and fixed customs dating from Apostolic times, if not preserved to us in Holy Scripture. These, and their celebration, would of course be reserved to the higher orders of the Church; while there evidently was a tendency to hold love-feasts in a less regular manner. "It behoves us," says St. Clement, "to do all things in order which the Lord has commanded us to perform at stated times. He has enforced these offerings and services to be performed (τάσδε προσφορὰς καὶ λειτουργίας ἐπιτελεῖσθαι) and that not thoughtlessly or irregularly, but at the appointed hours and

---

[1] "The Church and the Age," First Series, p. 275.
[2] Ep. ad. Cor. I. xl.

times. Where, and by whom He desires these things to be done, He Himself has fixed by His own supreme will; in order that all things, being piously done according to His good pleasure, may be acceptable to Him. They, therefore, who present their offerings at the appointed times are accepted and blessed; for, inasmuch as they follow the law of the Lord, they sin not."

In Church art, at all events, it seems that a sense of mystery and awe,—a pious reticence which for the present seems to have vanished from the Christian consciousness—was strong enough, at first, to prevent representations of the Lord's act of typical Self-Sacrifice. Representation of His actual fulfilment, in Death, of that and all other types of His Death, was long delayed; even to the sixth century, in which the first Eucharistic celebration-picture is found. That is in St. Vitale, and dates from the latter years of Justinian, about A.D. 550;[1] while the earliest known crucifixion-picture is that of the Rabula, Laurentian or Medici MS., dated A.D. 587 by its writer. The increasing demand for Representation, Personification, and the sight of doctrines which Faith was failing to hold, was prevailing over the Church by that time.

The subject of the Agapæ, and the disorders to which they sometimes gave occasion, even from St. Paul's time, is admirably treated by M. Raoul Rochette.[2] These repasts may account, he thinks, for the relics of cups and platters, knife-handles and egg-shells, &c., found in Christian sepulchres.[3] He

[1] St. Vitalis was archbishop in 541.
[2] Mém. de l'Institut. Inscr. et Belles Lettres, T. xiii. p. 715.
[3] Boldetti, lib. ii. xiv. tab. 5, 59, 60.

implies, moreover, that old Etruscan custom or instinct may have made survivors bury with their dead
many objects they had used in life. The disorders are
matter of recurrent complaint, from Apostolic times
downwards. [1] " I know many," says St. Augustine,
" who hold luxurious drinking bouts over the dead ;
and setting dainty meats before corpses, bury themselves (in intoxication) above the buried, and make
their own voracity and drunkenness a matter of religious observance." [2] St. Ambrose, again, speaks of
drunken revels in the crypts, and exclaims against the
folly of men who thought drunkenness could be a part
of sacrifice. [3] That great development of church decoration by symbolical and historical painting and
mosaic which has St. Paulinus of Nola for its most
prominent institutor, was connected, as he says, [4]
with his wish to give an untaught congregation subjects of religious meditation during vigils or festivals,
when no special service was going on in church. The
picture teaching was no doubt developed in his day,
for country-people; as it undoubtedly was for the
pilgrims to Rome after the ninth century.

Be that as it may, one of the earliest representations of the Eucharistic offerings is certainly that of
the central-sixth-century mosaic of St. Vitale. On
one side of it Abel is standing with hands raised in
prayer, clad in tunic and cloak. He has just issued
from a house. It is possible that this, with the

[1] 1 Cor. xi. 20.

[2] ' Novi multos esse, qui luxuriosissime super mortuos bibunt, et
epulas cadaveribus exhibentes super sepultos se ipsos sepeliant, et
voracitates ebrietatesque suas deputent religioni." (De Moribus
Ecclesiæ, ch. xxxiv.)

[3] De Elia et Jejun. c. xxvii.

[4] Poema xxvi. al. xxxv.

streaked sky of the mosaic, may indicate a morning
or evening sacrifice. At all events, the presence of
Abel connects the other figure of the Priest-King,
Melchisedech, with the idea of the Sacrifice of the
Lamb; of the death of the sinless for sin, which is
involved in the very idea of sacrifice, and therefore
with the Death of our Lord. Melchisedech stands
before a small oblong altar-table, totally unlike the
Roman altar at which Abraham is sometimes represented.[1] On it are a chalice, and two loaves of
bread. His hands are raised in prayer, not in the
act of blessing, and he is clad in a penula worn over a
long tunic and girdle. This mosaic is obviously of
great doctrinal interest, when considered as connecting the symbolic Bread and Wine with the symbolic
Lamb, and substituting the former for the latter. It
is also an important illustration of the principal and
sustained effort of Christian ornament, to impress the
fulfilment of the Old Testament by the New as deeply
and widely as possible on the mind of the people.

The Fish so constantly introduced in the Callix
tine and other pictures of Eucharistic (or at least
memorial) repasts, must be connected in thought
with the anagrammatic use of the word $i\chi\theta\dot{v}s$ for our
Lord, as well as with His words in St. John v., or the
last repast of Gennesaret in the last chapter of that
Gospel. How thoroughly that occasion was connected with the Last Supper may be well understood
from the words of Bede *ad locum* (in Joannis xxi.)
"Piscis assus, Christus passus." A glance at the
plates of De Rossi's "Roma Sotteranea" will show how
this theme is followed out on the walls of St. Callixtus.

---

[1] Sarcophagus of Junius Bassus, Bottari, tav. xv.

A certain probability of repainting attaches to this catacomb in the minds of many antiquarians. Still, on careful inspection of Mr. Parker's best photographs, the supposed retouches themselves appear to the writer, in most cases, of great antiquity; and if, as that gentleman is inclined to think, repaintings took place in the time of St. Paulinus of Nola, the original subjects must have been faithfully repeated, and the fifth century gives, at all events, a highly respectable antiquity to these records.

Martigny argues, from what he considers a general consensus of the Fathers expressed in Bede's rhyme; and also on a quotation from St. Augustine,[1] that the Agape is to be considered identical with the Eucharist, and the bread and fish the same objects as the bread and wine; the Body and Blood of Christ in the Transubstantiative sense. This is, of course, arbitrary; but an important painting remains to be described, which has already been alluded to in these pages. Its subject is the mystic Fish bearing a basket of loaves on its back. They are not decussated or crossed, as is most frequently the case in these pictures, but bear a central mark; which connects them, as Martigny thinks, with the Eastern or Jewish offerings of cakes made from first-ripe corn, which were called mamphula, or Syrian bread. The Fish bears also another object in the basket which is supposed to represent a bottle of wine. It may probably be so, but the pictures in De Rossi and Dr. Northcote are so evidently and markedly restored as to be of doubtful authority; and a good photograph or really close drawing from

[1] Tract xii. in Joannem vi.

L 3

the original fresco is greatly to be desired. But the reference to St. Jerome, " None richer than he who bears the body of the Lord in a basket woven of twigs, and His blood in a vial of glass,"[1] corresponds in the most interesting and impressive manner with the painting. There can be no doubt that it represents the Lord offering the Bread of Life to mankind.

These paintings are in the crypt named from St. Cornelia; near it is the Agape of seven persons, with bread and fish, in seven baskets—having reference, of course, to the feast of Gennesaret, and also to the miracle of the seven loaves.[2] It should be remembered, in dwelling on this and the former emblem, that the anagrammatic Fish, though a symbol of the greatest interest and antiquity, is not a Scriptural emblem, but a grammatical accident. Our Lord never likened Himself or His Flesh to fish as to bread ; and His own use of the fish in parable makes them representative of His Church, and by no means of Himself. Nevertheless, His act of blessing and breaking the fish, on three distinct occasions, must always connect them, at least by association, with the Eucharistic banquet.

The decussated Loaves re-appear on the sarcophagus of Junius Bassus, as offered to Job by his friends. They are also carried to Daniel by Habbacuc, on the sarcophagus found near the altar of St. Paolo F. M. at Rome.[3] The Manna and the Rock are also, and more properly, connected with sacramental imagery. But it is a somewhat gratuitous

---

[1] Ep. ad Rustic. n. xx.

[2] There is, it should be remembered, an Agape of six in the catacomb of SS. Marcellinus and Peter; Bottari, tav. cxxvii. and woodcut in Martigny.

[3] See chapter on Sculpture, and Martigny's woodcut, s.v. Sarcophages.

supposition that they were originally carved with that view. So also with reliefs of the Miracle of Cana. In mediæval times, since Giotto's picture in the Arena chapel, if not earlier, it has always been held to possess an Eucharistic signification, and to have been so intended by its author; and thus it no doubt is.[1] But in the very frequent and early representations of the Miracle, it must be observed that the Saviour does not raise His hand in the act of blessing, as the artist might have been expected to make Him do, had there been any design of connecting the miracle with the Last Supper. He is not so represented on the ivory tablet of the Duomo of Ravenna,[2] nor on the beautiful silver urceolus, given in wood-cut by Martigny.[3] It is impossible to recognise any meaning in these works, as documents of a certain date, except such ideas as their authors clearly meant to convey; and there is great improbability and unreason in crediting the artists of Ravenna or Byzantium in the sixth century with knowledge of, or care for, the realist definitions of the Middle Ages. There can be no doubt that the last miracle of the Galilean lake, and its feast of bread and fish, occurring so soon after the institution of the Eucharist, must have special relation to that event. Yet it has as vivid a connection to all appearance with the first miraculous draught of fishes, and the first charge to St. Peter; both of which were repeated, as if to restore the fisher-brethren to the well-remembered days of their first faith. But to suppose it was a re-institution of the Eucharist,

[1] See Prof. Ruskin's account of that building in the Arundel Society's papers.
[2] See Bandini, De tab. eburneâ. Florence, 1746.
[3] S. V. Eucharistie, and supposed of the fourth century.

changing bread and wine into bread and fish :—to take it for granted that the Church of the second or third century took this for granted—on the strength of the Callixtine paintings of Agapæ, is altogether gratuitous.   To attribute a reserve of meaning to the paintings is something very like claiming the right of reading our own meaning into them.   By the historical enquirer, paintings, like other documents, must be held to mean what they say. To the imaginative or polemical student they may mean whatever it pleases Heaven and himself.

It is not likely that the questions which have arisen as to the authenticity of most of the Catacomb paintings will ever be absolutely decided, though they may lapse as the paintings perish.   It may still be said that these works maintain the same reverent and mysterious view of the Central Act of Worship as seems also to have been adhered to in the writings of the first ages:—the pictured love-feast serving instead of any representation of the consecration of the Elements.   As to the supposed Callixtine picture of the celebrating priest and Oranti, the actual meaning of the figures seems somewhat uncertain, as well as their genuineness.   It seems that, as far as graphic representation went, the early Church refused to set forth the celebration of her mysteries before the public eye; nor does it seem a thing to be rejoiced at that this reserve should ever have been waived.   It remains for us to trace the developments of subject in art, which give evidence of the setting of all the currents of popular attention and emotion towards the manner of Our Lord's Death and its special sufferings.

CHAPTER IX.

THE CRUCIFIX.

IT is necessary to distinguish, in treating this important feature of early if not Primitive Church decoration, first, between its symbolic and realistic treatment, secondly, between Crucifixes and Representations of the Crucifixion. It may be said to be one of the few subjects of Art in which Religion should not avail herself of the assistance of Art to the full stretch of technical power. Whatever be the value of the higher gifts of imagination, in realizing the event and its bearings, the literal working out of all its details in a picture is certainly to be avoided : and in many cases, ancient and modern, detail has not been avoided, but rather pursued as an object. The highest subjects of course call forth the greatest energies of the painter or sculptor, and therefore betray most decisively and painfully the frailties or even degradation of his mind. How many Crucifixes or Crucifixions seem to have been looked on by their producers simply as anatomical studies; how difficult it seems for the artist to avoid dwelling solely and entirely on the physical Agony of the Redeemer; how easy, and how strangely pleasant, to appeal to what are called the popular emotions by writhing limbs and streams of blood. It is not that these are modern offences in particular, for we find them from the very first, though in the earliest instances the Blood of the Lord is dwelt on, apparently, with sacramental allusion.   There may be said to be three stages of realism in the treatment of this great subject: and it might have been well, perhaps, if the Church could have rested in the earlier. The first is the combination of the Lamb with the ornamented or emblematic Cross; the second is the clothed and crowned Crucifix, symbolical of the Priesthood and Kingdom of the Sufferer, and representing the event of Christ's Death for man, and not the piercing of the body of Jesus of Nazareth.   The third stage of representation is that in which actual details are dwelt upon to appeal to emotion; and teach the beholder, too literally, to look on Him Whom he has pierced.   These classes of representation range as widely as the countless degrees of religious imagination or executive power; and in proportion as the one or the other prevails in the artist, his work is successful, in the artistic sense, or in that of religious teaching.   Either his imagination of the event will prevail over all his technical skill in execution, or it will not.   If it does, it may prevail over either a low or a high degree of skill and power. One is the case of Angelico, or Fra Bartolomeo, where belief and devotion are great, and executive power is not so great.   The other is best exemplified in the Crucifixion of Tintoret in the Scuola di San Rocca at Venice; where the subject is indeed beyond human reach, but the effort at realization is alike so colossal in power, and so pure from self-display or taint of meaner motive, as to claim the

same feeling of reverence from highly-taught, perhaps over-educated Christians, which simpler souls
may have felt harmlessly and rightly before the rude
mosaics or frescoes of earlier ages. In proportion as
self-display enters into the mind of the artist, or as
he begins to forget his subject in his work, it will
probably gain in realism, and lose in symbolic power.
His soldiers will be well disciplined and his populace outrageous, his Pharisees malevolent, and his
disciples mournful: but if he be not a Christian in
heart after all, those who look at his work will feel
that it is but a capital picture of soldiers, crowd, and
Pharisees. Where, as in Tintoret's case, a mind of
vast originality and a hand perfectly trained become
the exponents of an intense imagination, possessed
with a sense of the reality of the scene and the event,
as a fulfilment of Prophecy, or at least a culminating
point in all men's history; the result may well be,
as in his picture it is, one of the great achievements
of the world.

The distinction between the Crucifix as an instru
ment of devotion, and a picture of the Crucifixion
as a scene, is one of principle as well as convenience.
Every variety and combination of the arts of sculpture, mosaic, painting, and engraving has been
applied to this great subject from the earliest times;
and to all parts of it. But the modern Crucifix and
its use form no part of our subject. Within the
limits of our period, all representations of the crucified Form of our Lord alone—as well as pictures,
reliefs, and mosaics, in which that Form is the central
object of a scene—may be considered alike symbolical; without historical realism, or artistic appeal

to emotion. There is doubtless a divergence in the direction of realism; and appeal to feeling by actual representation is begun, whenever the human figure is added to the symbolic Cross.[1] The use of the sculptured, moulded, or enamelled crucifix or crucifixion in early times, is a development of that of the cross, and the transition between them may have been a certainty from the first; but the rude efforts of earlier days, with which alone we have to do, can neither call on the imagination by vivid presentation of the actual event, nor awaken passion by appeal to the sense of beauty, nor distress by painful details of bodily suffering. While the primitive rules of representation were adhered to, as they are to this day in the Greek Church, the picture or Icon dwells on the meaning of the event rather than on its resemblance, and shadows forth, rather than represents, the God-Man in the act of death for man. These rules were first infringed by, or naturally collapsed in the presence of, increased artistic power. The paintings of Cimabue and Giotto, and the reliefs of N. Pisano, brought the personality of the artist into every work, and introduced human motive and treatment, in the artistic sense of the words. To those whose minds

[1] De Rossi (vol. ii. tav. v. p. 355) gives a Cross, with two lambs apparently contemplating it, below one of the usual pictures of the Good Shepherd. Aringhi, "Rom. Subt." ii. 473 (see his index, s.v. Crux): "Crux, cum Christo illi fixo, neutiquam effigiari olim solebat." The Crucifixion he calls "mysticis res coloribus adumbrata. . . . emblematicis figuratisque modis; sub innocui videlicet agni juxta crucis lignum placide consistentis typo." See Bottari, tavv. xxi. xxii. See, however (ib. tav. cxcii.), the crucifix found in the tomb of St. Julius and St. Valentine in the Catacombs, which so much resembles the mosaic crucifix of John VIII. that it can hardly be of very early date. It is generally assigned to Pope Adrian, about 880.

are drawn to ascetic thought and practice, it has always been natural to meditate, and to communicate their thoughts, upon the bodily Death of the Saviour of mankind. This was done by Angelico and other painters naturally and freely before the Reformation; since that period a somewhat polemical and artificial use has been made of this line of thought; and painting and sculpture have been applied to embody it accordingly, in the Roman Catholic Church.

It may be remarked, before retiring within our proper limits of time, that the use of blood by Giotto and his followers down to Angelico, has doctrinal reference to the Holy Communion, and to Scriptural promises of cleansing by the blood of Christ.[1] Giotto is less inclined to dwell for terror's sake on the bodily suffering of the Passion, than to dwell with awe on its mystery as a sacrifice for Man. But the rise of mediæval asceticism, and its attribution of sacramental efficacy to bodily pain, carried painters along with it as well as other men. And in later times, when Christian feeling on the subject was lost, many men seem to have considered the final scene of the Redemption of Man chiefly as a good opportunity of displaying newly-acquired powers of facial expression and of a knowledge of anatomy.

If Hallam's division of periods be accepted, which makes the end of the fifth century the beginning of the Middle Ages, the public representation of the Crucifixion may be said to be a mediæval usage in

---

[1] As in the Crucifixion over the door of the convent of St. Mark's, Florence, where the blood issues from the feet, in a conventional form, as a crimson cord, which is twined strangely beneath about a skull. Ruskin, "Mod. Paint." vol. ii. p. 125.

point of time. Further, Martigny[1] claims for France the honour of having possessed the first public crucifix painting which ever existed; for which he refers to Gregory of Tours,[2] and which he says must have been at least as old as the middle of the sixth century. But he says above, probably with great correctness, that all the most eminent Crucifixes or Crucifixions known were objects of private devotion; instancing the pectoral Cross of Queen Theodolinda, and the Syriac MS. of the Medicean Library at Florence, both hereafter to be described. The official or public use of the Cross as a symbol of Redemption begins with Constantine, though of course it had been variously employed by all Christians at an earlier date.[3] Crucifixes, according to Guericke, did not appear in churches till after the seventh century. Such images, probably, in the early days of the Church, would produce too crude and painful an effect on the Christian imagination; and to that of the more hopeful Pagan they would be intolerable; not only because his mind would recoil from the thought of the punishment of the Cross, but from superstitious terror of connecting the Infelix Arbor with a Divine Being. This feeling is very frequently referred to, and is described in Dr. Liddon's Bampton Lectures,[4] in relation to the Palatine Graffito, a wood-cut of which will be found in this volume.[5] "It is the scrawl of some Pagan slave in the earliest years of the third

[1] Dict. des Antiq. Chrétiennes, p. 190, s.v.
[2] De Glor. Martyr. i. 23.
[3] See chapter on the Cross.
[4] Page 397, ed. 1868.
[5] See p. 6.

century. A human figure with an ass's head is represented as fixed to a cross, while another figure in a tunic stands on one side, in the customáry Pagan attitude of adoration ; underneath runs a rude inscription : " Alexamenos adores his God. "

This is a work of heathen malevolence : but Christian teachers may have refrained from any addition to the Cross, as a symbol of divine humiliation and suffering, from purely charitable motives. The Cross itself may have been felt to be temporarily unwelcome to persons in certain stages of conversion. If we set aside the various Monograms of His name, and the emblematic Fish, which is an anagram of it, there are but two classes of representations of Our Lord—those which point to His Divinity and lordship over all men, and those which commemorate His Humanity and sufferings for all men. The earliest of the former class is the Good Shepherd ; the earliest of the latter the Lamb ; and both are combined in the painting given by De Rossi.[1] The symbolic Lamb, as will be seen,[2] conneets the Old Testament with the New, and unites in itself all types and shadowings of Christ's sacrifice, from the death of Abel to St. John's vision of the slain victim. It is well said by Martigny to be the Crucifix of the early times of persecution, and its emblematic use grows more significant as time advances. The Cross is first borne by the Lamb on its head, in the monogrammatic form, about the latter half of the fourth century.[3] The simple Cross occurs

[1] Vol. ii. tav. v.
[2] Gen. iv. 4, xxii. 8 ; Exod. xii. 3, xxix. 38 ; ls. xvi. 1 ; 1 Pet. i. 18 ; Rev. xiii. 8.
[3] Bottari, tav. xxi. v. 1.

thus in the fifth century.[1] In the sixth century the
Lamb bears the Cross,[2] and rests sometimes on
a book, sometimes at the foot of an altar,[3] above
which is the Cross; and then it is represented " as
it were slain," with evident reference to the Pas
chal feast.[4] Towards the end of the sixth century
the Wounds of the Cross are represented on the sides
and feet of the Lamb. The Lamb is raised on a
throne, itself bearing resemblance to an altar-table.[5]
The famous Vatican Cross[6] is the sixth-century type
of symbolic representation. A medallion of the Lamb
bearing the Cross, and with a nimbus, is placed at
its central point of intersection, and it is aecom-
panied by two half-length figures of our Lord, with
the cruciform nimbus, at the top and foot of the
vertical limb. Two others at the horizontal ends
are supposed to represent Justin II. and his Empress
Sophia. The upper half-length of the Lord holds a
book in the left hand, and blesses with the right;
the lower one holds a roll and a small Cross. The
embossed lily-ornaments are of some beauty, and

[1] Bottari, tav. xxii.
[2] Aringhi, ii. lib. iv. p. 559, " Roma Subterranea."
[3] Campiani, "Vetera Monumenta," vol. i. tab. xv. p. 26; vol.
ii. tab. xv. p. 58.
[4] lbid. vol. ii. tab. xv. xlvi.
[5] Ciampini, " De Sacris Ædificiis," tab. xiii.
[6] For which, and for the Cross of Velletri, see Cardinal Borgia's
monographs, Rome, 4to, 1779 and 1780. The Cross of Velletri,
which Borgia attributes to the eighth or tenth century, contains
the symbols of the four Evangelists. The Vatican Cross is photographed in M. St.-Laurent's paper in Didron's Revue Archéologique
(vol. xxvi.). The result reflects great credit on the accuracy of
Borgia's illustration; and M. St.-Laurent speaks highly of Ciampini, as does Mr. Parker. The integrity and accuracy of the elder
Roman antiquaries is of great importance, as their works are valid
testimony on the subject of Catacomb paintings in their day.
Great destruction has since taken place.

there is an inscription on the back.[1] As it is impossible to determine which is the earliest representation of the Crucifixion or Crucifix now in existence or on trustworthy record, a few of the oldest known may be briefly described here. They will be found in woodcut in Angelo Rocca,[2] though the copies have been made by a draughtsman skilled in anatomy, who has quite deprived them of the stamp of antiquity which their originals undoubtedly possessed. The first and second are said by Rocca to be the workmanship of Nicodemus and St. Luke. The first is evidently of the time of Charlemagne. The Crucified is clothed in a long tunic, and bears a crown of radiating bars, closed at top, rising from the circlet. A chalice is at its feet, and A ω is on the title overhead. This appears to be a copy of the great Lucca Crucifix, to be described immediately. If the separate Crucifix be systematically made use of in the Church of England, we would plead earnestly for the employment of this symbolic form of it; which both represents the manner of the Lord's death as far as is desirable, and also insists on His Divinity and Office of Priest and King of all men. The head of the second of these Crucifixes, attributed to St. Luke, is crowned and surrounded by a nimbus. It is almost entirely naked,—the waist cloth, at least, seems to have been purposely contracted: this of itself would place it at a later date.

The third example is historical; it is called the Crucifix of John VII., and is or was a mosaic in the old

[1] Which Borgia reads thus :

" Ligno quo Christus humanum subdidit hostem
Dat Romae Justinus opem " (et sociat decorem ?).

[2] "Thesaurus Pontificiarum Rerum," vol. i. p. 153.

Basilica of St. Peter's. Rocca dates it 706. It bears
the cruciform nimbus with the title I.N.R.I. It is
clothed in a long tunic, the form and folds of which
are most graceful; and bears a great resemblance to the
painted Crucifix found in the Catacombs, assigned to
Pope Adrian III., 884. The fourth is the celebrated
Crucifix of Charlemagne, given to Leo III. and the
Basilica of St. Peter's, and dated 815; it is clothed in
an ample waistcloth, the wound in the side is represented, and the head surrounded by a cruciform
nimbus. Four nails are used in all these Crucifixes.

A Crucifix is described by the Rev. F. H. Tozer
which, as he thinks, has a decided claim to be considered the most ancient in existence, and which he
saw in the monastery of Xeropotami at Mount Athos.
It is a reputed gift of the Empress Pulcheria (414-453),
and has been spared, no doubt, for that reason. It
is a supposed fragment of the true Cross; and consists
of one long piece of dark wood and two cross-pieces,
one above the other, the smaller intended for the
superscription. The small figure of our Lord is of
ivory or bone. Near the foot is a representation of
the Church of the Holy Sepulchre; in gold plate, and
set with diamonds and sapphires of extraordinary
size and beauty. Below that, the inscription Κον-
σταντίνου Εὐφροσύνης καὶ τῶν τέκνων. Another
exists at Ochrida in Western Macedonia, disused
and of unknown history. Mr. Tozer considers that
it belonged to a disciple of Cyril and Methodius,
and may probably be connected with the latter. He
mentions a third, also probably connected with the
Apostles of Bohemia, in the Museum of Prague,[1]

---

[1] See Murray's Handbook of South Germany.

and another as existing in Crete.[1] These are the only Crucifixes he knows of as existing in the Greek Church. The Iconoclastic controversy, he observes, took the same course with the Crucifix as with other representations, painted or carved; and when it died away into compromise on the distinction between Icons and images, the Crucifix was treated as an image. This does not necessarily apply to pictures in MSS.; but the carved form may have been the more easily dislodged in the Iconoclastic controversy of 720, because it had not been long introduced, since it did not exist till the end of the seventh century. " To the human perception of the Greeks,[2] there may have arisen a feeling that in its more rigid and solid form the Image was nearer to the Idol. There was a tacit compromise" (after the period of Iconoclasm); "nothing appeared but painting, mosaics, engravings, on cup and chalice" (this, of course, accounts for works like the Cross of Velletri, the Diptych of Rambona, and others), "and embroidery on vestments. The renunciation of sculpture grew to a rigid passionate aversion . . . as of a Jew or Mohammedan." There can be no doubt that the first step in a progress which has frequently ended in idolatry was made in the Quinisext. Council,[3] or that in Trullo, at Constantinople in 683. It is the challenge to Iconoclasm. It decrees that, as the antitype is better than type or symbol in all representation, the literal representation of the Lord shall take the place of the symbolic Lamb on all emblems of His sacrifice, and ordains thus :—" We pronounce,

[1] See Pashley's Travels.
[2] Milman's "Latin Christianity," vi. 413.
[3] The author can remember no representation of the Crucifixion as existing either at the Convent of Mount Sinai, or that of Mar Saba.

that the Form of Him who taketh away the sin of the world, the Lamb Christ our Lord, be set up in human shape on images henceforth, instead of the Lamb formerly used."[1]

A very early Crucifix of the sixth century seems to be mentioned in the following passage (which is produced by Binterim,[2] without reference, but which he may have seen in some unpublished record). He is speaking of the church of Hoye, in the bishopric of Liége, destroyed by the Huns in the fourth century, and restored A.D. 512, at the time of the first synod of Orleans. This church "is rebuilt by its townsfolk, and extended lengthways towards the east, to the steps of the choir, under the crucifix; the ancient altar, however, being still left there."[3] Further, he quotes Ægidius as stating that Robert, Provost of Liége, was buried under the Crucifix. This only proves the existence of Crucifixes at the time of the writers, especially as the original altar is spoken of as remaining, without mention of Cross or Crucifix, at the end of the choir which contained it. Had the name or date of the author of the passage quoted been known, it would have been of great importance; but it may be, and its Latin might indicate that it is, from some late chronicler, familiar with the appearance of the church, and using the words as meaning no more than "under the present Crucifix, or rood above the altar-screen." Dr. Binterim urges no argument as to the

---

[1] Τὸν τοῦ αἴροντος τὴν ἁμαρτίαν κόσμου, 'Αμνοῦ Χριστοῦ τοῦ Θεοῦ ἡμῶν, κατὰ τὸν ἀνθρώπινον χαρακτῆρα, καὶ ἐν τοῖς εἰκόσιν ἀπὸ τοῦ νῦν, ἀντὶ τοῦ παλαιοῦ ἀμνοῦ, ἀναστηλοῦσθαι ὁρίζομεν.

[2] Denkwürdigk. iv. part i. 48.

[3] "A suis civibus re-edificatur, et in longum versus Orientem extenditur usque ad gradus Chori sub crucifixo, altari tamen antiquo semper remanente," etc.

date of the German change from Cross to Crucifix, and the passage may be let pass.

The "Santo Volto," "Vultus de Luca," or Crucifix of Lucca (corrupted by William Rufus, for imprecatory purposes, into the "Face of St. Luke"), is carved in cedar-wood, and is attributed to Nicodemus, and supposed to have been conveyed miraculously to Lucca in 782. It is said to be of the sixth century, and is certainly one of the earliest Crucifixes now remaining. It bears the Lord crowned as King, and vested in a long pontifical robe as priest, and thus combines symbolic treatment with realism, perhaps in the way afterwards intended by the Council in Trullo. The idea is that of the Crucified King of men, and the work is an assertion of the combined Deity and Humanity, and of the submission to death, of the Lord of humanity. A Crucifix greatly resembling this was found during some operations at Christ Church, Oxford, and is now preserved in the Bodleian; it was probably an outer ornament of some Evangeliarium. We understand M. St.-Laurent to consider these copies to date from the twelfth century.[1]

The steps of the progress from symbolic to literal representation will be noticed immediately; but two more Crucifixions of great and undoubted antiquity (the first having a claim to be considered the most ancient in existence) remain to be briefly noticed.

[1] Iconographie de la Croix et du Crucifix; Didron's "Annales Archéologiques," t. xxvi. and t. xxvii., a most valuable and exhaustive summary of this subject, admirably illustrated. See also Dr. Heinrich Otte's article, "Zur Ikonographie des Crucifixus," "Jahrbücher des Vereins von Alterthumsfreunden," &c., heft 44, p. 214.,

M

Both confirm, to a certain extent, the remark insisted
on or suggested by many Roman Catholic writers,
that the private use of the Crucifix in devotion dates
from very early times. The first is in the famous
Syriac Evangeliarium of the Medicean Library, at
Florence, and is widely known for the probably
unique detail of the soldiers not casting dice, but
playing at the world-old game of "Mora" on their
fingers, for the garment without seam.[1] The whole
MS. is one of the most interesting documents in the
world, with many illuminations, performed with
that indescribable grimness of earnestness, which
was the root of Eastern asceticism, and which still
lingers in the handiwork of the stern Arcagnuoli, or
the brothers Orgagna. Assemanni calls it "the oldest
codex in the library;" and it is described by Prof.
Westwood, in his "Palæographia Sacra," and dated
586 by its writer, the monk Rabula. The Crucifixion-
picture is composed with instinctive skill in two
groups, upper and lower. At the top are the sun and
moon; one a face, the other a crescent. The upper
group, which is semicircular or rather cycloidal in its
shape, consists of the three Crosses, supported on
their right by the Virgin Mother and another female
figure, on the left by three more women. The soldiers,
with the spear and the sponge, stand on each side,
next to the central and largest Cross. Over the head
of the former is the name λο<ΙΝΟC. The Lord wears
the long robe; the thieves have waistcloths; and large
drops of blood, in conventional form, are falling from
their hands. Four nails are used throughout. At the

[1] It is represented in Assemanni's "Catalogus Bibl. Medic.,"
Florence, 1742, tav. xxiii.

foot of the Cross the upper and lower group are joined by the soldiers playing for the coat. In the centre, below the Cross, is a Holy Sepulchre, represented in all early Byzantine and Italo- or Gothic-Byzantine work, as an upright structure of much the same shape as a sentry's box. It is supported on the left by a woman, the Blessed Virgin, and an angel; on the other by St. John, another Apostolic figure in the act of blessing, and other adoring women. The base of the composition, as it were, is formed by a group of soldiers, overthrown by the stroke of visible substantial rays from the sepulchre; the stone also lies on the left. The designer seems to have thought much of the fact of its being rolled away, and he has accordingly drawn it as a disk like a grindstone.[1] Grotesque and archaic as it is, this work is composed exactly like Orgagna's or Michael Angelo's "Last Judgment," Titian's "Assumption," or Raffaelle's "Transfiguration"—i.e. of two great upper and lower groups, tied together and supported on both sides; nor could any work better illustrate the lingering of Byzantine tradition in sacred subjects. A full description is given by Professor Westwood.[2] Of the four Crucifixions given by Gori,[3] that at p. 203, called the "Diptych of Rambona in Picenum," is the most ancient and extraordinary. It contains a medallion of the First Person of the Trinity above, with the sun and moon below on the right of the cross, personified as figures bearing torches. There are two titles,

[1] It may possibly be intended for a round shield.
[2] In his "Palæographia Sacra," also by Dom Guéranger, "Inst. Liturgiques," vol. ii. app.
[3] In vol. iii. of his "Thesaurus Diptychorum," pp. 116, 128, 203, 216.

EGO SUM IHS NAZARENUS, in rustic capitals, with a smaller label, REX IUDEORUM, over the cross. The nimbus is cruciform, the waistcloth reaches almost to the knees, the navel is strangely formed into an eye. The Virgin and St. John stand under the arms of the Cross. But the distinguishing detail is the addition of the Roman wolf and twins below the Cross, with the words ROMULUS ET REMUS A LUPA NUTRITI, in rustic characters also. This wonderful ivory is now said to be in the Vatican Museum, and is in the most ancient style of what may be called dark-age Byzantine art, when all instruction and sense of beauty are departed, but so vigorous a sense of the reality of the fact remains as to render the work highly impressive—as in the Medici MS.

Professor Westwood[1] enables us to refer to a Crucifixion found in an Irish MS. written about 800. It is in the Library of St. John's College, Cambridge, and is partly copied from the Palæographia by Mr. Ruskin,[2] who selects one of the angels above the Cross as a specimen of absolutely dead and degraded art. This is perfectly correct, and the work is a painful object of contemplation, as it displays the idiotcy of a contemptible person instructed in a decaying style, rather than the roughness of a barbarian workman, like the carver of the diptych. The absurd interlacings and use of dots, the sharpening of fingers into points, and the treatment of the subject entirely as a matter of penmanship, without either devotional sense of its importance or artistic effect to realize it, make the MS. most disagreeably interesting as far as this miniature is concerned.

[1] " Pal. Sac.," pl. 18.   [2] " The Two Paths," p. 27.

The plea or hypothesis of Roman Catholic writers, that actual images of the crucified body of the Lord may have been used in the very earliest times for private devotion, is open to the obvious remark that none of them can be produced ; whereas symbolical memorials of the Crucifixion are found in regular succession, and in forms both mural and portable. Father Martigny argues that the Graffito may be a caricatured copy of some undiscovered crucifix used for Christian worship. Father Garucci's description of it,[1] and the remarks which accompany it, are most important, as they show "the more intelligent and bitter hostility of Paganism to the Church, since the apostolic martyrdoms a century and a half before, when converts had also been made in Cæsar's household." He shows also, incidentally, that it can hardly have been derived from any Christian emblem, as the ass's head connects it evidently with the Gnostic invective, which attributed to the Jews the worship of an ass. This Tacitus mentions,[2] and Tertullian[3] notices Tacitus' confusion between Jews and Christians, and appeals to his account of the examination of the Jewish temple by Pompey, who found "no image" in the Temple.[4]

The relics of the treasury of the Cathedral of Monza, described and partly represented in woodcut by M. Martigny, are valuable examples of the

---

[1] "Il Crocifisso Graffito in casa dei Cesari," is given by Canon Liddon in his Seventh Bampton Lecture, p. 397.

[2] Hist. v. c. 4.

[3] Apolog. 16.

[4] For proof of the confusion of the early Christians with the Jews by the Pagan world, Dr. Liddon refers to Dr. Pusey's note on the above passage in Tertullian, in the Oxford Library of the Fathers.

transition between symbolic and actual representation of the Crucifixion. One of the ampullæ
for sacred oil is said to have been presented by
Gregory the Great to Theodolinda, wife of Autharis,
king of Lombardy, probably some time soon after
590, and about ninety years before the Council in
Trullo. It is circular; and the head of the Lord,
with a cruciform nimbus, is placed at the top.
Below, to right and left, are the two thieves, with
extended arms, but without Crosses; and below
them two figures are kneeling by a Cross which
seems to be budding into leaves. Two saints or
angels are on the extreme right and left, and the
usual Holy Sepulchre below, with an angel watching it on the right in the act of benediction; while
St. John and St. Mary Magdalene are (apparently)
approaching it on the other side. Another vessel
bears a figure of the Lord, clothed with a long robe,
with the nimbus and extended arms, but without
the Cross. Finally, the reliquary of Theodolinda, so
called, has the crucified Form, with the nimbus
and inscription IC. XC., clothed in the long tunic,
with the soldiers, two figures apparently mocking
Him, and the Virgin and St. John on the right and
left. The clothed figure indicates symbolical treatment, since it must have been well known that the
Roman custom was to crucify naked; and Martigny
argues that the Graffito, which is clothed, must therefore have been copied from some Christian picture.
But from this time, or from that of the Council of
685, the artistic or ornamental treatment begins.
The earliest Crucifixions are narrative, not dramatic;
the Resurrection being frequently introduced into

the same composition, as if without it the subject would be altogether too painful for Christian eyes. And, indeed, till the first efforts of Pisan sculpture and Florentine painting, the importance of the event represented withdrew all attention from the personality of the artist. In works of after days the painter's power is all. Their range of excellence is as wide as the difference between the tender asceticism of Fra Angelico, the mighty sorrow of Michael Angelo, and the intense power, knowledge, and passion of the great canvas of Tintoret in the Scuola di San Rocco at Venice. The treatment of this picture resembles that of the most ancient works. All its consummate science is directed to bringing every detail of the scene into a great unity, while attention is expressly withdrawn from the face of the Lord, which is cast into deep shadow.[1] In all ancient work the Lord's face is abstracted and expressionless: any attempt to represent His bodily pain belongs to modern work of the baser sort, which forms no part of our present subject. For the details and accessories of the Crucifixion, whether things or persons, they have been for the most part enumerated and described. The nails are always four in number in ancient works, two for the feet and two for the hands. The crossed legs, and single large nail or spike, belong to the artistic period.[2] St. Cyprian, he says, had seen the punishment of the cross. The suppedaneum, or rest for the feet, occurs in the crosses of Leo III. and of Velletri, not in the

---

[1] See Ruskin, "Modern Painters," vol. ii.

[2] Martigny refers to St. Cyprian (De Passion. Dni. inter Opuse. p. 83, ed. Oxon), as speaking of the nails which pierced our Lord's feet, in the plural number.

Diptych of Rambona. The Graffito indicates its presence. It seems to have been occasionally left out, in deference to those passages in Holy Scripture which refer to the disgrace or curse attaching to one "hanging" on the tree. The title of the Cross, which is given with slight differences in St. Matt. xxvii. 37, Mark xv. 26, Luke xxiii. 38, John xix. 9, varies greatly in different representations. It is omitted in the crosses of Lucca and Velletri. Early Greek painters reduce it to the name of Christ, IC.XC, or substitute the A and ω. The sign Φ (φώς) occurs, as well as LVX MVNDI, frequently accompanied by the symbols of the sun and the moon, as a red star or face and crescent, or in the Rambona ivory as mourning figures bearing torches. They are introduced as emblematic of the homage of all nature, or in remembrance of the darkness at the Crucifixion. The Blessed Virgin and St. John appear in the Medicean MS. and very frequently in older works; the soldiers rather less so, though they occur in the above MS. and in the reliquary of Monza. The typical figure of the first Adam rising from the earth as a symbol of the resurrection of the body, with the Hand of Blessing above indicating the Presence of God, is given in . Ciampini.[1] The skull, whether human or that of a lamb, placed at the foot of the cross, either as an emblem of sacrifice or in reference to the place Golgotha, is of late use; and is almost the only late addition of symbolic detail. The rare addition of the soldiers casting lots *on their fingers* is said to be found in an ivory of the eighth century from Cividale in

---

[1] De Sacr. Acdif. tabl. xxiii. p. 75.

Friuli.[1] The only other representation of it is in the Medici MS. The wolf and twins are in the Rambona diptych alone. The types of the four Evangelists are on the back of the Cross of Velletri, in the Gospel of Egbert of Trier, and on numerous Crosses of later date.

Some additional inscriptions have been mentioned, as well as the addition (in the Vatican Cross) of medallion portraits. Considerable liberty in this matter seems to have been allowed in the earliest times, as is indicated by Constantine's introduction of the words of his Vision; and still more strongly in an instance referred to by Borgia, in Anastasius,[2] of a cross given by Belisarius to St. Peter—" by the hand of Pope Vigilius "—of gold and jewels, weighing 100 lbs., "on which he wrote his victories."

But even the Vatican Cross yields in interest to two German relics of the same character, lately described and well illustrated.[3] The first of these is the Station-Cross of Mainz. It is of gilded bronze, of the Western form (commissa), and rather more than one foot in height. Herr Heinrich Otte refers it to the end of the twelfth century, a date far beyond our period. But its interest is paramount; more particularly from the evident intention of the designer to make it embody a whole system of typical instruction, and to leave it behind him as a kind of sculptured document, or commentary, connecting the Old and New Testaments. Thus, at the middle or

[1] Mozzoni, "Tavole Cronologiche della Chiesa Universale," Venezia, 1856-63.
[2] Tom. i. n. 2 ed. Vigilii.
[3] In No. 44 of the "Jahrbücher des Vereins von Alterthumsfreunden im Rheinlande," p. 195, Bonn, 1868.

intersection of the arms of the Cross, the Lamb is represented in a medallion, his head surrounded with a plain nimbus. On the back of the Cross in the same place there is a square plate, with an engraved representation of Abraham offering up Isaac, the angel, and the ram. Round the latter is the beginning of a hexameter line—*Cui patriarcha suum*—which is completed round the medallion of the Lamb in front, thus: *Pater offert in cruce natum.* In like manner, four engravings on each side at the extremities of the Cross refer to each other, and are described by corresponding halves of hexameters. The New Testament subjects are all in front, with the Lamb in the centre, as antitypes; the Old Testament or typical events or persons are at the back. Thus on the spectator's left at the back of the Cross is an engraving of Moses receiving the Tables of the Law on Mount Sinai, with the words *Qui Moysi legem.* Corresponding to it on the right front is the Descent of the Holy Spirit, with *dat alumnis Pneumatis ignem.* The remainder as under—

HEAD.	MOTTO.[1]
Back—Elijah carried up to Heaven	Qui levat Eliam.
Front—The Ascension	propriam sublimat usiam (ούσίαν).
Back—(right hand of spectator) Samson, and gates of Gaza	Que portas Gaze.
Front—(left ditto) The descent into Hades	vis aufert claustra Jehenne.
FOOT.	
Back—Jonah and the Whale....	Qua redit absumptus.
Front—Resurrection	surgit virtute sepultus.

[1] *Elias and Ascension.*—He who uplift Elias, raises on high His own Substance. *Gates of Gaza and Descent.*—The power

The decorative scrollwork is rather sparingly disposed, with great judgment, and on the spike, ferule, or metal strap, probably intended for fixing the Cross on a staff for processional or other purposes, is an engraving of the probable designer and donor. The graphic power and exceeding quaintness of the Scriptural engravings are those of the finest miniatures of the twelfth or thirteenth century.

The second of these most interesting works, inferior as a work of art from its barbaric wildness, and the preference for ugliness so often observed in Northern-Gothic grotesque, is of even greater interest as a transitional Cross; especially when viewed in relation to the changes enforced by the decree of the Council in Trullo. This is the Station Cross of Planig, near Kreuznach, of the same size and form as that of Mainz, but referred by Otte to the tenth century. The ancient symbol of the Lamb is preserved on the back of this Crucifix, which is of bronzed copper, and displays the human form in front, as in many other Romanesque Crosses. On this combination—perhaps a compromise between the feeling of older times and the more modern spirit of the Quinisextine Council— Otte quotes Durandus: " For the Lamb of God ought not to be represented in the chief place on the Cross : but when the Man is placed there, there is no objection to depicting the Lamb on the lower part or on the back." [1]   He also

which destroys the gates of Gaza destroys the bolts of Gehenna. *Jonah and Resurrection.*—The Buried One rises by the same power as the devoured.

[1] " Non enim agnus Dei in cruce principaliter depingi debet : sed homine depicto, non obest agnum in parte inferiori vel posteriori depingere." (Rationale, lib. i. c. 3, n. 6.)

gives the express words of Adrian I., in his letter to
Tarasius, Patriarch of Constantinople, in 785 : "Therefore we give orders that the true Lamb, our Lord J. C.,
be represented on the images in the human form,
instead of the Lamb as of old." [1]   He refers also to
a splendid work on Rhenish antiquities [2] for the Essen
and other roods, which much resemble those of
Kreuznach and Mainz; combining the Lamb with
the human form, and adding personifications of the
sun and moon which remind us of the Diptych of
Rambona; and the symbols of the four Evangelists,
as in the Crucifix of Velletri.   Space forbids us to
give accounts of these most interesting relics, but
the subject appears to be treated with exhaustive
fulness and illustrated to perfection in the two
German works referred to.   The Planig-on-Nahe
rood, however, is entitled to a briefly-detailed description.   In front is the Crucified Form, severely
archaic in treatment; the long hair is carefully
parted and carried back; the head is without nimbus;
and the limbs are long, stiff, and wasted, the ribs
being displayed, as is so commonly done in mediæval
Crucifixes, to complete the illustration of the text,
" They pierced My hands and My feet: I may tell
all My bones."   A triple serpentine stream of blood
runs from each hand, and also from the feet, being
there received in a cup or chalice, the foot of which
is a grotesque lion's head.   The back of the Cross
bears on its centre the Lamb with cruciform nimbus;

---

[1] "Verum igitur agnum Dominum nostrum J. C. secundum
imaginem humanam a modo etiam in imaginibus pro veteri agno
depingi jubemus." (De Consecr. Dist. iii. c. 29 ; Labbe, vi. 1177.)
[2] "Kunstdenkmäler des Christlichen Mittelalters," by Ernst
aus'm Werth, Leipzig (Weigel), 1857, taf. xxiv.–vi.

below it is a medallion of the donor, "Ruthardus Custos;" and four other bas-reliefs, now wanting, occupied the four extremities of the arms, and almost certainly represented the four Evangelists. As in the Diptych of Rambona, the navel resembles an eye.

Scarcely inferior to these is the tenth-century miniature of a single Crucifix with the title IHS NAZAREN REX IUDEORUM; the sun and moon are above the Cross-beam, within circles, and represented with expressions of horror, seated in chariots, one drawn by horses, the other by oxen. It is impossible to omit the Crucifixion-picture from the Gospel of Bishop Egbert of Trier, 975—993,[1] now in the Stadtbibliothek there. Here the Lord is clad in a long robe to the ankles; the robbers are also clad in loose tunics girded so close to the form as to give the appearance of shirt and trousers. Above, are the sun and moon hiding their faces. The Cross has a second Cross-piece at top, forming a Tau above the western Cross. The robbers are on Tau Crosses; suspended, but with unpierced hands; the passage in the twenty-second Psalm being referred to the Redeemer alone. Their names, Desmas, the penitent, and Cesmas, the obdurate, are above their heads. The Virgin-mother and another woman stand on the right of the Cross, St. John on the left. The soldier "Stephaton" is presenting the sponge of vinegar;[2] two others are casting lots below. This detail reminds us of the great Florentine miniature of the

[1] Mooyer's "Onomasticon Chronographicon Hierarchiæ Germanicæ," 8vo. Minden, 54.
[2] Longinus is always the lance-bearer. See Medici (Laurentian) Crucifix, *supra*.

monk of Rabula, excepting that the game of Mora is there substituted for dice. These works are somewhat beyond our period: yet as a chapter on Crucifixes must contain some account of the things whose name it bears, and the first eight centuries supply us with so few examples of what are popularly called Crucifixes, a short inroad into early mediævalism may be allowed. The Iconodulist transition, formally made at the Council in Trullo, was well suited to the Northern mind, and to the sacramental theory of pain; but it fell in also with that tendency to *personification* advancing on symbolism, which the Western races inherit, perhaps, from ancient Greece; and which Mr. Ruskin, in his late Oxford Lectures, points out as the idolatrous tendency of Greek art. With Cimabue and Giotto, and from their days, artistic skill and power over beauty are brought to bear on the Crucifix, as on other Christian representations, for good and for evil. Of the cautious and gradual compromise of the Greek Church we have, already spoken.

CHAPTER X

THE LOMBARDS.

THE important distinction between definition and development, of objects of faith and doctrine, is marked, as might be expected, by modifications in Church Art. After the Council of Nice, certain symbols, as the A ω, the Cross as representing the Second Person of the Trinity, and the Dove for the Third—mark the effect of the definitions of the Great Council. In the next two centuries we observe, and have partly described, the advance from the Monogram, or from the Good Shepherd; and we have followed the advance from those symbols to the Crucified Form, as representations of the Saviour; and have implied that such a change points to new habits of thought concerning Him. It would not have taken place, unless men's minds had turned to the persevering contemplation of His Death rather than of His Life, and of the Manner and Sufferings of His Death rather than of its Efficacy. The extraordinary distresses and depression of the Christian world, which made Death a familiar and welcome subject of meditation for the whole Church, seem to have been the chief cause of this transition. It may be said to be the work of the dark ages, so called as ages of affliction; because it synchronised with them, it was completed by the time they were over, and it was in a great degree the reflection of their darkness. Parallel with this change from Primitive to Mediæval faith, and from Primitive to Mediæval art, is another great development in both, which has had an almost equal effect on the religion of the whole Christian Church; and which certainly brought art to bear on men's personal religion and faith with extraordinary power, though with dubious or evil result. This was the worship of the Saints, and of the Blessed Virgin as Chief of Saints, and finally, as a Divine Person. Speaking generally, it may be said that this misdirection of the prayers and spiritual hopes of mankind makes the main and crucial difference between Primitive and Mediæval faith; and this book is happily not concerned with the endless and distressing task of following its progress beyond the sixth or seventh century

The dawn of the earliest Renaissance, or revival of art, through the means and under the auspices of the Christian Faith, is like an Eastern sunrise, beginning with a false dawn while it is yet deep night. A faint reflection appears in the east, and departs, and for a while all is as dark as ever. The rule of Theodoric at Ravenna, and his willing encouragement of Græco-Roman and Byzantine workmen there, gave an appearance of revival to the expiring genius of form and colour, which died away and vanished with him. It was not till the greater desolations of the Lombard conquest were fulfilled, till Autharis and Theodolinda were seated on the throne of Alboin, that it was found that the new conquerors and colonists of Northern Italy possessed a

genius of their own, and were barbarians who could
learn and improve upon the lessons they found in
ancient models. This extraordinary race of men
have furnished almost a majority of the chief
masters of Christian art, if not poetry; and a Chronicler of their own blood has written the early
history of his people, as far as he himself knew it.
He claims a Scandinavian origin for them, yet considers German to be the generic name which they
shared alike with the Gepidæ and the Eastern and
Western Goths. Like Jornandes, who speaks of the
North as the quiver[1] of races and forge of nations, he
has a general idea of the shores of the Baltic and
the Northern Ocean (*Septentrionalis plaga*) as the
original hive of Goths, Wendels, Heruli, Rugii, and
àll the younger races of Europe. But his geogra-
phical information is vague, and goes but little
further north than Scandia or Gothland; an island
or peninsula which he conceived of as sufficiently
extensive to be the birthplace of his nation. He
thinks the Northern cold favourable to health and
population, having, perhaps, seen with sorrow that
the Italian sun had diminished the energies of his
countrymen, and made them an unequal match for
the West Franks. He had shared in the retributive
calamities which befell them from Pepin and Charlemagne.[2] He had lived at the Court of the three
last Lombard kings at Pavia, being a gentleman of

---

[1] Vagina nationum et officinâ gentium. De Rebus Geticis, c. 4.

[2] See Muratori's Preface. It is useless to revive the extinct
controversy, whether the Lombards were Brandenburghers (see
Cluverius), or Northmen (as Grotius). Sismondi says, "Ils se
croyaient originaires de la Scandinavie, mais depuis 42 ans (before
Narses' invitation to Alboin in 567) habitaient la Pannonie:"
which seems sufficient.

the blood of Alboin, with whom Leuphis (?), his great-grandfather, had crossed the Eastern Alps. He was taken prisoner by Charlemagne after the final defeat of Desiderius or Didier; and was long imprisoned in France, for faithful adherence to the latter. On his final deliverance or escape, he became a Benedictine of Monte Casino, where he seems to have written his chronicle and many ingenious copies of Latin verses, to the praise and glory of his patron, and the not inconsiderable wonder and amusement of their infrequent students. " I have framed a list of his (St. Benedict's) miracles one by one, in separate couplets of elegiac metre, as follows," says the Deacon :—

> "Where, O holy Benedict, shall I begin thy triumphs?
> Thy heaps of virtues, where shall I begin?" [1]

and so on for about a hundred and forty lines. Also a hymn in Iambics, not unlike Prudentius. The introduction of his chronicle is enough to show that he was neither careless of knowledge like a barbarian, nor incurious like an ascetic, but a man who sought and accumulated information, and had formed habits of observation and inference. He appears to have heard of reindeer; he speaks of his ancestors as inhabiting some Arctic region, and being accustomed to the use of snow-shoes, or perhaps skates : and this, and their skill in the manufacture of arms, seems to establish their Scandinavian origin. It is a curious coincidence, supposing this great race to be descendants of the hammer-men of the North,

---

[1] " Singula ejus miracula per singula disticha Elegiaco metro hoc modo contexui :—

> " Ordiar unde tuos, sacer O Benedicte triumphos?
> Virtutum cumulos ordiar unde tuos?"

cunning in all iron-work, that they should have shown such early and vigorous taste for sculpture. Yet it seems likely that a nation of smiths should make the easy transition from hammer and anvil to hammer and chisel. They were probably accustomed to rude carving in wood. Like the Franks and Ostrogoths, they showed their superiority to the Huns and lower races of barbarians by willingness to learn, even from the Romans whom they despised. Their final conversion to orthodox Christianity may be placed in the time of Autharis and Theodolinda, whose Baptism both, by immersion and aspersion, in a large laver or "pelvis," was commemorated in an extraordinary mosaic, of which a plate will be found in Ciampini's "Vetera Monumenta."[1] It seems as if they had but few ideas on the subject of art beyond the making of goblets from the skulls of their enemies, before they passed the Noric Alps, in the neighbourhood of Forum Julii or Friuli. One singularly grim relic of that kind the Deacon tells us he has himself seen—the identical "Scala," or goblet made by Alboin from the head of Cunimund, and mounted in gold.[2] "Let not this seem impossible to any man. I speak the truth in Christ. I have seen King Rachis holding that cup in hand, to display it to his guests on a certain feast day."[3] This early history of Turismond and his knighthood of Alboin is very remarkable; as one of the earliest instances of chivalric institutions, and also of the highest chival-

---

[1] Tab. iii. part i. p. 20.
[2] De Gestis Longobardorum, II. 28.
[3] Hoc ne cui videatur impossibile : veritatem in Christo loquor, ego hoc poculum vidi, in quodam die festo, Rachis (sic) principem, ut illud convivis suis ostentaret, manu tenentem.

ric feeling, in the midst of ferocity and brutality. The name and memory of Alboin seem to have been especially dear to his descendants in the Deacon's time; and his occasional acts of clemency are specially dwelt on by his Chronicler. But the great progress for the better in Lombard civilization may be best estimated by comparing the foul and murderous story of his valiant life and death with that of the first and, indeed, the second wooing of Theodolinda. She was daughter of Garibaldus (of all names in the world),—King of the Bajoarii or Bavarians. Autharis of Lombardy is courting her: he comes disguised as his own ambassador to her father's Court, to ask her in marriage. She pours out his wine at the feast; he takes her hand and passes it gently over his own face. She consults her nurse on the subject of such a strange liberty; and is told that none but the King, her future husband, could have dared to take it. The pretended ambassador is honorably escorted to the frontier of his own land; and as he crosses it, he swings his heavy battle-axe and drives it deep in a pine-trunk, saying, "Such a blow deals the King of Lombards." Meanwhile it is prophesied to Agilulf, who rides in his train, that the King's bride shall be his bride. Happier and better times begin with the reign of Autharis and Theodolinda, and on his death the voice of her nobles and people invites her to remain on the throne, and choose another spouse. She consents, and her peers do her homage in succession, with some feudal ceremonial which includes kissing her hand. And her choice is made known for the first time to its object, Agilulf of Turin or Taurini, by her bidding him proceed to her lips, for he was the chosen of Lombardy and of herself; her Lord and King.[1] The story is certainly charming; and the lady appears to have been still more so, almost throughout her long life. At a period like the present, when the civilizing influence of Christianity is roundly denied, and its precepts of self-denial and purity pronounced on the whole mistaken and deleterious, Christian writers may be permitted to call attention to the difference between the history of Alboin and Rosamond, and that of Agilulf and Theodolinda. It is certainly as if the savage conqueror had determined the conditions and character of his race, when he spared Pavia after his three years' siege, moved by the black monks' prayers. At all events, in less than twenty-five years occupied in the settlement of Northern Italy, the change of character in the rulers of the conquering race is very strongly marked.

The earliest specimens of Lombard art still in existence, or on record, date from the reign of Theodolinda. Her second marriage took place in 599; according to Gibbon;—the year of Gregory I.'s accession to the Popedom: and his earnest and pathetic appeal to her husband and herself, setting

[1] The story of Theodolinda's wooing is thus related in Rose's "Biographical Dictionary," vol. i. p. 149 : "Without announcing her intentions, she requested the pleasure of his (Agilulf's) company at her court. She took with her an escort to meet him as far as Somello. When they met, she called for a cup of wine, and having drunk half of it, she offered the other to the Duke. On returning the cup, he kissed her hand as a mark of respect; when, turning to him covered with blushes, she said, 'That is not the salute I ought to expect from my lord and husband.' She then acquainted him with the wishes of the Lombards, and her own choice—and the Duke became a king."

forth the misery of Italy, and their power for good
or evil, seems to have been the beginning of an
influence over them which must have been as beneficial as it was uninterrupted. Some curious and most
interesting vessels, which once contained sacred oil,
sent by Gregory to the Lombard queen are still preserved in the treasury of Modœtia or Monza, with the
reliquary which accompanied them. Both are described in our Chapter on the Crucifix ; and the vessels
are represented in Martigny's Dictionary under that
word ; and on a larger scale and with greater clearness
by M. Grimoard de St.-Laurent.[1] Another relic of
the same age, of world-wide reputation, is the famous
Iron Crown ; this, with the plain diadem worn by
Theodolinda herself, is represented in Muratori's
edition of Paul the Deacon.[2] But a still more interesting record of that age is his plate of the bas
relief (tabula marmorea) which once stood over
the door of the ancient Duomo of Monza, dedicated
to St. John Baptist by the Lombard king and
queen. A basrelief we presume it to have been,
though the original building (entirely renewed in
1396) was Byzantine, and some of the figures bear a
certain resemblance to the mosaics of Ravenna. It
seems to have filled the tympanum of the great
doors. There is little composition or arrangement
of the symbols and figures. Agilulf kneels in prayer
on the spectator's left, wearing a long tunic apparently over his mail, and what seem to be *rowelled*
spurs. There are jewelled crosses over royal crowns,
and an eagle with an ampulla. Theodolinda is
offering her crown on the other side ; there are other

[1] In "Annales Archéologiques," vol. xxvi.
[2] "Scriptores Italici," vol. i.

Crosses resting on chalices, and the singular and in part unique symbol of the Hen and Chickens. In such a place, one cannot but suppose that this is an allusion to St. Luke xiii. 34,—in which case the Chioccia, or silver-gilt hen of Theodolinda (still preserved in the Cathedral treasury) must have the same meaning, rather than a mere reference to the archpriest of Monza or the seven Lombard Princes. The lower range is flanked by St. Peter with the keys and St. Paul bearing a sword: in the centre is the Baptism of Our Lord with an attendant angel, the water rising pyramidically up to the middle of His Body. on either side, the Blessed Virgin and (most probably) St. John the Evangelist. This carving must have been of the greatest interest, as a specimen of Byzantine work done under Lombard patronage; as the figure of Theodoric at Pavia, and many Ravennese carvings and mosaics, were produced for Ostrogoths.[1] The Deacon appeals to this, or to another carving, in Theodolinda's palace, as an interesting record of the dress of his ancestors, and their manner of cutting their hair short behind and wearing longer front and side-locks. "Their garments," he says, "were loose and of linen, such as English Saxons are wont to wear, ornamented with borders (institis) woven in divers colours. They had sandals open almost to the end of the great toe, and kept on by lacing with leathern thongs (laqueis corrigiarum alternatim). But

[1] Paul the Deacon, iv. 22. This latter was certainly a mosaic (mensa tessellis ornata), and it, or another similar portrait of Theodoric, is mentioned by Procopius, de Bello Gallico, xxiv., as "Ex lapillis compacta, minutis admodùm, et versicoloribus fere singulis." Its head fell away just before Theodoric's death, the middle at Amalasuntha's, and the legs and feet crumbled at the coming of Belisarius.

afterwards they began to wear hose (hosis uti) : over which when on horseback they used to put on " tubrugi birrei "—which last singular expression seems to denote red or tan-leather overalls.[1]   But it is of importance to observe so early an example of the Lombard insistence, in pictures, on the dress and arms of their own life.   They were evidently from the first determined to have an art-school of their own.   The church of St. Michele at Pavia, mentioned by Paul the Deacon as a sanctuary in 661, is one of their earliest works, and must be placed in the seventh century, with the Church of St. Ambrose of Milan.   Their naturalism and in-sistence on fact, their vigorous imagination of truth, and wild play of fancy in fiction, their delight in action, motion, and contest, their taste for hunting and battle, their irresistible or unresisted taste for the humorous grotesque, are described by a master-hand.[2]   But Professor Ruskin also notices in this passage (a knowledge of which is almost essential to a good understanding of Italian-Gothic or Romanesque architecture) how rapidly the Lombard character toned down, as it were, under their new civilization and in their new climate.   That their conversion to the Faith had even more to do with the change, we can see no reason whatever for doubting.   But in the seventh century the condition of the Lombard artist seems to have been one of continued excitement, the feeling of one of a conquering race which has just won its land.   "The Arab feverishness," says Pro-fessor Ruskin, "impels the Lombards in the South,

---

[1] Birrei = $\pi\upsilon\rho\rho\alpha\acute{\iota}$.   Muratori.
[2] In Append. 8 to Vol. I. of "The Stones of Venice," and there gra-phically contrasted with the Byzantine work of St. Mark at Venice.

showing itself, however, in endless invention, with a refreshing firmness and order. The excitement is greatest in the earliest times, most of all shown in St. Michele of Pavia, and I am strongly disposed to connect much of its peculiar manifestation with the Lombard's habits of eating and drinking, especially his carnivorousness. The Lombard of early times seems to have been exactly what a tiger would be, if you could give him love of a joke, vigorous imagination, a strong sense of justice, fear of hell, knowledge of northern mythology, a stone den, and a mallet and chisel. Fancy him pacing up and down in the same den to digest his dinner, and striking on the wall, with a new fancy in his head, at every turn; —and you have the Lombardic sculptor. As civilization increases the supply of vegetables, and shortens that of wild beasts, the excitement diminishes; it is still strong in the thirteenth century at Lyons and Rouen; it dies away gradually in the later Gothic, and is quite extinct in the fifteenth century."

But the most complete and important example of the earlier Lombard style[1] is St. Zenone at Verona. The excitability and grotesque humour of the older workmen are still there, in considerable force; but the characteristic of the sculpture which covers the whole façade of the Church, and is lavished on every part of its interior, is historical realism. The instruction which is conveyed in the Book-Temple of Venice by means of mosaic, at Verona is given in sculpture. Mr. Ruskin's Oxford Lectures on

---

[1] Called Romanesque from the round arches which it derived from Old Rome, as Byzantine takes its name from Byzantium, New Rome or Constantinople.

Sculpture contain an excellent photograph of this wonderful Church front; particularly happy in its absence of heavy shadow and clearness of detail; even to the castings of the wonderful bronze doors which anticipate Ghiberti. They show an imagin ative realism in their rendering of Old and New Testament history, like nothing which precedes them, excepting only the mosaics of Sta. Maria Maggiore. The choice of subjects is particularly interesting, inasmuch as we find the ancient Scriptural cycle of the Catacombs almost complete in it, though expanded into a pictorial History of the Redemption of Man from both Testaments. There is less pure symbolism, and more attention to type and pro- phecy :—the Good Shepherd is no longer to be seen, nor the Vine, nor the various emblems of Dove or Lamb which shadowed forth the relation of Man to God in the earliest days of faith, with yet unde- veloped doctrine. But Adam and Eve are sent forth from Paradise, as on the sarcophagi—Cain fells Abel with a short bludgeon; Abraham sits under the tree with the Three Guests; and in another compartment, the Angel is staying Abraham's hand (armed with a formidable Gothic war-sword, straight and pointed), from sacrificing his only son. The Brazen Serpent is also crucified on a Tau Cross. But the most curious instance of derived treatment, connecting the new barbaric Christianity with the old classic teaching, is the Lombardized Noah; standing in his square " area " or chest, as of old, but now tossed on a rather stormy sea, in a tabernacled and gabled structure, and stretching forth his hands to a dove, of the size of an albatross, and drawn with the skill of one who must often have watched the falcon's flight. The Divine Lamb is on the keystone of the round arch which forms the high porch; and in the low gable, or pediment above, is the Hand of Blessing. Tall Corinthian pillars support this porch, based on lions or griffins. In the lowest course of sculpture on the façade, now entirely destroyed by wanton mischief, was once the strange allegory called the Chase of Theodoric; the hunter striking his quarry, and himself watched for by the Evil One. Within the church, quaint grotesques, and knights in combat, alternate with Scriptural subjects: the transition from devotion to jest seems to have been as easy to the first Lombards, as to Florentines in Giotto's day, and centuries after. It is through this Church of St. Zenone and the Veronese Gothic in general, that the relationship of the thirteenth-century work of Florence, and the after glories of the early Renaissance, can best be traced to their real origin.

After the close of the ninth century darkness settles over Rome for ages more, and mosaic seems to have been attempted no further. The name of Beno de Rapiza occurs in the eleventh century, in a charter of 1080.[1] An inscription on one of the rude paintings of the legend of St. Clement, in the Church bearing that Saint's name in Rome, records that it was his donation and his wife's: EGO BENO DE RAPIZA CVM MARIA VXORE MEA PRO AMORE DOMINI ET BEATI CLEMENTIS. The pictures in this church are eleventh century; with the exception, perhaps, of the paintings on the outer wall of the south aisle, representing the Ascension, the

---

[1] Parker, "Church and Altar Decorations," p. 58.

Crucifixion, and the Descent into Hades, which appear to be considerably earlier. There is with them a Madonna apparently of the seventh century, about the same time as the mosaic picture in the apse of St. Agnes.

The family of Cosmati were the great Roman mosaicists of the thirteenth century and worked also in cities of northern Italy. The name of Buschetto is connected with the Cathedral of Pisa in the eleventh and twelfth centuries : those of Niccola and Giovanni Pisano with the sculpture of the thirteenth. In these great Italians the Lombard energies began to be trained by the study of ancient models of Greek art ; and it is with them that the true Revival or Renaissance of art begins. This book does not enter on the subjects of Gothic or Mediæval art, further than to assert what will be universally admitted—that the primitive, typical, historical, and symbolic teaching was not discontinued, but overlaid and obscured by legendary painting ; by the increasing attention paid to subjects connected with the Passion of our Lord and the Last Judgment ; and by the rise of the lay or artistic spirit. Art ceased to be conventual, because monks were no longer the only artists. But art was still religious ; first because its chosen subjects were of a religious character, and secondly because the painters were men of definite Christian belief. However non-religious, or anti-religious, or abominably sensual, or profane, art may have since become, her historical connexion with the Christian Faith cannot be disputed.

It seems to us that the same tradition of Christian graphic art remains through all the Lombard works, though changed by innovations in subject. History and doctrine were still taught in form and colour ; the illuminated church stood instead of the painted Evangeliary, for men who perhaps could not read, or whose reading, like children's in our own day, was greatly assisted by pictures. It needs but little acquaintance with ancient MSS. to understand how difficult, through the varieties of hand, character, and contraction, the art of reading must have been, even to the comparatively few who knew lines and letters at all. Meanings imperfectly apprehended from the written page might often be mastered with the help of the inlaid walls or sculptured porches and columns ; and the poor would have the assistance of sermons or catechizings, which would probably instruct them in the Scriptural account of their own condition and hopes ; at least while the clergy cared to teach it them, or until mere legend had superseded it.

To inquire how far this really took place would re quire volumes of somewhat disputable statement. But there can be no doubt that a body or substratum of Christian history and doctrine was always taught in Italy and Germany ; nor yet that art was employed to express and impress it, as in former days. Men could not worship Mary without some instruction concerning the Son of Mary, nor adore the Saints without know- ing Whose Saints they were. The advancing cultus of the Blessed Virgin has been traced in the Roman mosaics in our chapter on that subject : for a fuller account of it, illustrated both from history and from other monuments of early art, we must refer to the late Rev. Wharton Marriott's valuable work.[1] The effects

[1] "The Testimony of the Catacombs."

on painting and sculpture of the ever-increasing devotion to the Mother of the Lord, and of the easier and
more familiar worship of patron Saints, appear to us
specially lamentable. Not only severity, but earnestness, seems to have been gradually withdrawn from
religious art; Church painting was conventionalized
more and more; the Virgin became a Queen of
Heaven, and the hagiology of Saints a mythology of
inferior deities, with special tastes and employments.
It was often found easier and more attractive to the
painter to range at will in legend, and indulge princes
and people with unattested miracles and martyrdoms,
than to continue in the ground of Scriptural narrative, and walk in the old paths of symbolism or
history. As the people's taste went after Legends
and Last Judgments, Infernos and Assumptions, the
painters showed themselves no wiser or stronger
than the people. Their work was often paid chiefly
by abbots and priors, who were compelled to minister
to the people such religion as seemed to please them
best. They would often require religious pictures
which were, or represented, incredible nonsense. It
was a lamentable consequence that the painter lost
faith in religious work. He had to paint what he
did not really believe : and in consequence, the subjects of his art seemed less and less to him, and he
could but rest on its technicalities. Many would
(for a time) live happily on the subtle and delicate
pleasures of colour and form, not caring what they
painted : as Botticelli or Benozzo Gozzoli. But as
soon as it was understood that the end of art was
pleasure, without reference to religion, evil enjoyment and sensual subjects were certain to break in

overpoweringly, and they did so. The course of our own days is not a very different one; but the object of this book is not polemical. Whether art be openly or consciously dedicated to the service of God or not, it will depend, after all, on the character of the artist whether its effects be Christian or atheistic, godly or godless. No Theist can feel what is most rightly called the inspiration of art, without asking whence it comes, and answering himself that, being so good a thing, it must come from the Giver of all good gifts, and be one of the choicest of the ordinary or natural gifts of the Spirit. He who thinks thus of his work may yield to natural passion, or stumble over that impalpable barrier which divides the artist's taste in beauty from the sensualist's. But he will return and repent; and until he has finally cast off the Giver, he cannot use the gift purposely for suggestive temptation. Michael Angelo yields to, or boldly asserts, natural passions from time to time: but no man ever yet was led to impurity or lowered in tone of honour by studying him. And why not? In the end, because the vehement and misled master desired through all, and in spite of all, to serve Christ with his great gifts.

There is a connection, last worked out in Dr. Woltmann's admirable Life of Holbein, but not unnoticed by former writers, between the Church art of the fourteenth and the sixteenth century—between the Reformation and the post-Reformation workers, between Orgagna and Holbein. It goes back, indeed, to the mosaics of Torcello,[1] or even to the unknown painting of Methodius for Bogoris of Bulgaria. It

[1] See Index, s. v. "Last Judgment."

consists in the habit of dealing with thoughts of
Death; in attempts to realize the final change, the
separation of soul and body, with all its pangs and
dismal outward signs; and in the efforts to realize the
Final Judgment as a scene. All attempts of this kind
fall, naturally, under the head of the Grotesque; because strangeness and imperfect conventionality must
necessarily be the result, where a subject beyond
human thought is essayed by human hands and conceptions. But in the hands of powerful men their
impression is powerful at all times. There can be no
doubt that such representations were an innovation;
not earlier than the eighth century, or probably than
the eleventh; beginning at a time when all adherence
to the ancient Scriptural cycle of the early frescoes
and carvings had long ceased. Yet the subject of the
Judgment is not unscriptural, while St. Matt. xxv.
and the book of the Revelation are part of the Canon.
It seems that that increasing attention paid to illustrations of the Apocalypse, which has been noticed in
the chapter on Mosaics, would necessarily lead artists
to try to represent those parts of it which involved
the strongest personal terror and warning: and such
attempts once made, would have great power on the
minds of barbarians accustomed to scenes of horror
and desolation; and perhaps would have an un-
confessed attraction for polemical disputants, who
desired to terrify their opponents with Hell as the
penalty of their errors, if not to doom them to it
finally. Certain it is that the Fire-stream or River
of God's Wrath, and the worms which die not, are
strangely and rudely inlaid at the west end of the
Duomo of Torcello. Whether that church dates

from Attila, or from Alboin's invasion (both which seem improbable)—or from after the destruction of Altinum in 641 by the Lombards, or from the general restoration in 1008, mentioned by the Marchese Selvatico—the mosaics must be part of its original ornaments.[1] But from this mosaic of Judgment there begins a succession of such like representations; down to Giotto's frescoes at Padua, or Orgagna's in the Campo Santo of Pisa; and from Orgagna again to Holbein's Dance of Death, or of the Dead. As we by no means desire to have this subject perpetuated in our Sacred Buildings—mainly because the Primitive Church refused it, under circumstances which might seem to point specially to its use—there is no reason for dwelling on it at length: but one or two special observations may be permitted.

In the first place, the Torcello representation is still symbolic. The Fire and the Worm are ideas drawn from the written word of Holy Scripture; but they are accepted as they are given, and only, as it were, repeated verbally in the painting. The work is Eastern, ascetic and contemplative: its severity is sharpened by the sense of corruption in the Christian life itself, by painful strife with heresy and schism, and by external distress. The treatment of the subject

---

[1] See "Lectures on Christian Art and Symbolism," by the author of this work, pp. 88–95. A critic in the *Saturday Review* calls attention, with much irritation, to the contradiction between passages, where two of these dates are suggested. It really arises from the fact that it is impossible to say whether any original church was built at Torcello by those who fled before Alboin in 568. If so, it formed a part of the duomo of the next century; with its mosaics, if any. At all events, those which are there now must be of the same date as the original part of the present church, and may be earlier.

develops in Lombard or Frank hands, and becomes
wildly grotesque, horrible, grand in despair and agony
of expression, loathsome in details of torment; as
Giotto's work, in a great degree, and still more in
Orgagna's, who seems to have thrown himself into
his Infernos [1] with a sort of enjoyment which casts
a disagreeable kind of firelight on the faith of the
Middle Ages. One is inclined to think that men
who handed their neighbours over, in deliberate
thought, or even in elaborate jest, to eternal
torment; or who played with the idea of so doing,
cannot have had much conviction of its reality, or
of the fearfulness of actual judgment of men for
their deeds. Orgagna might perhaps plead the example of Dante for placing his political or private
enemies in the Inferno; but it is clear, if any
attention whatever is to be paid to Vasari, that he
stood accused of a kind of personal malice, which
was never attributed to the author of the Divine
Comedy. A personal Inferno, or anticipation of
the Judgment of God, by either poet or painter,
really appears to be an act of presumptuous wicked-
ness; which He may doubtless pardon, but which
ordinary men are bound to protest against. There
does, and must, remain in all spiritual thought of the
future, a certain fearful looking for of indignation
which no faith or definite form of religion ever denies
or avoids. The Christian Church of the first three or
four centuries seems certainly to have dwelt less on

[1] In the Campo Santo, at Pisa: that in Sta. Maria Novella in
Florence has been repainted, it is believed by Ghirlandajo
(Vasari, vol. i. p. 204.—Andrea Orgagna); that in Sta. Croce
has perished.

this subject than on any other popular creed. But it was never denied or ignored. The sense of future justice and judgment is human, inevitable, and irresistible ; and it is, to say the least, inaccurate, to talk as popular writers do now, about Christian priests having fabricated a penal doctrine, which every priest on earth would gladly deny, if he could, in the name of his Master. However, this penal doctrine is a subject unfit to be dwelt on by art, as the temporal inflictions of disease, famine, or legal punishment are unfit for her :—but if it must be set forth, the grim vagueness and terrors of the Torcello mosaic are sufficient. There is great difference between emblematic pictorial repetition of the Lord's words, letting them mean what He meant by them, and painting law-officers in hell, for having been engaged against one.[1] One might suppose that this kind of revenge indicated levity or scepticism rather than deliberate malice, and probably amounted to little more than the profane oaths in which the last generation of English gentlemen indulged so freely. Still, the elaborate painting of a picture like the Inferno of Pisa is a proceeding far more deliberate than any verbal curses ; and it must remain, while the plaster and colours last, one singular monument out of many among the moral contrasts of mediæval character. It is humbling to reflect that the author of the mighty Presence of the flying Death, and the great angels of Judgment, could endure to labour over such

---

[1] See Vasari, Orgagna, 210. ed. Bohn. Whether this fresco be the work of Orgagna or the Lorenzetti of Siena has nothing to do with this volume. (See Crowe and Cavalcaselle, vol. i. ; also Vasari, Orgagna, 310, ed. Bohn.)

filthy and hideous details of torment. Things which
are unnameable ought at least to be unpaintable.
Something may be attributed to what are called the
habits of the time, and its butcheries of public
execution and private murder; and much to the
deadly enmities of Florence. To this day her glorious
architecture bears the ancient tokens of a city divided
against itself, house against house; marked by the
gloomy strength and heavy windowless rustications
of the outer walls of her palaces, meant to defy siege,
and harbour garrisons for offence and oppression.
Orgagna died before 1376–7; and two years after
that date broke out the desperate struggles of the
Albizzi and the Parte Guelfa, with the Ricci and
other Ammoniti or disfranchised families—followed
by the contest of the middle classes against the
Minor Arts and the Ciampi. The names of Silvestro
da Medici, Filippo Strozzi the elder, Benedetto
Alberti, and not the least of Michael Lando, the wool-
carder who saved the state, are among those of the
chief actors of the time.

It is singular, and certainly points to the uncon-
trollable, yet sometimes fatal fierceness of Italian
temper, that Michael Angelo himself was guilty of
the same profane folly as Orgagna, in painting his
enemies or foolish critics among the condemned, in
the Last Judgment of the Sistine. And as almost
every weakness or error of the great masters has been

---

[1] The remarkable passage in Hallam's "Middle Ages," vol. i.
pp. 240–249, ed. 1846 (chap. iii. part i.), may be read with advantage on this point. It speaks of the "dark long-cherished hatreds,
and that implacable vindictiveness which distinguished the private
manners of Italy. . . . For revenge she threw away the pearl of
great price, and sacrificed even the recollection of liberty," &c.

religiously imitated, while their great deeds are inimitable and unrecognized, this absurdity has been repeated by no less excellent a follower than Cornelius of Düsseldorf and Munich; who showed his zeal for the Papacy by introducing a corpulent caricature of Luther among the lost, in the great fresco of the Ludwig's Kirche in the latter city. Few artistic errors can be more demoralizing to the painter, or better calculated to make a thoughtful spectator infer that he believes in no future state or judgment whatever.

Orgagna's subject of the Triumph of Death may be taken as heading the long list of Dances of Death or of the Dead, or " Danses Macabre," led by the great Egyptian ascetic Macarius, who presides in Orgagna's work.[1] That at Lucerne on the old wooden bridge is still in existence ; and there is an elaborate one preserved in the French " Histoire des Arts du Moyen Age."[2] But the Dance of Death is always associated with the memory of Hans Holbein, who, though his name is less generally beloved, and less popular than Raffaelle's in sacred-decorative art, is greater as a guide and model, from his matchless invention and energy of graphic power. It is better, too, to close this work with some account of a part of his labours ; first from his connection, through Orgagna, with the earliest pictures of Judgment, and so with the early mosaics of the Apocalypse ; secondly because, as the first and greatest of Protestant painters,

---

[1] The derivation of the word Macabre is uncertain. Dr. Woltmann thinks that " Machabæorum chori" is the real etymology.

[2] Chap. viii. p. 35. De Sommerand. Album 5⁰—7⁰ série. Illustration of a " Danse Macabre " in a MS. belonging to Anne of Bretagne (sixteenth century), " Où est démonstré tous états estre du *bransle* de la mort."

he marks a final stage in the history of Sacred or Religious Art; when it became polemical as well as theological. For the first three or four centuries, in the time of the Biblical cycle, Church art repeats and strives to impress the teaching of Holy Scripture. As doctrine is defined, art becomes theological. As developments of doctrine are demanded by the people, and accepted, and enforced by the failing rulers of the Church, she becomes ecclesiastical; and is claimed accordingly by the Roman system, as a kind of property or private engine of its own. With the Reformation, art is made polemical on both sides:—and its first employment thus, or perhaps rather the most noticeable of its early applications in this direction, is the work of Hans Holbein. For his are the great wood-cuts which express to our minds at this day, as to the minds of all the German people at his period, the thoughts of the religious laity of northern Europe on the subject of the Reformation. The three works of his, the Dance of Death, the Indulgence-mongers, and Christ the True Light, seem to claim precedence in description, even before the great Passion subjects, from that vast mass of Scriptural illustration in all forms, which exercised his immeasurable imagination.

His Dance of Death, or of the Dead, comes first, with its Last Judgment. It is not with the frescoes on the cloister walls at Basle that we are concerned, but with that wonderful series of wood-cuts of his drawing (cut probably by Lützelburger the admirable "form-schneider") which will carry down his name for ever in connection with the contrast of Death and Life. Two or three of these cuts have been repro-

duced for Prof. Ruskin by the exceeding skill of Mr.
Burges, and are facsimiles utterly undistinguishable
from the original print.[1] As in all the more solemn
Dances of Death, Holbein's is accompanied by his
foreshowing of the Judgment of Mankind. And he
alone seems to have formed, and to acknowledge the
thought, that though condemnation be real, and
Tophet assuredly prepared of old, it does not become
a painter to let his imagination run riot on horrors
he has not seen. And as in the great Pisan fresco,
Hell seems to have the better, and few are saved, so
in the last of Holbein's wood-cuts, the just alone
stand before their Lord rejoicing. Yet he goes on
warning throughout, by one threatening text after
another, that the sinner risks dying in his sins,
even to infinite loss or perdition unless he repent.
"What will ye do in the end thereof?"[2] is the motto
of the whole work. But there is a tone of half humorous reflection through it all, on the grand equality
of Death, so just and mighty, subtle and searching.
There is no democratic spitefulness, though the difficulty and piteousness of the great change to the fair
and luxurious is steadily dwelt on. But the starving
hind and his worn-out horses are in deadly terror at
the grim unknown, who strides to them across the
heavy furrows, bringing rest, " bringing pleasant time
to weary team;"[3] and the poor pedlar, with his
heavy pack, is hurried off as pitilessly, and goes as
unwillingly, as the stern old noble who turns on the
Destroyer, sword in hand, and rejoices once more in
fierce unavailing battle. Indeed, in some of the later

[1] See "Fors Clavigera," No. 4.
[2] Gedenk das End—Memorare novissima.
[3] "Bobus fatigatis amicum tempus agens."

verses, which are supposed rightly to express the painter's mind, Death speaks kindly to his valiant victim, " Come thou with me, good sword and true." But go we all must, quoth the painter; and each will go from his daily life, from ploughing or grinding at the mill; and undoubtedly, ye shall go from the midst of your sins, if ye *will* practise them.   O, king and emperor, cardinal and pope, burgher, soldier, old crone and little child, painter, scholar, apothecary, ploughboy, thief; and you, all-privileged Fool—you must depart for good or evil.   And therefore—what? Do not, as Orgagna says, turn hermits and live on hind's milk, but do justly, love mercy, walk humbly in Christ's name ; and above all, fear not.   There lingers in Holbein's mood the same defiance of death which the Lombards learnt from their Scandinavian fathers. It is the spirit of the wanderer, Viking or Varang, who rose up ready to seek another land ; and faced the last enemy like an earthly foeman, with scornful welcome; meeting the inevitable as Antar the Arab met his enemies, "even as the ground receives the first of the rain."   Allowing for changes of period, race, circumstance, and instruction, there is much in this which is nearly allied to the spirit with which Christians of the Martyr-ages seem to have looked on death.   Willingness to depart, through hope in Christ, is more pronounced, of course, in those who were preaching His name within memory of actual witnesses who had seen and handled, than in men accustomed to be told that Alexander VI. and Leo X. were Vicars of Christ.   Yet the early symbolisms of the anchored ships or unyoked chariot, the flower-wreaths, and winged creatures rejoicing in liberty, and the absence of inquiry about the sensations and phenomena of their change : the general and undefined hope in Christ for all who repent and believe in Him, seem to have been nearly the same in the martyrs of the Empire, as in the martyrs of the Curia.

The invention of wood-cutting and copper-engraving has had this important bearing on church decoration, that it has withdrawn the *absolute* necessity for wall-paintings of the Sacred Histories. Not only are there more books, but those books may be illustrated, and appeal vigorously to the learner's imagination : and this not only here and there, at great expense, through manuscript illumination, but by all the countless devices of the Press, with at least some excellence, and at the cheapest rate. This seems to us in no sense to diminish the value of instructive decoration in churches, only to make it more necessary that the Primitive standard and a list of subjects involving Primitive doctrine, should be thoroughly recognized in our own Church. But if Holbein were a far less remarkable man, he would be remembered in Religious Art, perhaps for ever, by the originality and power of his Protest in wood-cut.[1] The True Light dates 1524, and Holbein was in London in 1527, the year before Dürer's death.

---

[1] The word "Protestant" has many meanings in our own day, varying greatly with the matter which a person may protest against. Aggressive infidelity claims the title, for the purpose of exciting popular passion against High Anglicanism. In one man's mind, Protestantism seems to mean personal religion; in another's, personal irreligion. Speaking as Christians, we use it in the sense of the ancient Christian brotherhood of the early English Reformation, about 1526. There is a Protestantism of the German and English Reformation, and another of the French Revolution ; the one against the Pope, the other against the existence of God. And it is time for Anglicans, in their turn, to protest against atheistic assumptions of Puritan language.

Six years before, the tale had come to Antwerp of
Martin Luther's imprisonment, and had provoked
the great Nuremberger's prayers and lamentations
over his supposed danger.   We have Dürer's protest
in that bitter and pathetic outburst [1]—it is that of
personal belief in Christ as God and Lord ; nor do we
recognize the word Protestantism in its negative sense.

Holbein's declaration of what he held, and what he
did not hold, in the day of spiritual trial and confusion, is recorded in the Indulgence-shop and the
True Light.   In the one, the sale of pardons is
going on.   Those who can pay for forgiveness of
sins are paying, and money down is the strict order
of the day : those who cannot pay are left in their
sins : there they may stay unforgiven.   The real
sting of the picture is not that the rich man is fined
for his offences, or that the monk gets the money ;
but that the poor man, for as much as he has not to
pay, shall *not* be frankly forgiven.   But Holbein's is
no merely negative Protestantism ; for on the other
side, and apart from the dealer, the " Offen Synder,"
the repentant man, self-convicted, and avowing his
sin, is following David and Manasses, who kneel
before Christ, and is making his prayer, not unheard.
This is the practical side of the Reformation, and a
simple assertion of personal reliance on the Redeemer
for forgiveness.   In the True Light, we have the
speculative side of the renewed faith, as it appeared
to painters, burghers, and nobles, weary of the Papacy
but by no means weary of the Faith.   The Lamp of

---

[1] See Mr. Scott's " Life of Dürer."   The passage is found in
Weale's folio work, London, 1846.   See *Contemporary Review*,
vol. ii. p. 398.

Truth divides the picture in two. By it stands the Lord, with willing followers crowding to Him, of all sorts; laity, clergy, and women. He is opening their eyes, and they receive sight from Him. On the other side, popes, cardinals, monks, and doctors are leading each other away from the Lord among dark mountains, which remind one of the fate of the Hypocrite in the Pilgrim's Progress, who stumbled and fell, and rose no more. Plato and Aristotle are the leaders of the blind; the former has just fallen into a pit, and the other, turbaned like a " malignant" Turk, is following him straightway. This is the protest of energetic lay-thought; of newly-gained knowledge of nature; of fresh enterprise and desired learning, against the Aristotelian limits and barriers of thought. " Men saw," as Mr. Maurice has said, ". that the popes were governed by the doctors, and the doctors by the Categories." The Categories were classifications of all things for the purposes of formal logic, and men found that they themselves, and a vast number of newly found thoughts and things, could not be thus arranged and dealt with *secundum artem* any longer. They rose and said: On many new things we must have truth, if God will. We must have new arrangements of new phenomena, and inferences will follow from them. Let us look at facts as we find them; either at human facts of old, at the Greek language, at its literature, and at the remnants of its art; or more particularly at the present facts of nature; at all which God has given us to know on earth of earth. In evil hours and for evil reasons, through worldly interests which could not be avowed, and for selfish or panic terrors which should not have been felt, Theology was set against Knowledge; and the quarrel has never been healed. But for all that it never should have existed; and firm ground will be reached for its adjustment, when rival professors of spiritual and natural science shall mutually concede to each other (as in many cases they are beginning to do) that both the results of physical experiment, and the facts of spiritual experience, are after all true and real things.

With Raffaelle and with Holbein the higher symbolism and the historical testimony of Church art seem both to have passed away, or to have run wild; on the Roman Catholic side into polemical assertion of the Deity of Mary, and of prayer to Saints and Angels, aided by every kind of luscious appeal to beauty; or into the unscrupulous exploitation of the doctrine of the material purgatory, by general representation of souls in torment. The German Catholic-art revival, though the work of highly instructed and conscientious men, has not altogether escaped this; but there can be no doubt that it has done infinitely more good than harm. On the Protestant side, art has run astray into foolish unmeaning allegory; and altogether fallen into disuse and suspicion as a means of Christian instruction. If a course of subjects, directed to illustration of the Primitive Faith and the fufilment of prophecy, and to reverent realism of the events of Holy Scripture, were either defined and laid down, or tacitly accepted for Church decoration —to be treated of course as the different genius of different artists should direct them—that would be the foundation of an English school of high-aimed art. It may be visionary to hope for one;

but it must be said that loftiness of aim appears to be at present the great want of English artists. The contemplation of the highest subjects of human thought can at least do them no harm.

Two papers, one on Liturgical Books, the other containing some remarks on Miniatures and Illumination, have been added to the Index of Subjects of Primitive Art. They hardly form a part of this book, considered as an account of the decorative principles and records of the Early Church. The works of Professor Westwood, so frequently referred to, are the best source of information which is generally accessible. But it is probably the case that most persons who are interested in early art, and read this book, would, rather than not, have a few few facts on the subject of early caligraphy and book-ornament: and the addition has been made accordingly. The arts of illumination and of architectural carving, preserved in the dark ages, and fostered in their mediæval infancy under shade of convent walls, always remained in full practice. They had their chief professors still, in monastic workshops and scriptoria, while fresco, oil-painting, and sculpture broke into artistic liberty, and then advanced to the license of the later Renaissance; so that for a time art passed into the service of pleasure instead of religion.[1] But this work would be incomplete without some brief allusion to a deeply interesting relic of the Later Middle Ages, which not only throws a favourable light on the Christian teaching of the

[1] Those times of transition are best commented on in Prof. Ruskin's works, especially in volumes iii. and v. of "Modern Painters;"—best described, perhaps, by Messrs. Crowe and Cavalcaselle, and in the works of Kügler, Lübke, and Woltmann.

German peasantry in very early ages, but preserves and repeats many of the subjects of the Catacombs and Sarcophagi, with reference to Messianic type and prophecy—we mean of course the Passions-Vorstellung of Ober-Ammergau. Its music and *mise en scène* are its only modern features ; and it possesses the deepest interest from the light which it throws on the lay-religion of the German peasantry. So many accounts have been given of it that we can but refer to the Rev. Malcolm McColl's as the standard one; and to a highly interesting article signed Karl Blind in " The Dark Blue Magazine." [1] The latter points out its truly Catholic or non-Papal character, which was certainly and fully maintained when the author visited it in 1871. Those who would understand it fully should read the article on German literature in Prof. Max Müller's " Chips from a German Workshop," which points out a thing difficult to understand, the German maintenance of pure Scriptural teaching, in spite of ignorance and neglect, before the Reformation. He attributes it to the lower clergy, and—to their great credit—to the fraternization of the preaching friars with the people against the higher clergy. " The people were hungry and thirsty after religious teaching. They had been systematically starved or fed with stones. Part of the Bible had been translated for them ; but what Ulfilas was free to do in the fourth century was condemned by the prelates assembled at the Synod of Trier in 1231. Nor were the sermons of the itinerant friars in towns and villages always to the taste of bishops and abbots. Brother Bert

[1] July 1871.

bold (died 1272) was a Franciscan. He travelled about the country, and was revered by the people as a saint and a prophet. The doctrine he preached, though it was the old teaching of the Apostles, was as new to the peasants who came to hear him as it had been to the citizens of Athens who came to hear St. Paul. The saying of St. Chrysostom, that Christianity had turned many a peasant into a philosopher, came true again in the time of Eckhart (d. 1329), and Tauler (1361). Men who called themselves Christians had been taught, and had brought themselves to believe, that to read the writings of the Apostles was a deadly sin. Yet in secret they were yearning after that forbidden Bible. They knew that there were translations; and though those translations had been condemned by Popes and Synods, the people could not resist the temptation of reading them."

The character of German Catholicism is still moulded, after all changes, by the reading of the Law, the Prophets, and the Gospels. Nor could anything prove this more vividly than the Ammergau exhibition, which is in fact an acted homily on the connection of the Old and New Testaments; of type with antitype, and Messianic prophecy with the Messiah. The same subject supplied motives of ornament for the Catacomb-paintings and carven tombs. Paulinus of Nola's motto[1] would be a suitable motto for the performance, theologically speaking. It begins;—as the history of Redemption begins;—as the Catacomb-cycle begins;— as the time-honoured Sacramental instructions of

---

[1] "Lex antiqua novam firmat, veterem nova complet."

Bishop Wilson begin—with the fall and corruption of man and the institution of sacrifice; it ends with the Crucifixion and Resurrection. The Fall, the Promise of the Redeemer, and the Sacrifice of Isaac, are its first tableaux from the Old Testament; and they are followed at once by the opening of the Passions-spiel proper, with the Lord's Entry into Jerusalem. The Rock and the Manna are compared with the Lord's Supper; the thirty pieces of silver, and the sale of Joseph are set over against each other. Daniel's condemnation to the Lions followed by the Lord before Pilate; Moses, Aaron, and the Scapegoat by the "Ecce Homo;" the Brazen Serpent by the actual Crucifixion; Jonah by the Resurrection; the passage of the Red Sea, by the Ascension, as the return of our Forerunner where He was before. All these illustrations of type and prophecy, with others, are in the Passions-spiel; and nearly all the subjects will be found in the Primitive cycle. The doctrines of Incarnation and Sacrifice govern both: and both illustrate the convergence of the Christian-mind of all races and ages on the central and primæval doctrine of Salvation in the life and death of Christ for Man. In spite of evil, man hopes for all things through the Lord's life and death; he has had that hope from the beginning of evil; and Christian art and symbolism are one great means of its expression. It never fails, it reaches all minds. It labours for ever at its manifold answer to the great question, "Cur Deus Homo," from the earliest paintings of the martyrs' graves, through Ravenna and the fall of old Rome, and the rise of Byzantium; through the irruption and conversion of the Lombard race; through

the Pisan and Florentine outburst of intellect, and
poetry, and graphic powers, from Nicolo Pisano
and Cimabue to Michael Angelo; and from Bellini
to Tintoret and Veronese in Venice;—even to its last
regularly descended offset, the multitudinous pageant
of the Bavarian Highlands. This adds to primitive
subjects the actual representation of the Crucifixion,
and so far rests on sixth-century precedent. But no
one word in it that we ever heard speaks of prayer
to Mary or to Saints, of the deity of Mary, of purgatory, or of legend. Each scene of the New Testament was preceded by its typical scene from Hebrew
history, expounded in recitative or choric hymn, with
noble voices and modest gesture: and the argument
was still the Whole Humanity for man's sake, to
atone for and do away with evil. Its logical gist or
argument was exactly that of Bishop Wilson's first
chapter on the Holy Communion, reasoning from the
Fall to Sacrifice for sin, and from typical sacrifice to
the conclusive sacrifice.

Few scenes—at least in Europe—can better illustrate the difference between things of the senses,
which seem so real, and yet change hour by hour,
and things of the spirit, which endure—than the
ancient Passion-play, set forth in the solemn presence
of the blue pine-woods of the Ammer-thal, under the
frown of its steep unchanging hills. Unchanging as
men call them, they crumble and alter under storm
and frost, and the quaint ceremonial marks new
decades, and actors and audience pass away from the
shows of things into silence and reality. What is there
that will last?—At least, the Argument of the Play
alters not, for the word of the Lord endureth for ever.

CHAPTER XI.

THE modern system of divided labour possesses great advantages for production, and perhaps for scientific research, though men's minds appear to be often somewhat cramped and narrowed by exclusive study. It has been remarked—we believe by Mr. Fitzjames Stephen—that the principle of division of labour is now being carried on so quickly in almost every department of thought, that it seems probable that we may at last arrive at a state of things in which the claim to any other sort of knowledge than a microscopic acquaintance with some particular department of some one branch will be regarded as an absurd presumption. This, he apprehends, and so do we, would have very little tendency to elevate and enrich the minds of the possessors of these separate stores of mutually un-intelligible discovery. But in fine art, where the inventive faculty has so much to do with combination and composition, separate and exclusive studies have already done harm enough. They have led to the great decorative difficulty of the present day, that architects on one hand, and painters and sculptors on the other, are always at variance in Church ornament. The necessity that a great architect should also be a sculptor, and indeed a painter, has already been expressed, not in vain, by Professor Ruskin in this country; but we are glad to refer to Dr. Lübke's and Herr Burckhardt's "Geschichte der Renaissance" for a parallel observation. Ghiberti's remark, on the all-embracing Giotto, is quoted;[1] and the authors observe on it that "the many-sidedness of the earlier artists, which is quite a riddle to our age of division of labour, was of extraordinary value in architecture .... when architects were also sculptors, painters and carvers in wood; accustomed to express form in every way."

Venturing no further at present on this grave matter, than to express the hope that our architects will at least become students of organic form, and more especially of colour; and that our painters will remember that the construction of a building is *its* organic form, which they are to express and embellish under the architect's direction, and not to thwart him by disguising—we still take leave to set down here a few distinctions and reflections for the popular mind, which may help the building public, subscribers, promoters, and well-wishers to Church art, to understand what they really wish for or ought to desire; and how much of that they ought to have according to their funds; that is to say, according to their willingness to sacrifice money to education, spiritual and temporal.

It seems to us, in the first place and of course, that the decoration of every consecrated building should be planned from the first by the architect in subject, colour, and form, or thoroughly arranged by him,

---

[1] Quando la natura vuole concedere alcuna cosa, la concede senza veruna avarizia. "When it pleases Nature to grant a thing, she bestows it without any manner of grudging."

with painters and sculptors, as to its execution; and with employers and clergy, as to its subjects and purpose. The practical object of this book has been to suggest to clergy and laity the ancient standard and list of subjects represented in the first six or seven centuries. But whatever choice may be made in the matter, we think there are a few remarks to be made about things to be understood on both sides. Let us start with the assumption that subjects of Church ornament have been arranged between subscribers, architect, artists, and clergy; and that a style has been selected. Then, for internal decoration, we think it at least convenient to begin with the consideration of colour. For the selected style, whatever it may be, determines in a great measure where the sculpture is to come ; and the powers and acquired knowledge of the architect will be shown in its proportions and arrangement. But he should know, and ought to be able to convey the idea to his patrons, how much colour he will have, and where, and on what means he will rely for introducing it.

Colour, as we take it here, is either solid or transparent ; you either see light through it, or you do not. You must either get the charm and glow of varied hue into your stone building through painted windows, which is using transparent colour ; or obtain them by fresco or mosaic, or opaque glass work on the walls, which is using opaque colour.[1]

Now—architects will excuse the utterance of truisms for popular use—

[1] Transparent pigments may, of course, be used in wall-painting. All we can regard here is, that the wall is not transparent, only reflecting light, while the window transmits it.

First, in northern, or high-gabled, or "vertical" architecture—French, German, or English—more light is, on the whole, desirable than in a round-arched, Roman, or "horizontal," or low-gabled building—for the round arch is Roman, and so is all that is built therewith. All such work is derived from the vaultings of baths and cloacæ.

Secondly, and in consequence, your windows will be more important features, in construction and decoration, in Gothic than in Byzantine or Roman-esque; and in French Gothic than Italian Gothic.

Thirdly, you will have to make up your mind whether the colour shall come in through the win-dows, or be laid or inlaid on the walls; that is to say, whether you will call chief attention to the one or the other. Both cannot go first as vehicles of colour; they must be harmonized, and that by subduing the one in favour of the other. I have known the other principle asserted; of exaggerating hue in wall-paint-ing, because brilliant windows were used in the same building; and that by an able architect of great and deserved name; but I remain totally unable to under-stand him, so far.

Fourthly, in Northern Gothic you will have to insist on the windows for colour; and as they there-fore, infallibly, will draw the eye to them, you must put your most important subjects, the principal arguments of your art-preaching, in your principal windows. And your walls should not be made to rival them, but toned down to equal richness, with less brilliancy.

Fifthly: If your architecture is to be that of the hotter countries of Europe, where excess of light is to be avoided, rather than where every ray of it must be courted, you will have small windows and large surfaces of wall. In this case you will rely on your spaces of wall for colour and subject; the colour of your church will be opaque; you will use fresco or mosaic; and have to deal with the far greater difficulties of treatment which are involved in their use. But in any case the help of an educated painter or professional colourist is highly necessary, unless the architect be one himself.

On this subject, we are inclined to think that decorators, as a rule, seem hardly sensible of the value of the natural tints of the materials they employ. One of the great beauties of Saracenic structure is its banded architecture, as observed in Cairo and Damascus; in red and white, or red, black, and white material. It has been well imitated in this country, as in Mr. Butterfield's chapel at Balliol College, Oxford; but internal colour as well might be bestowed on the cheapest buildings, by lining them with red and white bricks in the barred form, and simply omitting the plaster. Great attention, we hope, is now being bestowed on moulded brick and terra-cotta ornament for such interiors. Mere repetition of patterns in paint is not satisfactory; and until fresco-painters are more numerous, and fresco-colours more decidedly permanent, there is reason for effort to do all which can be done with the natural hues of brick, stone, and tile. The author would prefer them, in all cases, to merely decorative forms without symbolical or historic meaning. Moreover, in our large and smoky cities, he hears strong complaints against all paint whatever; it fouls and will not clean. Those who have seen the little chapel at Lynmouth, North Devon, will see how much can be done at slight expense in a land of granite and red sandstone, without a touch of paint or a line of gilding. The latter means of orna ment would take a book to itself; and the mention of paint opens up the whole subject of interior decoration, religious and domestic. But thus much he may say to church-builders—spare paint and plaster altogether; study the star-and-cross pattern of the Doge's Palace, and try it in limestone and sandstone, or even in good red and white brick. Compare it with the barred Egyptian work: have bands if you will, or pattern if you will, but beware of both together. The repetition of an easy idea is the secret of simple pattern, where no high thought is expressed; and the popular eye is too indolent to follow pattern, if interrupted and complicated by stripes and stars. Gilding, as the richest form of ornament, should be on the leading lines, and direct the eye. But we have not yet seen how much may be done by incrustation and the use of tile-mosaic and opaque glass. There is no reason why moulded tiles should not be used as freely as moulded bricks: on walls as well as pavement. And, with really good designs, symbolic or other, an honestly-built church, lined with these materials and rejoicing in well-arranged hues of its own structure, ought to be felt to be successful and beautiful, whether light and clearness, or dark ness and richness, be its tone of colour-decoration.

Again, if the artistic effect of the whole thing is not to suffer grievously and continuously, some understanding ought to exist as to the use of violent colour in temporary decorations, such as flowers, hangings, altar vestments, and the like. If colour is used in the ceremonial of our Christian worship, it must be used well or ill. If well, it proves that time, thought, and artistic effort have been faithfully devoted to God's service; and it gives a lofty and true pleasure to all. If ill, it at least vexes or distracts those worshippers, few or many, who are not protected by colour-blindness, real or acquired. To have a large light church with all the colours of the rainbow in its windows, as in a Norman Gothic cathedral—to add to this fresco and mosaic, excellent of their kind, but adapted from the colours of Venice or Ravenna, contending desperately with showers of transmitted hue at every gleam of morning or evening sunshine—and then to put in altar-cloths and hangings in different styles and tints, with mediæval vestments, variegated flowers, and gilding regardless of expense—supposing, moreover, that the colours employed include the metallic greens and acrid mauves and magentas of modern glass work and weaving;—this is to make a picture by sitting on a set palette. Whereas if you will have plenty of grisaille in your windows, and study harmonies of one or two colours in them, rather than contrasts of many—if you will avoid violent greens as you would deprecate a steam whistle in an orchestra; if you would try what could be done in a small window with olive-greens and ivy-greens, white and yellow *alone*, allowing sparks of the emerald tint, or one touch of crimson, in fear and trembling—then, at all events, the immediate effect would be chastened and softened. Such windows, too, especially if placed low on church walls, would not interfere with the opaque colours of the interior. The use of rich brown. varied to purple, and olive to green, with a small quantity of crimson, excluding all other colour, is much to be desired. In blues all violent mazarines and "university" colours are to be avoided, except in their faded form, in which indigo takes part: but even the deep hues of Ravenna mosaic are unsuited for window colours, through which light passes; though the varied play of their own hue is so very striking.

The present writer has just had the pleasure of contemplating the progress of some tolerably well-guided, though very quiet church decorations for Easter. He has been struck with the good effect of green ivy or even box wreaths, studded with white and yellow immortelles in little bundles. He observes that daffodils alternating on green with primroses have a delightful effect. He has succeeded in excluding any colours from the reredos except white, two or three greens, and pale crimson azaleas. He is thankful to have seen the altar of a well-beloved church not loaded with tier on tier of ill-arranged nose-gays like an inn sideboard. And it occurs to him that any part of a congregation (more especially any sister-hood, numbering among them ladies well trained in embroidery or painting) might greatly assist the decorations of chancels and altars all over England by framing a good set of rules for natural-flower ornament; founded on the succession of ordinary and "country" blossoms, such as they can best obtain, as

" The daughters of the year,
Each garlanded with her peculiar flower,
Dance into the light, and die into the shade."

He cannot help thinking that throughout the ordinary year crimson and white should be the only colours of flowers used on the altar. Of course, every variety of shade and hue in one colour should be used. Red berries and white immortelles, in not too large quantity, would supply the need in Autumn, if scarlet geranium, white aster, or chrysanthemum, or Christmas-rose, failed. Violet or even blue, well combined or mixed with black (violets, dark hyacinth or pansies), would be substituted for crimson in Lent. Yellow, white and orange would be a chord of colour to admit the early spring flowers—and red roses and white pinks would last the summer through. Green leaves, he thinks, will be better round or behind the altar than upon it, unless in fringes to distinguish the white flowers from the snowy coverings. The quantity of blossoms is highly unimportant, if they be rightly massed and opposed to each other, and he would plead for a few vessels of white opaque glass or alabaster to contain them. Great mingled bunches of hyacinths, primroses, peonies, wallflowers, anemonies and daffodils will doubtless be observed at this season—stuck in brass chimney ornaments, and backed by thickets of box and laurel; disguising the reredos of many an English church, and vying with masses of candles to eclipse or hide the vessels of the Eucharist altogether.

It is supposed, of course, in these remarks, that flowers are admissible on, or above, or around Anglican altars, or credence tables. It seems strange that when whole churches have been decorated with flowers time out of mind, their presence in that part of the church should call for protest or legal interposition. The actual state of law on the subject is hard to define; but treating the question as a matter of archæology, there is no doubt that flowers were the ornaments of the earliest Christian sepulchres, and that the earliest sepulchres were frequently used as altar tables for the celebration of the Lord's Supper, whatever rite may have been used. The use of red and white flowers, or of violet and white in Lent, seems equally harmless and appropriate.

If it were possible to employ ladies in mosaic work instead of embroidery, the results of their labours in church ornament would be more perceptible to the grosser sex, and, as the author thinks, more valuable. Educated labour of this kind will assuredly increase rapidly in value; for if churches are ever to be decorated on the Venetian model, having the principal events of the Old Testament at the west end, and their fulfilment in the New, to the east;—or, if in others, the ancient symbolisms are to be set forth that men may remember that their Church and her services are really not things of yesterday, but an inheritance from Apostolic days—then art work of high character must be cheapened, for it will be needed in great quantity. The evidence of Messrs. Watts, R.A., and Armitage, R.A., before the late Royal Academy Commission, is very weighty and apposite on this subject. Both assert, with immaterial differences, that designs of high merit would be willingly supplied by some of our leading artists at a moderate rate; and that each might be executed by students (properly trained, we presume, either in the school of the Royal Academy, or in the higher grades of the departmental instruction) under the superintendence of some one competent man.   The only reason, Mr. Watts thinks, why the taste for mural decoration in churches and schools does not rapidly increase in the country is because such things are not enough seen ; they are only executed where the public do not see them.   " To employ students upon them, and to scatter them abroad as much as possible, is what is wanted in the first instance.   The Royal Academy should, by way of developing taste, do something towards placing before the eyes of the public at large the best specimens of art. . . . The students of the Royal Academy who made good designs and gained medals should be given a set of designs, and, with a certain small allowance, required to carry them out on the walls of some public building."

We cannot but hope that somewhat of a British school of fresco and grand mosaic may arise from the national contribution to the decoration of St. Paul's Cathedral.   The preliminary difficulties are very great; strong rivalries must necessarily be involved ; and personal friendship and interests must hamper great works now, as heavily as in the days when Ghiberti was set up against Brunelleschi, or when Bramante pitted Raffaelle against Michael Angelo. But in those days, at all events, the immortal labour was accomplished ; and we will hope for the best now.

Another means of national progress in graphic art, specially adapted to Gothic or Romanesque architecture, and to which the great mediæval churches owe most of their sculpture, is the formation of a class of artist workmen ; by proper instruction in drawing and modelling, which is now accessible, we are most thankful to say, in all our cities and considerable towns. No one has spoken so eloquently on this point, nor with such practical acuteness and fulness of suggestion, as Prof. Ruskin, in his dissertation on the *Nature of Gothic*.[1] The following observation appears specially important with relation to the large number of artizans and their sons who might in time form schools of ornamental sculpture which might adorn not only our cathedrals, but our country churches:—" It is perhaps the principal admirableness of the Gothic schools of architecture that they thus receive the results of the labour of inferior minds ; and out of fragments betraying imperfection in every touch, indulgently raise up a stately and unaccusable whole. To every spirit which Christian architecture summons to her service, her exhortation is, do what you can and frankly confess what you are unable to do : neither let your effort be shortened for fear of failure, nor your confession silenced for fear of shame."

It certainly seems to the writer a possibility that English artisan-art may yet culminate in works like the stony hawthorn of Bourges, or the bossy figure-sculpture of St. Zenone. We shall not see it :—yet art would lose all its interest for lovers of our England, if it were not for the hope that it will yet do something to teach and elevate the poor, and all the others " whose souls cleave to the dust" either for want of means, or for greed of money. To get men lifted into the art-world seems in fact as great a matter even as the production of great isolated works

[1] In " The Stones of Venice," vol. ii., 2nd period, chap. i. p. 158.

of art. And it certainly does appear, that if any places be specially fitted to convey the teaching of beauty to poor English people much in need of it, it is the churches which are their own; whose doors invite them continually, from which no man can be shut out; which appeal by painting or sculpture, without letter or line, straight to the heart and understanding.

One suggestion only we have to make about sculpture; and that especially to artist-workmen and their employers—to be specially careful and sparing of deep cutting and black shadow, in diffused lights like those of most of our own great churches. New builders ought to remember the singularly unconsidered truism that their buildings cannot be old, or have the deep-marked features of age, all at once. Let them be patient, and have large faith in time and dirt. We really have often noticed, in the many criticisms on new buildings which have reached our ears in the last decade or so, that a class of critics exists who seem to think a thirteenth-century cathedral can be built with the grey honours of all its ages, in a few years' work in the nineteenth. They decline to remember that the thirteenth-century Gothic, when it was new, looked new; and that it would not have been impressive by reason of historical connections and hoar antiquity to us, if we had seen its first stones laid. So we hear very good modern Gothic virulently abused, not because it is ill-designed or ill-cut, but because it does not produce all the same varied associations of thought which old and historical work necessarily does, whether it be good art or bad. Every builder worth his salt, works for posterity; others shall enter into his labours, as he has gained his inspiration and his science from those who have gone before.

The Slade Professor's "Aratra Pentelici"[1] ought to be read with great attention on this subject, and the beautiful thirteenth engraving carefully studied. Perhaps no other work can give so clear and prompt understanding of the immense power of good drawing, as distinguished from deep cutting. Depth and shadow of relief, the mere vulgar pleasure of seeing white against black, are very unimportant indeed when balanced against power and rightness of line. The bas-relief is to all intents and purposes a light and shade picture; and it is as wrong to force the pitch of shade, without good reason, in the one as in the other. Moreover, time and its stains always act in favour of the artist's light and shade, as the projecting parts get worn white with exposure, and dust accumulates in the hollows. Another and highly important reason for shallow cutting in exterior carvings, is its far greater solidity and the enduring nature of the work. Far too much modern English Gothic bears witness sadly, by its premature decay, to the zealous and misapplied ambition of the workman; who has honestly wished to do his work thoroughly, or indulged vanity in his manual skill, and so under-cut everything to obtain dark shadow (when an outline incised round each object would make it tell quite sufficiently), treating stone as if it were as tough as bronze, to its certain destruction in years or even months. Steady practice of animal-drawing,

[1] Prof. Ruskin, Fifth Lecture, pp. 164–175.

where the slightest incisions mark the play of broad surfaces of muscle, would probably be the best discipline to cure the pupil of too constant search for edges and shadows.

This book has reached a sufficient length, and the writer is unwilling to encumber it here with remarks on several works of modern artists, which appear to him to give evidence, in various grades of sacred art, of power of high character and degree.[1] But one painting he has been allowed to see, to which the public is now admitted, and which seems to him a work of the gravest import. It is the chief result of five years' labour;—by one of the men strongest to labour in all toiling England. It is Holman Hunt's picture, called "The Shadow of Death." Our Lord rises from toil in the late afternoon, in the carpenter's shop at Nazareth, stretching His arms lightly on each side with a natural gesture of slight fatigue; and the slant rays of the early sunset, bathing a wonderfully realised landscape of the thymy terraces of the Galilean hill-sides, enter the wide open window, and cast the shadow of the Crucified on the opposite wall. The Virgin-Mother kneels below at an open chest, which contains the presents of the three kings who had come to the brightness of His rising. She may be recalling words of theirs, or thoughts of that time, and asking Him about the fulfilment of His Father's business. We must altogether decline description or criticism of any part of this picture, and most of all of the face with which He looks towards her. But it falls

---

[1] For this he may refer to an essay in the First Series of ".The Church and the Age," pp. 154, 155.

in with what we have already said[1] to make one observation on this great work :—that, beyond any others with which we are acquainted, it unites in harmonious realism the two great schools or styles of ideal representation of the Son of Man. On both sides of the Alps there has always been the classical or quasi-traditional ideal of Him, which endowed Him with the greatest beauty of face and form which the artist could picture to his invention, or embody by his graphic skill. On the other hand, among Byzantines in the East and German Goths in the West, the ascetic ideal has been followed, which passed from melancholy grace to grimaces of feature and unsightly emaciation or convulsion of body. Mr. Holman Hunt's great skill and experience, and a peculiar happiness, in this instance, in the selection of his model, have enabled him to produce a face of supreme beauty and power, and a form alike ascetic and athletic ; where brilliancy of skin and low condition of flesh produce all necessary effect of delicacy on the long, grandly-formed and sinewy limbs of the Fairest of all men. To an archæologist the appearance of this picture is an era : what it is to the painter only a skilled painter can tell. Whatever it is or may become to the Christian spectator, this work is the thought and object to which five years' labour has been dedicated by the first painter of sacred subject which this generation has produced.

[1] See the chapter on the Catacombs, and the Index article on Portraits of the Lord.

THE ASCENSION. FROM MS. OF THE MONK RABULA.

INDEX

HISTORICAL AND EMBLEMATIC SUBJECTS

OF

Sacred Art in the Primitive Church.

A and ω.

Of these symbolic letters the ω is always given in the
minuscular or " small " form. They are generally ap-
pended to the Monogram of Christ, or suspended from
the arms of the Cross, whether from the St. Andrew's or
decussated symbol, or the later upright or penal Cross.
For the first see De Rossi, Inscr. No. 776 ; for the
latter Bottari, tav. xliv. This is a sixth or seventh
century Cross in the Catacomb of St. Pontianus, and
is given in photograph of its actual present condition
by Parker.

These letters are found, with or without the Monogram, on
all kinds of works of Christian antiquity ; on sepulchral
monuments, especially those of ancient France (see Le
Blant's " Monuments Chrétiennes de la Gaul," *passim*) ;

on cups (Boldetti, from Callixtine Catacomb, tav. iii. 4, p. 194) ; on rings and sigils (*v.* Martigny, " Dict. des Ant. Chrétiennes," s. v. Anneaux) ; and on coins (Do. Numismatique), immediately after the death of Constantine.

Their use amounts to a quotation of Rev. xxii. 13, and a confession of faith in Our Lord's assertion of His own Infinity and Divinity.   See Prudentius, Hymnus Omn. Hor. 10, Cathemerinon, ix. p. 35,

> " Corde natus ex parentis ante mundi exordium,
> Alpha et ω cognominatus, Ipse fons et clausula
> Omnium quæ sunt, fuerunt, quæque post futura sunt."

No doubt the symbol was more common after the outbreak of Arianism ; but it seems pretty clear from the above-mentioned cup in Boldetti, and from the inscription by Victorina to her martyred husband Heraclius (Aringhi, i. 605), that it was used before the First Nicene Council. It will be found (see Westwood's " Palæographia Sacra ") in the Psalter of Athelstan (703) and in the Bible of Alcuin, both in the British Museum.

Abel, Cain and

See Bosio, III. v., p. 159, on a sarcophagus from the Cemetery of Lucina, and not unfrequently in bas-relief, Bottari, tav. cxxxvii.   Abel offers the Lamb ; and Cain ears of corn, or a bunch of grapes.   The presentation of the Lamb by Abel may doubtless have been an Eucharistic symbolism in the mind of the artist : whether the grapes are substituted for the corn in the above-quoted picture with the same idea seems doubtful.

Abel in the act of Sacrifice.

With Cain, see Bottari, tav. cxxxvii. 51, and vol. iii. p.

41.[1] See Mosaics of Ravenna, by Parker, and Chap. vii. on the Sacramental Picture in St. Vitale, of Abel and Melchisedech.

ABRAHAM.   Bottari, tav. xv. Sarcophagus of Junius Bassus, also xl. cxi. xxxvii. &c.

Most frequently with Isaac, in the interrupted Sacrifice, as in St. Vitale at Ravenna, where the Visit of the Three Angels is also represented.   Both Abraham and Isaac are generally clad in tunics; in Bottari, tav. lix., Abraham wears a long tunic, and Isaac the pallium.   In tav. clxi. Abraham is clad in high-priest's robes.   As might be expected, this is a very frequent subject in the Catacombs : occurring in the earliest and least disputed parts of the Callixtine.   It is of course repeated throughout all Christian illustrative art, in all MSS. &c. &c. ; and finally, is one of the first pictures of the Ammergau representation.

ADAM AND EVE.

Among the earliest subjects of Christian sculpture : on the sarcophagus of Junius Bassus, Bottari, vi. tav. xv., also on that in tavv. xxxi. xxxvii. xl. No. 2.   Sometimes, as Aringhi, pp. i. 613, 621, 623, the ears of corn, or the mattock, are delivered to Adam, the distaff or lamb to Eve.   The motto of Jack Cade, " When Adam delved and Eve span," may be connected with mediæval repetitions of this treatment.   The serpent appears in Bottari, tavv. xxxi. li. and lxxx.

AGAPE.   See chapter on Sacramental Representations.

AGNES, ST.   See chapter on Mosaics.

[1] This seems rather dubious : two young men are offering, one ears of wheat, the other a lamb, to a seated Person, not advanced in years. Another face is dimly seen behind—possibly Adam's, as Bottari interprets.

ANCHOR.

A frequent emblem on tombs, conveying the idea of rest in hope. De Rossi ("De Monum." ἰχθύς, p. 18) thinks that it is used as a symbol of the names Elpis, Elpidius, &c. &c. The mystic fish is often added to it. See Bottari.

Its form is constantly associated with that of the Cross. See De Rossi, vol. i. pl. 18, 20.

ANGELS.   See Cherub, chapter on Symbolism.

The Abbé Martigny admits that few, if any, representations of Angels are to be met with before the fourth century. The genii and winged boys (Aringhi, ii. p. 29, 167), see also Bottari, ii. tavv. lxxiv. and xciii., and the catacombs of St. Prætextatus, &c. &c. cannot be thought to have represented the heavenly hierarchy in the mind of their painters or their first spectators. The figures in the fresco in St. Priscilla (D'Agincourt, Peinture, pl. vii. n. 3) may represent the Angel with Tobias: but Mr. Parker's photograph of the present state of the fresco makes this a matter of the merest conjecture. Again (Aringhi, ii. 297) there is a picture of a wingless Angel of the Annunciation. In Sta. Maria Maggiore (fifth century), and in St. Vitale at Ravenna in the sixth, the Three Angels are appearing to Abraham. From early times of Neo-Roman or Byzantine art, two Angels supporting a medallion have been a symbol of the special presence of the First Person of the Trinity. This is the case in St. Vitale, and also in the well-known diptych of Rambona, representing the Crucifixion. See Gori, "Thesaurus Diptychorum." Angels wear the pallium, and are often represented as of gigantic stature, like the Apostles. This simple distinction between mortal and supernatural presences extends into the Byzantine and even Gothic art of Venice. Ruskin, "Stones of

Venice," vol. iii. p. 78. "Aratra Pentelici," p. 75, and plate.

ANNUNCIATION.

Found in the Cemetery of St. Priscilla, Bottari, tav. clxxvi., and in the fifth-century mosaics of Sta. Maria Maggiore, on the Arch of Triumph. Ciampini, "Vetera Monumenta," vol. i. tab. ii. p. 200. D'Agincourt gives a sixth-century miniature from the Laurentian Library at Florence. Peinture, pl. xxvii. No. 2. In a diptych published by Bugati, a tradition is repeated, which is familiar to most visitors to Nazareth, where the Well of the Virgin is named in accordance with it. It is that the Annunciation took place, not in the house of the Virgin, but when she had gone forth to draw water.

APOCALYPSE. See chapter on Mosaics, and Rio, "L'Art Chrétienne," Introd. p. xliv.

APOSTLES.

In the earliest Church-art the Apostles may be said to be represented without personal distinction or characteristics. SS. Peter and Paul are the first to be specially designated, the first in particular by his keys. Martigny names two examples which he places in the fourth century; one of these is in Bottari, tav. xxi. 5; for the other he refers to Perret's plates, vol. i. p. 7. The date of both is somewhat uncertain, as the drawings are virtually restorations, and the unhappy removal of the sarcophagi from their places in the cemeteries makes their real period matter of the vaguest conjecture (see chapter on Catacombs, &c.) On a vase of uncertain date (Bottari, i. 185), St. Peter is receiving one key from our Lord. He is apparently presenting them before the Lamb in the mosaic of Sta. Maria in Cosmedin at Ravenna.

The Apostles are frequently symbolized as twelve doves or sheep, often representing the Church of believers (with reference also to Luke x. 3 : " I send you forth as lambs among wolves.") See Ciampini, " Vet. Mon." vol. ii. tav. xxiv. for the great mosaic of St. Apollinaris ; and Parker's photograph for those of SS. Cosmas and Damian and St. Prassede at Rome. The same is repeated on various sarcophagi (Bottari, tav. xxviii. &c.), and very frequently a thirteenth Lamb is placed on a rock in the centre, often bearing the Cross on its forehead, and having the four rivers of Paradise flowing from beneath its feet. The twelve doves were painted to represent the Apostles in St. Paulinus's church at Nola : and the mosaic cross of St. Clemente at Rome is well known (Bottari, vol. i. p. 118). In their human form, they are present on almost all the sarcophagi, and wherever the miracles of Our Lord are represented. (See Bottari, xxi. xxv. xxx. et alibi). The two Baptisteries at Ravenna are magnificent examples in mosaic ; the dome of each being occupied by the Twelve, separated by palm-trees. Or they are arranged by pairs, in remembrance of our Lord's having sent them forth "two by two before him" to preach the Gospel. Their dress is almost always the striped pallium and tunic of old Rome. The specially ecclesiastical robes of later Byzantine art, extending to the eleventh century and beginning of mediæval art, are not part of our present subject-matter.

APPLES.   See De Rossi, " R. S." vol. i. tav. xxx.

ARK.   See Church.

For the symbolic Ark or square Chest in the Catacombs, and in the doors of the Lombard St. Zenone at Verona, see Bottari, *passim,* and chap. x. on the Lombards.

Ascension of Our Lord.

Found in the MS. of Rabula, see woodcut, p. 306, and
s. v. Evangelists, symbols of. Like the events of the
Passion, this great subject is not touched in the Catacomb frescoes, and rarely, if ever, on sarcophagi,
though of constant occurrence in mediæval Church art;
which may be said to begin, in principle, with especial
calls of attention to the final sufferings of our Lord.

Baptism of our Lord. See chapter on Sacramental subjects of art.

Bethlehem.

Represented in several ancient mosaics as the mother-city
of the Gentile Church, as distinguished from "Hierusalem," from which the sheep of the Hebrew covenant
are issuing. See, for the great picture of St. Apollinaris in Classe at Ravenna, Ciampini, V.M. ii. 24,
and pp. 153, 173. There is a Nativity with Adoration
of the Shepherds in Bottari, tav. xxiv. but the cattle-
shed of modern art is substituted for any attempt at the
cave or buildings of Bethlehem. Jerusalem and Bethlehem both appear on the singular Cup of the Vatican
collections, Northcote, No. 32.

Bird (as symbol).

The birds represented in the earliest Christian art are
generally distinguishable by their species, as Dove,
Peacock, Eagle, &c. This is often the case in early
sarcophagi and frescoes of the Catacombs, and is specially
remarkable in some of the early Lombard work of the
North of Italy (see Ruskin, "Stones of Venice," Appendix, vol. i. Byzantine and Lombard Carvings). But
in the earliest tombs (see Aringhi, vol. ii. 324, &c.
De Rossi almost passim, Bottari, tav. clxxiv. &c.) birds

assignable to no particular species are introduced, clearly with symbolic purpose. They may occur often with the palm-branch, and be taken as images of the released soul seeking its home in heaven. Aringhi recognizes this in a passage of some beauty (ii. 324). He takes the lightness and beauty of the bird as a symbol of the aspiration of faithful spirits. He refers to Bede, who says, "Volucres sunt qui *sursum cor* habent, et cælestia concupiscunt," looking on the bird as a sign of the resurrection. Note the curious analogy of the Psyche-butterfly, and of Hadrian's dying address to his soul, "Animula, vagula, blandula," as to a winged thing of *uncertain* flight. Caged birds are occasionally found in paintings, &c. (Boldetti, tav. vi. p. 154), and may represent the soul imprisoned in the flesh, imprisoned martyrs, &c.

The symbolism of the Cross by a bird's outspread wings is St. Jerome's ; and Herzog, we believe, refers it also to Tertullian. It may have occurred to many. For the pairs of drinking birds in Veneto-Byzantine art, see Dove, Peacock, &c. and chapter on Mosaics.

BLIND, Cure of.

As one of the Miracles of Mercy, this is very frequently represented on the sarcophagi, Bottari, tavv. xxix. xxxii. xlix. also xxxix. A single blind man is generally represented, intended probably for the man blind from his birth. But in tav. xxxix. the two, Bartimæus and his fellow-sufferer, are represented. At tav. lxviii. an engraving is given of the cure of a single blind man, which, from its Raffaellesque though imperfect drawing, has somewhat the appearance of a late restoration ; and which represents the afflicted person as of the same full stature with our Lord. In nearly all other representations of this miracle the human sufferers are of purposely dwarfed size. This naïve method of calling attention to the Divinity of the Healer was continued to the earlier days of Venetian art: see Angel, supra.

BREAD. See in text p. 217, 222.

For representations of bread or loaves as part of an Agape, see De Rossi, "Roma Sott.," vol. ii. tavv. xvi. xviii.; also Parker's Photographs of the Callixtine Agapæ, for the actual present state of these paintings. For the Miracle of the Loaves, see Bottari, tavv. lxiii. and lxxxix. For the Fish bearing loaves, see De Rossi, I. tav. viii. The bread represented either in the pictures of Agapæ, or in those of the Miracle (as Bottari, tavv. lxxxv. clxiii.) is generally *panis decussatus*, crossed cakes, like those made on Good Friday at present.

CALF.

Irrespectively of its meaning as the symbol of an Evangelist (see that word), the image of the calf or ox is held by Aringhi (lib. vi. ch. xxxii. vol. ii. p. 320) to represent the Christian soul, standing to Christ in the same relation as the sheep to the shepherd. He also takes the calf or ox to represent Apostles labouring in their ministry, quoting various Fathers, and finally St. Chrysostom's idea, that the oxen and fatlings spoken of as killed for the Master's feast are meant to represent prophets and Martyrs. The calf or ox, as a sacrificial victim, has been taken to represent the Lord's sacrifice; for which Aringhi quotes a comment on Num. xviii. These similitudes seem fanciful, and pictorial or other representations hardly exist to bear them out. A calf is represented near the Good Shepherd, in Buonarotti (" Vetri," tav. v. fig. 2); and Martigny refers to Allegranza (" Mon. Antiche di Milano," p. 125) for an initial letter at Milan, where the animal is represented playing on a lyre : typifying, he thinks, the subjugation of the human nature to the life of the faith. He also refers to St. Clement of Alexandria ("Pædag." lib. i. c. 5) for a comparison of young Christians to sucking calves (μοσχάρια γαλάθηνα), connected perhaps in the Father's mind in the same way as in his own ; though, as Bishop Potter remarks in his note (ad loc.) no such comparison exists in Scripture. The plate in Allegranza is of considerable interest, being from a "marmo" belonging to the ancient pulpit of St. Ambrogio. The calf is lying down, and turning up its forefoot to hold the lyre, or "antica cetra." It is engraved in the loop of an initial D. The preceding "marmo" is a representation of an Agape, from the posterior parapet of the pulpit; and Allegranza considers the calf to be a symbol connected with the Agape. See above, Clem. Alex. "Pædag." i.5. The Lyre, as an instrument, has been held typical of the human body in its right state of harmony with, and subjection to, the divinely-guided soul. For Calf in connection with Cherub, see chapter on Symbolism, and s. v. Evangelist.

CAMEL.

A picture of a camel occurs in Bottari, tavv. lxiii. and lxxi., among the animals which surround the symbolic Orpheus, or Shepherd collecting his Flock ; and with the Magi, on a fragment of a sarcophagus in the Lateran Museum, in a Nativity, above the Ascension of Elijah.

CANA, Miracle of.

Representations of this miracle frequently present themselves in Christian art. It was early supposed to be typical of the Eucharist ; indeed, Theophilus of

Antioch, so far back as the second century, looks on the change of the water as figurative of the grace communicated in baptism (comment in Evang. lib. iv.) Cyril of Jerusalem (Catech. xxii. 2) says it represents the change of the wine into the Blood of the Lord in the Eucharist; and this idea has been applied, with eager inconsequence, to the support of the full dogma of transubstantiation. The miracle is represented on an ivory, published by Mamachi, Bottari, and Gori, which is supposed to have formed part of the covering of a throne belonging to the exarchs of Ravenna; and is referred to the seventh century. The writer saw it in the sacristy of the Duomo, in June 1871. Bandini ("In Tabulam eburneam Observationes," 4to. Florentiæ, 1746) gives a plate of it. In Bottari, tavv. xix. and xxxii., our Saviour, wearing the ordinary tunic, and toga over it, touches or points respectively to three and two vessels with a rod. In tav. li. five jars are given, as also in lxxxviii.; four in tav. lxxxix. The vessels or hydriæ are of different and generally humble forms, on these sarcophagi. Bottari remarks that the sculptors may have been hampered by knowing the water-vessels to have been large, containing a "metretes." But those on Bandini's ivory are gracefully-shaped amphoræ. Here the Lord bears a Greek cross on a staff, and motions with the other hand to the bridegroom, or a servant, who is carrying a cup to the master of the feast, gazing steadily at it, and extending his left hand towards the Saviour. The first quoted of these plates (xix. and xxxii.) of Bottari's, are from sarcophagi found in the Vatican, and of high merit in an artistic point of view. The later ones, not much inferior, are from the cemetery of Lucina, in the Callixtine Catacomb; or from a sarcophagus dug up in 1607, in preparing foundations for the Capella Borghese at Sta. Maria Maggiore.

CAR, CART, CHARIOT, &c.

Herzog ("Real-Encyclopädie für protestantische Theologie u. Kirche," 8vo. Gotha, 1861, s. v. "Sinnbilder") mentions a sculpture in St. Callixtus, which contains a chariot without driver, with pole turned backwards, and whip left resting on it. This, as he says, appears evidently intended as a symbol of the accomplished course of a life. In Bottari, tav. clx., two quadrigæ are represented at the base of an arch (covered with paintings of ancient date) in the second cubiculum of the catacomb of St. Priscilla on the Salarian Way. The Charioteers carry palms and crowns in their hands, and the horses are decorated with palm-branches, or perhaps plumes; which connects the image of the chariot with St. Paul's imagination of the Christian race (1 Cor. ix. 24; 2 Tim. iv. 7). (See Martigny, s.v. "Cheval.") Guénébault refers to a sculpture from an ancient Gothic or Frank tomb at Langres ("Univ. Pittoresque France," pl. xlv.) and to a cart or waggon on one of the capitals in the crypts in St. Denis (pl. lv. vol. ii. in A. Hugo, "France Pittoresque et Monumentale"). In Strutt ("View of the Inhabitants of England," Lond. 1774, 4to. vol. i. p. 5. fig. 6.) there is a chariot of the 9th century, so presumed. See also D'Agincourt. Peinture, pl. clxiv. No. 14, and pl. clvii. In the catacomb of St. Prætextatus (see Perret, "Catacombs," vol. i. pl. lxxii.), there is a somewhat powerful and striking representation of the chariot of Death, who is taking a departed woman into his car.

CASK. (Dolium.)

CHURCH. (Symbols of.)

Early representations of the Church of Christ are very numerous, and may be divided into (A) personifications and (B) symbolisms; both of the highest antiquity.

Those derived from 'Holy Scripture may be taken first.
(*A*) 1. The Lord's comparison of Himself to the Good
Shepherd, constantly represented in the Catacombs,
and supposed to be the most ancient of purely Christian
emblems in painting or sculpture, has generally united
with it, pictures of two or more sheep at His feet,
besides the one carried on His shoulders. The word
" fold " represents the Church, exactly as the word
" church " the congregation of Christ's people. (Lamb,
Good Shepherd, &c.) The fresco in the Callixtine Catacomb (Bottari, tav. lxxviii., and Aringhi, vol. i. lib.
iii. ch. xxii. p. 327, ed. Par. 1657), of the Shepherd
sitting under, trees, and surrounded by sheep, or sheep
and goats, as here, may be taken as one example out of
many. See also that at tav. xxvi. In another (Bott.
vol. ii. tav. cxviii.) the sheep are issuing from a small
building, seeming to stand for a town, at whose gate the
Shepherd stands, or leans on His staff. The sheep
of the Gentile and of the Jewish Churches are distinguished in the mosaic from St. Apollinaris in Classe,
where two flocks are issuing from separate towns or folds,
Hierusalem and Bethleem, and moving towards our
Lord. In many mosaics in Rome and Ravenna, He
stands in or by the banks of the mystic JORDANES,
with His sheep, and with the stag for the Gentile Church.
In a mosaic at St. Sabina's, Rome, the two Churches
are represented by two female figures, standing, each
with an open book in hand. (See also Aringhi, lib. iii.
c. xxii. p. 327.) Over one is inscribed " Ecclesia ex
circumcisione," and St. Peter stands above her ; the
other is named "Ecclesia ex gentibus," and above her is
placed St. Paul. (See Gal. ii. 7.) The same subject
occurs in a compartment of the ancient gates of the
Cathedral of Verona, treated with somewhat of the
quaintness of Lombard fancy, but quite intelligible.

The twofold Church is represented by two women, shaded by trees; one suckling two children, the other two fishes. (Fish.)   Martigny gives a woodcut from Father [1] Garrucci, Hagioglypt. p. 222.   It represents two lambs looking towards a pillar, which symbolizes the Church, and is surmounted by the Lamb bearing on his back the decussated Monogram of Christ.   From it spring (apparently) palm branches ; and two birds, just above the lambs, may be taken for doves.   The figures of St. Peter and St. Paul, with their division of the Church into Jewish and Gentile, seem to be represented in the fresco given by De Rossi (vol. ii. Tav. d'Aggiunto A.); but are almost destroyed by the opening of a tomb, which has been broken into through the fresco, as so frequently happens.   There can be no doubt that the Oranti, or praying female figures in the Catacombs, are frequently personifications of the Church.   (See Bottari, tav. xxxviii., Orante with doves placed next to the Good Shepherd.)   In the corners of the square ceiling of the well-known Crypt of Lucina, in the Callixtine Catacombs (De Rossi, R. S. tav. x.) the Orante alternates with the Good Shepherd.

2. A few representations exist of Susanna and the Elders as typical of the Church and its persecutors, Jewish and Pagan.   Martigny names three sarcophagi as the only certain examples of this subject in old Italian art. For one he refers to Buonarotti, " Vetri," p. l.   Of the two others, one is from the Vatican, the other from St. Callixtus.   They are found in Bottari, tavv. xxxi. and lxxxv. sarcoph. from St. Callixtus.   In Southern Gaul they are more numerous (Millin, " Midi de la F." pl. lxv. 5 ; lxvi. 8; lxviii. 4).   All these are bas-reliefs containing the Elders as well as Susanna ; and the third represents them as eagerly watching her from behind trees.   Martigny gives an allegory in woodcut drawn

[1] Parker's Photographs.

from vol. i. pl. lxxviii., of M. Perret's work, of a sheep between two wild beasts: " Susanna" and " Sinioris" are written above.

3. The Woman with the Issue of Blood has been considered as a type of the Gentile Church, which would account for the frequent representations of that miracle to be found on ancient sarcophagi. See Bottari, tavv. xix. xxi. xxxiv. xxxix. xli. lxxxv. ix. cxxxv. So St. Ambrose (lib. ii. in Luc. c. viii.). She is always of small stature, like the other subjects of our Lord's miracles.

(B) Symbolisms of the Church (it is not generally observed how important the distinction between symbolism and personification is) begin with the ark of Noah ; passing by easy transition to the ship of souls and the ship of Jonah in the storm. It is singular that our Lord's similitude of the net is rarely found illustrated by the graphic art of early Christendom. The idea of the Lord's drawing forth the sinner from the waters, as with a hook and line (see Bottari, xlii., De Rossi, &c.), seems to have prevailed over that of the sweeping net. The net is perhaps assigned to St. Peter in the Vatican sarcophagus represented (Bottari tav. xlii.). A small net is used on one side of the bas-relief (Net, Fish, Ship, Jonah, &c.).

The ark is very frequently used as a type of the Church militant. On tombs it is held to imply that the dead expired in full communion with the Church. In Bottari, tav. xlii., an olive-tree stands in the ark, in the place of Noah. It is of a square form, a chest in fact (Bottari, tavv. xl. cxx. clxxiⁱ. &c.); and in tav. cxviii. it is placed in a boat or ship. The dove appears with the olive branch in almost all these, or is represented by itself : in Bottari, tav. cxxxi. it is placed on the poop of the ship of Jonah. In tav. xxxvii. Noah stands in a square chest on the shore, receiving the dove

P 3

in his hands; Jonah is being thrown from a boat into the sea next him.   This is one of the most frequent of all symbolic works in the Catacombs, no doubt on account of the Lord's own comparison of Himself to the Prophet. For representations in the Catacomb of Callixtus and elsewhere, see De Rossi and Bottari, passim.   The ship " covered with the waves," is represented in Martigny, from a fresco lately discovered in St. Callixtus.   A man stands in the waist, or near the stern, of a sharp-prowed vessel with a square sail, such as are used in the Mediterranean to this day.   The waters are dashing over her close to him, and he is in an attitude of prayer; far off is a drowning man who has made shipwreck of the faith. The vessel in full sail (Boldetti, pp. 360, 362, 373) is also common as the emblem of safe-conduct through the waves of this troublesome world; that with sails furled, as quietly in port resting after her voyage (as in Boldetti, pp. 363, 366), is the symbol of the repose of individual Christians in death.   An even more interesting symbolism is where not only the ship is painted as analogous to the Church, but the actual fabric of a Church is made like a ship.   This was the case with some of the early Romanesque churches, where the apse which completed the basilica had the bishop's throne placed in the centre, as the steersman's place, with semicircular benches below for the clergy; so that a real and touching resemblance followed.   See the memorable passage in Ruskin's " Stones of Venice," vol. ii., on the ancient churches of Torcello, the mother-city of Venice, and a passage in the Apostolical Constitutions (ii. 57)[1] to the same effect,—the bishop being likened to the steersman, and the deacons to seamen.   " First, let the building be

[1] καὶ πρῶτον μὲν ὁ οἶκος ἔστω ἐπιμήκης, κατ' ἀνατολὰς τετραμμένος . . . ὅστις ἔοικε νηΐ. Κείσθω δὲ μέσος ὁ τοῦ ἐπισκόπου θρόνος παρ' ἐκάτερα δὲ αὐτοῦ καθεζέσθω τὸ πρεσβυτέριον, καὶ οἱ διάκονοι παριστάθωσαν . . . ἐοίκασι γὰρ ναύταις καὶ τοιχάρχοις.

turned lengthways to the East,[1] . . . it is like a ship.
And let the bishop's throne be set in the midst; and on
each side of him, let the presbytery be seated: and let
the deacons stand beside: for they are like to sailors
and their petty-officers."[2] The ship placed on the
back of a fish is found in a signet illustrated by
Aléandre ("Nav. Eccles. referent. Symb." Romæ, 1626;
see also s. v. Fish). A jasper given by Cardinal Borgia
("De Cruce Velitern." p. 213 and frontispiece) places the
Lord in a galley of six oars on a side, holding the large
steering oar. This rudder-oar—or rather two of them
—are inserted in the rudest ship-carvings, where other
oars were omitted.

COCK.

Representations of this bird occur frequently on tombs
from the earliest period. When not associated with the
figure of St. Peter, as Bottari, tav. lxxxiv., or placed on
a pillar, as Boldetti, p. 360; Bottari, tavv. xxxiv. xxiii.
&c., it appears to be a symbol of the Resurrection, our
Lord being supposed by the early Church to have broken
from the grave at the early cock-crowing. A peculiar
awe seems always to have attached to that hour, at
which all wandering spirits have through the Middle
Ages been supposed to vanish from the earth. "Hamlet,"
and the ancient ballad, called "The Wife of Usher's
Well," occur to us as salient examples of a universal
superstition. Prudentius' hymn, "Ad Galli Cantum"
("Cathem." i. 16), adopts the idea of the cock-crowing
as a call to the general judgment ("Nostri figura est
judicis"), and further on (45 seqq.) he says:—

"Hoc esse signum præscii
Noverunt promissæ spei
Qua nos sopore liberi
Speramus adventum Dei."

Or, "somewhat long-shaped and turned to the East."
[2] τοίχαρχος, the boatswain, who gave orders to the "wall," or
bank of oars on each side.

And again, 65 seqq.:—

> " Inde est, quod omnes credimus
>   Illo quietis tempore,
> Quo gallus exultans cauit,
>   Christus redisse ex inferis."

See Aringhi, vol. ii. pp. 328–9, for a complete list of animal symbols. Fighting-cocks (see the passage last quoted) seem to symbolize the combat with secular or sensual temptations. The practice of training them for combat has probably always existed in the East, and certainly was in favour at Athens (cf. Aristoph., $Av.$ αἶρε πλῆκτρον, εἰ μαχεῖ). For a symbol drawn from such a pastime, compare St. Paul's use of the word ὑπωπιάζω (1 Cor. ix. 27). See Bottari, tav. cxxxvii. Two cocks accompany the Good Shepherd in Bottari, tav. clxxii. (from the tympanum of an arch in the cemetery of St. Agnes).

CORN, ears of.

Corn is not so often used in early Christian art as might be supposed. (Bread, Loaves, &c.) The thoughts of early iconographers seem to have gone always to the Bread of Life with sacramental allusion ; as Bottari, tav. clxiii. vol. iii. et alibi. In Bottari, vol. i. tav. xlviii., the corn and reaper are represented in a compartment of a vault in the cemetery of Pontianus. Again, in vol. ii. tav. lv. the harvest corn is opposed to the vine and cornucopia of fruit (Callixtine Catacomb). The more evidently religious use of the ears of corn is in various representations of the Fall of Man. On the Sarcophagus of Junius Bassus (supp. A.D. 358), Bottari, vol. i. tav. xv. 9, Adam and Eve are carved ; the former bearing the corn, in token of his labour on the earth (see Bread).

CROSS. See text.

CRUCIFIX and Representations of the Crucifixion. See text.

DANIEL in the Lion's Den.

> One of the most common as well as the most interesting
> subjects of the earliest art. Like the deliverance of the
> three children in the Furnace, it is evidently chosen in
> times of persecution and suffering for the Truth. It is
> found in the earliest frescoes in the Callixtine Catacomb,
> and on most of the sarcophagi. See Bottari, passim.
> Daniel is generally placed between two lions, and some-
> times he is receiving food from the prophet Habbacuc,
> as in a curious sarcophagus at Brescia, of which Dr.
> Appel gives a woodcut: in another (Bottari, tav. xix.) he
> is represented in the act of administering the balls of
> pitch and hair to the Dragon, according to the narrative
> of the Apocrypha.

> DEATH, symbolically represented either by birds, denoting
> the deliverance of the soul from evil (see Bird), or by
> a vessel with furled sails (see Ship), or by an unyoked
> chariot (see s. v. Car). The skeleton forms of death
> are unknown to primitive Christian art; but the
> wreaths and ornaments of flowers on the early tombs
> were willingly adopted from Gentile decoration. The
> skulls and worms in the Judgment of Torcello, eighth
> or eleventh century, are the earliest examples of the
> terrors of death. With Giotto's crowned skeleton at
> Assisi, and the Triumph of Death by Orgagna at Pisa,
> a whole pictorial course of ascetic exhortation begins,
> which took a new form with Holbein and the transalpine
> Dances of Death or the Dead, Danses Macabres, &c.,
> &c. See Text, Chapter X.

> DOCTORS, dispute with. See Bottari, tav. xv. Tomb of
> Junius Bassus, A.D. 358, and tavv. xxx. and liv. from the
> Callixtine Catacomb. Also tavv. cxlvi. clxxviii.

Our Lord is generally represented as seated on a cathedra in the centre; in the Callixtine pictures with rolls or books at His feet. On the sarcophagi, the figure raising its veil, and representing the firmament, is at His feet.

DOLIUM or Cask. See Boldetti, pp. 164, 368. Bottari, tav. lxxxiv., &c. and Parker's Photographs, for present state of paintings.

Seven men with a Dolium or wine-cask, and two other such vessels, are here represented. Abbé Martigny (Dict., s. v.) collects various interpretations of this not uncommon symbol. It may be the empty cask, the body laid up at rest when the soul has departed; the wine may be the blood of martyrdom. But Martigny is inclined to suspect a play on the word Dolere; and quotes an inscription from Mamachi, IVLIO FILIO PATER DOLIENS, which seems conclusive.

DOLPHIN.

An ornament adopted from Gentile art, as are the Peacock, and, in a great degree, the Vine and Dove (see Fish). On the Tomb of Baleria or Valeria Latobia (Bottari, tav. xx.), it is supposed to symbolize conjugal love. Combined with the Anchor-Cross, it may symbolize either the Crucifixion, or the soul's adherence to the Faith. See Martigny, "Dauphin," Dict. Ant. Chrét.

DOVE.

Like the Lamb and the Fish, the Dove has several meanings, all of early date. In its highest use, as the symbol of the especial presence of the Holy Spirit, it is found in all representations of the Lord's Baptism, as in the Baptisteries of Ravenna, in that of the Catacomb of St. Pontianus at Rome, and passim. (See chapter on

Sacramental subjects of art.) It is also represented as hovering over the Lateran Cross. (See plate in Archbishop Binterim's "Denkwürdigkeiten," v. i.) Our Lord's words in Matt. x. 16 propose the dove as an emblem of Christian meekness, and it is used to symbolize other virtues, probably as gifts of the Holy Spirit.

Its second symbolic meaning is certainly that of the faithful disciple, of whatever rank and condition. St. Paulinus of Nola, Ep. xi., declares that twelve doves were used to represent the Apostles in his Church; and the mosaic Cross (Bottari, i. p. 118) bears twelve doves also. A pair of doves is represented in Didron's "Iconographie Chrétienne," v. i., p. 396; also Gori, " Thes. Diptych." iii. p. 160, apparently contemplating the Tau-Cross and Monogram; a serpent is twined round its lower limb. If this latter is an allusion to the Brazen Serpent as uplifted on the Cross, it must be connected with the undoubtedly sacramental emblem of two doves with the chalice, which passed from Roman into Veneto-Byzantine art, and seems to have become merely ornamental, peacocks and nondescripts being constantly used in the same way. For the symbolic meaning of the Peacock, however, see that word. Doves are constantly represented on sarcophagi and added to inscriptions. In the monuments of Southern France they occur constantly, see Le Blant, " Inscr. Chrét. de la Gaule," and the letters A ω are very frequently added.

For the Dove of Noah, see Bottari, &c. passim, and in Chapter IV. woodcut.

DRAGON. See Serpent, and under Daniel, Bottari, xix.

DUCKS.

Are frequently represented in the MS. of Rabula (see Assemann's Catalogue of the Laurentian Library at

Florence) : and by one of the most beautiful of ancient mosaics—the small picture of birds from the Callixtine Catacomb. (Parker's Antique Photographs.)

EAGLE. (See vignette at end.)

It is probably an instance of the careful exclusion of all Pagan emblems or forms which had been actual objects of idolatrous worship, while merely Gentile or human tokens and myths were freely admitted, that the form of the Eagle appears so rarely in Christian ornamentation, at least before the time of its adoption as the symbol of an Evangelist. (See Evangelists). Aringhi (vol. ii. p. 228, c. 2) speaks of the Eagle as representing the Lord Himself: and this is paralleled by a quotation of Martigny's from a sermon of St. Ambrose : where he refers to Ps. ciii. (" thy youth is renewed like the eagle's ") as foreshadowing the Resurrection. Le Blant (" Inscr. Chrét. de la Gaule," i. 17, No. 45, in illustrations). Bottari gives a plate of a domed ceiling in the sepulchre of St. Priscilla, where two eagles standing on globes form part of the ornamentation. He refers it evidently to some general or legionary officer (vol. iii. tav. clx.). Triumphal chariots fill two of the side spaces, but they and the eagles can hardly be considered Christian emblems, though used by Christians.

EGG.

There seems some diversity of opinion as to the use of the Egg as a Christian symbol. Boldetti (p. 519) speaks of marble eggs found in the tombs of St. Theodora, St. Balbina, and others : these were of the size of hen's eggs. Egg-shells are occasionally found in the loculi of martyrs, and Raoul Rochette refers them to the Agapæ so frequently celebrated there (see Eucharist). But Martigny is inclined to think that the Egg signified the immature hope of the Resurrection. " Illa enim gallina divina Sapientia est ; sed assumpsit carnem, &c. Ovum ergo nostrum, id est, spem nostram, sub alis illius gallinæ ponamus." " For that hen is the Divine wisdom, but He took on Him the Flesh. . . . Therefore let us place our egg, that is, our hope, under the wings of that Hen." Aug. Serm. cv. 8. Migne, vol. xxxviii, p. 623. The use of eggs at Easter has no doubt reference to this idea : but whether the idea was really attached to the object or not, in a generally symbolic sense, seems still a dubious matter.

EGYPT, Flight into.

It is difficult, if not impossible, to name any earlier representation of this event than the bronze casting on the doors of St. Zenone at Verona, which is at all events one of the earliest known Christian works in metal.

ELIAS.

The translation of Elias, as a typical event relating to the Resurrection and Ascension of our Lord, is a very common subject of early art. See Aringhi, v. i. pp. 305, 309, 429, and Bottari, tav. xxvii. The prophet's mantle is always cast behind him, and he holds the reins of two or four horses. On the Station-Cross of Mayence, whose bas-reliefs are a body of doctrine, the translation of Elias is at the back of the Cross, opposed to the Ascension on the Front, with the following hexameter " Qui levat Eliam (at the back of the Cross), propriam sublimat usiam" [1] (in front).

Elias occurs with Moses in the mosaic of the Transfiguration at the Convent of Mount Sinai, and in the very important one of the same subject in St. Apollinaris in Classe at Ravenna. Few things in ancient picture-

[1] οὐσίαν.

instruction are more remarkable than the way in which the Doctrines of the Testimony of both the Law and the Prophets to the coming Redeemer, are insisted on in this great work.   See chapter on Mosaics.

A remarkable Ascension of Elijah in a Sarcophagus in the Lateran is evidently copied from a Pagan model of Helios in his chariot, as Dr. Appel observes.   See Art Library, S. Kensington (portf. 406, No. 41) and Martigny, p. 23.   Also Bottari, tavv. xxvii. and xxix.

ELIZABETH, ST.

There is a salutation, evidently modern, in the Cemetery of St. Julius (Pope) or of St. Valentine, on the Flaminian Way.   Bottari, tav. cxci.

ENTRY INTO JERUSALEM.

This event in our Lord's life is very frequently represented in the earlier art of the Christian Church, occurring on some of the first sarcophagi, though not, as far as the present writer knows, in fresco, or mosaic in the Catacombs or elsewhere, excepting in an ancient mosaic of the Vatican (Bianchini, "Demonstr. Hist. Sac." I. tav. ii. No. 17), and one from the basilica at Bethlehem (Count de Vogué, "Les Églises de la Terre-Sainte," pl. v.)   See woodcut in Martigny, s.v. Jerusalem ; the picture is of the twelfth century, probably from an older model.

The earliest MS. representation of it is probably that in the Rabula or Laurentian Evangeliary.   The treatment is almost always the same ; the Lord is mounted on the ass, sometimes accompanied by her foal, and the multitude with their palm-branches follow or lay their garments before Him (Aringhi, t. i. 277, 329, ii. 159, and passim), Bottari, tav. xxi.   His right hand is generally raised in the act of blessing.   In one of the oldest MSS. of the New Testament in existence, the Gregorian Evangeliary of St. Cuthbert (" Palæographia

Sacra") the Lord is represented mounted on an ass, and bearing a large whip, evidently with reference to the scourge of small cords used in the expulsion of buyers and sellers from the Temple. There is a certain variety in the examples taken from different carvings. In Bottari, I. tavv. xv. xxii. xxxix. Zaccheus is represented in the fig, or sycamore tree, behind the Lord, as if to call attention to the beginning of His last journey to Jericho. In the last example the sycamore and palm-branches are carefully and well cut. In I. tav. xl. the garments are being strewn before the Lord (as in the others). See also vol. II. tavv. lxxxviii. lxxxix., III. tav. cxxxiii. In one instance without Zaccheus the colt accompanies the ass; III. cxxxiv. The small stature of Zaccheus is often dwelt on. Or the figure may represent a person in the act of cutting down branches.

EPIPHANY. See Magi.

EVANGELISTS, Symbolic Representations of. (See vignette at end.)

We find from Aringhi, vol. ii. p. 285, that the four symbolic creatures are not, as might be expected, the original emblems of the Four Evangelists. The four rivers of Paradise are undoubtedly intended to represent the Gospel, and the distinct channels of its diffusion throughout the world; Gen. ii. These are found in some of the earliest specimens of unquestionably authentic Christian decoration; as in the Lateran Cross (see art. Cross), where the Lamb and Stag are introduced.

The four Books, or Rolls, are also found in early works, Ciampini, "Vetera Monumenta," I. tab. lxvii., Buonarotti, xiv. 2. In some instances, as in the Baptism of our Lord, in the cemetery of St. Pontianus (Aringhi, 275, 2; also at end of Bottari), the animals are introduced drinking in the Jordan. In this case either the mystic river is identified with the four rivers of Paradise, and made to accompany the ornamented Cross, representing the Gospels, as in the Lateran Cross. Or the Cross in St. Pontianus below the Baptism-picture, represents the Lord's Death, and Baptism thereinto. Mr. Parker gives an admirably clear photograph of the present condition of this important work, which he dates from A.D. 772. The Lateran relic is supposed to be similar to the Crosses of the time of Constantine. The adoption of the four creatures of the Apocalypse (iv. 6) as images of the Evangelists, does not seem to have taken place generally, or is not recorded on Christian monuments, before the fifth century. It involves of course the peculiarly impressive connection between the beginning of the visions of Ezekiel and the first sight of the unveiling of Heaven to the eyes of St. John. This is unmistakeable, although in the prophet's vision the living creatures were not only four in number, but each was fourfold in shape. "They four had the face of a man, and the face of a lion, on the right side; and they four had the face of an ox on the left side; they four also had the face of an eagle." While in the Apocalypse the first beast was like a lion, the second like a calf, the third had the face of a man, and the fourth beast was like a flying eagle. This connection is said by Mrs. Jameson ("Sacred and Legendary Art," p. 79) to have been noticed as early as the second century, though no representations are found till the fifth. Nor was it till long after the four creatures had been taken as prefiguring the Four Evangelists, that a special application was made of each symbol to each writer. This may be referred to St. Jerome on Ezekiel i. St. Matthew has the man, as beginning his Gospel with the Lord's human genealogy; St. Mark the Lion, as testifying the Lord's royal dignity; or as containing the terrible condemnation of unbelievers at the end of his Gospel; St. Luke the Ox, as he dwells on the Priesthood and Sacrifice of Christ; St. John the Eagle, as contemplating the Lord's divine nature. Ingenuity and devotion have done their utmost on this subject for centuries, with little result. An ivory diptych of the fifth century, given by Bugati ("Memoire di S. Celso"), is the earliest known representation of this emblem, which does not occur in the glass devices recorded by Garrucci, or Buonarotti. The well-known representation of the four Creature-symbols in the great mosaic of the Church of St. Pudentiana at Rome must, we think, be left out of reckoning altogether as an historic document. See Mr. J. E. Parker's Photographs, and the articles thereon in his "Antiquities of Rome" (text, p. 139). See also Messrs. Crowe and Cavalcaselle, "Early Italian Art," vol. i. chap. i. (remarks on the present state of the mosaic). The symbols are placed above a seventh-century Cross, and, on close inspection of the photographs, appear to have been repaired in fresco, or painting of some kind. The appearance of the whole mosaic in fact is that of a quantity of material of different ages, some doubtless very ancient, and of great merit, combined as a whole by a painter and mosaicist of the greatest skill and power in the sixteenth century. However, the use of the quadruple symbols is universal; East and West, and throughout the Christian world, in every kind of situation, and by use of all vehicles and methods. They are very frequently placed on Crosses of the seventh century, about the same time that the change took place from the Lamb at the intersection of the limbs of the Cross to the human form crucified. They occur on the Cross of Velitræ, and on an ancient German Cross mentioned in chap. ix. as the Station-Cross of Planig. But the most interesting sixth-century representation of them known to us is the quaintly, but

grandly-conceived, Tetramorph of the Rabula MS.
which represents the Lord at the Ascension mounting a
chariot of many wings and cherubic form (see woodcut).
It shows that the Syrian miniaturist had a most vivid
imagination, and the highest power of realizing his conceptions ; as appears in so many parts of that extraordinary work. The wheels of the chariot, as well as the
cherubic forms, connect the Vision of Ezekiel with the
Griffius of Lombard Church-art ; as at Verona. Mrs.
Jameson gives a very interesting Tetramorph, or cherubic
form, bearing the Evangelic symbols, from a Greek
mosaic. This symbol is certainly not of the age of
the earlier Catacomb paintings, and occurs first with fre-
quency in the tessellated apses and tribunes of Byzantine
Churches ; it is of course specially worthy of note as ex-
plaining the connection between the Vision of Ezekiel and
that of St. John. The four animals separately represented
occur passim, both in Eastern and Western Churchwork.
See Ciampini, "V. Mon." I. tab. xlviii. There are grand
examples in the spandrils of the dome of Galla Placidia's
Chapel in Ravenna, as in St. Apollinaris in Classe.

Extraordinary illuminations of this subject occur in the
  Evangeliary of Drogon, son of Charlemagne ; but the
  Hours of that Emperor and the MS. of St. Médard of
  Soissons also contain whole-page emblems of the Four.
  For these see Count Bastard, " Peintures des Manu-
  scrits," vol. ii. In St. Vitale at Ravenna the symbols
  of the Evangelists accompany their sitting figures. St.
  Matthew has the man, St. Mark the (wingless) lion ;
  the calf, also wingless, belongs to St. Luke, and the
  eagle to St. John. The nimbus is sometimes added,
  and sometimes the creatures bear the Rolls or Books
  of the Gospel (Ciampini, " V. Mon." II. tab. xv. in St.
  Cosmo and Damianus). See also ibid. ii. 24. for St.
  Apollinaris in Classe.

There is a very strange missal-painting referred to by
Martigny, where the human forms of the Evangelists in
Apostolic robes are surmounted by the heads of the
creatures. This occurs also, he says, in an ancient
Church of Aquileia.

Two examples are given in woodcut by Mrs. Jameson,
("Sacred and Legendary Art," p. 83). One is by Fra
Angelico; and the hands, feet, and drapery of the
other, which is not dated, seem too skilfully done to be
of early date. But the four creatures occur alike in
bas-reliefs on altars, or sacred vessels and vestments,
and even on bronze medals. It may be supposed
that where the Lord is surrounded by Saints and
Apostles, the bearers of books are intended for the
Evangelists, especially if they are four in number,
though on the Sarcophagus in Bottari, tav. cxxxi. only
three are represented, probably St. Matthew and St. John
with St. Mark, as companion and interpreter of St. Peter.
Four figures in the baptistery at Ravenna, holding books,
and placed in niches of mosaic arabesques, are considered of doubtful meaning by Ciampini, " V. Mon." I.
tab. lxxii. ; but Martigny is perfectly satisfied that the
Evangelists are intended by them.

FIRMAMENT.

The male figure observed in various representations, as of
the Dispute with the Doctors, Bottari, tav. xv. on Sarcophagus of Junius Bassus, A.D. 358, and tav. xxx. is
said to be meant for Uranus, or the firmament of
Heaven. It is always raising a veil or cloth over its
head; symbolical, we presume, of the Heavens raised
as a curtain.

FIR-TREE OR PINE.

See Aringhi, vol. ii. p. 632. 3. "Præter Cupressum
Pinus quoque et Myrtus pro Mortis symbolo, &c. Et

pinus quidem, quia semel excisa nunquam reviviscit et
repullulascit." See the threat of Crœsus to the people
of Lampsacus, Herodotus, vi. 37. These are rather
general or human reasons for choice of the pine as an
emblem of death, than as conveying any specially
Christian thought. But the Fir, or some tree much
resembling it, accompanies the figure of the Good
Shepherd, Aringhi, ii. 293, from the Cemetery of
St. Priscilla; also at pp. 75 and 25 : and is certainly
intended to be represented among the trees which
surround the same Form in vol. i. 577. This latter
painting is from the Callixtine, and is certainly an
adaptation from the common fresco subjects of Orpheus.
The Shepherd bears the Syrinx or reeds, but sits in a
half reclining position, as Orpheus with the lyre : and
various trees are surrounding Him. This association
of the Fir or Pine with the Good Shepherd, and of
both with Orpheus, would account for the introduction
of different species of "trees of the wood ; " the fir
being also characteristic of the mountains or wilderness
in which the lost sheep is found. Herzog thinks it was
placed on Christian (as well as other) graves as an
evergreen tree, and therefore a symbol of Immortality ;
which is by no means unlikely.

FISH.   (See Catacombs, Symbolism, Eucharist.)

The Fish is a symbol of almost universal occurrence in the
painting and sculpture of the primitive Church. Like
the Dove or the Lamb ; it is used in more than one
sense ; and its non-scriptural or anagrammatic meaning
is perhaps the most popular at the present day. In
Matt. xiii. 47 ; Luke v. 4—10 it is used in the
parable of the net, and our Lord there assigns it its
significance ; His parabolic use of it is frequently
imitated in early Christian Art, where the fishes in the

Church's net, or caught by the hook of the fisher, correspond exactly to the lambs of the fold, or to the Doves which also represent the faithful on many Christian tombs and vaultings. See Tertullian de Baptismo, sub init. " Nos pisciculi secundum ἰχθύν Nostrum in aquâ nascimur." This anagrammatic sense appears to have been in very early use, derived, as all know, from the initials of the words Ἰησοῦς Χριστὸς Θεοῦ Υἱὸς Σωτήρ. This appears to be recognized by St. Clement of Alexandria ("Pædag." iii. 106; see also St. Augustine, de Civ. Dei, xviii. 25), and to have been so well understood in his time as to have required no explanation, since he recommends the use of the symbol, on seals, and rings, without giving an explanation of its import. The other devices he commends are the Dove, Ship, Lyre, and Anchor. At so early a period as the middle of the second century, and under the continual dangers of persecution, the use of such a symbol for the Person of the Lord is perfectly natural, as it would attract no notice from the outer world : and in the same manner, for even more obvious reasons, the form of the Cross was frequently disguised up to the time of Constantine (see Cross). But the mystic senses assigned to this emblem by various Fathers often seem to the modern mind somewhat gratuitous and ill-founded. They strain their imaginations, apparently, to find reasons in the nature of things for what is simply an ingenious arrangement of initial letters ; seeming to assume that there must be real analogy between the Lord and the Fish, because the initials of the Name and titles of the One made the Greek name of the other. The pleasure derived from the anagram, or the facility it may have given for concealing Christian doctrine from the heathen, seems occasionally to have overcome the thought that the Lord Himself had used the Fish as an emblem of His.

Q

people only, not of Himself; of the Sheep, not of the
Shepherd.   Aringhi dwells more naturally on the
Scriptural meaning, and the various examples he gives
(vol. ii. p. 684, II. p. 620, also that from the inscription made in Stilicho's consulship, A.D. 400, vol. i.
p. 19), all speak in the same sense.   The lamp at II.
620 has the Monogram on the handle, and the two
Fishes on the central part.   He refers to the Dolphin
as King of fishes, speaking of its reputed love for
its offspring (see the tomb of Baleria or Valeria
Latobia, now in the Vatican).   Martigny states that
because Christ is man, He therefore is a Fish of His
own net: and gives prophetic significance, following
Aringhi, to the story of Tobias, and of the Fish which
delivered him from the power of the evil spirit.   He of
course accepts and follows the various attempted con-
nexions of the anagram with the Fish of the last Repast
at the Sea of Galilee, and sees in them the sacramental
representatives of the Body of our Lord; quoting St.
Augustine, Tract. cxxiii. in Joannem xxi. and Bede's
rhymed citation of the same passage, Piscis assus
Christus est passus (see Eucharist, Representation of).
These analogies are difficult to follow, especially when
we consider the scriptural use of the emblem from the
Lord's own mouth.

The Fish as the believer, St. Ambrose, L. iv. in Luc.
v., Hexemeron, v. 6, is more frequently represented on
the hook of the Gospel-Fisherman than in the net of
the Church.   Bread and fish are the universal viands of
the representations of earlier Agapæ, as frequently in
the Callixtine Catacomb.   The genuineness of some, at
least, of these paintings is generally allowed; and Dr.
Theodore Mommsen mentions in particular an Agape
with bread and fish, in the vault named after Domitilla,
the grand-daughter of Vespasian, on the Ardeatine

way, and near the ancient church of SS. Nereus and
Achilles. In this, so impartial and accurate an observer
as Dr. Mommsen has full confidence, as coeval with the
vault; though he thinks the case for the vault itself
being so early as 95 B.C. incomplete : and observes that
the painting of this subject, as of those of Daniel, Noah
and the Good Shepherd, is less excellent than that of the
Vine in the vaultings of the original chamber of Domitilla without the catacomb, which is quite like a work
of the Augustan age.

The use of this emblem is connected by Martigny with,
what he styles, the Secret Discipline, or teaching of
the early Church. There can be little doubt that
reverent mystery was observed as to the Eucharist;
and that in ages of persecution till Constantine's
time, no public use of the Cross, as a sign of the
Person of the Lord, was made. Till then the Fish-
anagram was perhaps in special and prevailing use,
and it may have yielded its place from that time;
the Cross being the sign of full confession of Jesus
of Nazareth; supposing the special use of the Fish
to have been concealment from the heathen. The
secrecy of discipline, or doctrine, after Constantine,
seems to have consisted mainly in the gradual nature of
the instructions given to catechumens, and in the fact
that for a time the chief doctrines of the Faith were
not brought before them.

FISHERMAN.

Our Lord or His disciples are frequently represented as
the Fishers of Men in ancient art. St. Clement of
Alexandria uses the simile for both. "Pædag." III.
106. See also Aringhi, II. 620. St. Augustine,
Tract. xl. in Joannem ; St. Ambrose, Hexemeron, v. 6.
Martigny gives a woodcut s.v. Pécheur, represent-

ing a man clothed in the skin of a fish, bearing a spata, or basket: which may, as Polidori supposes, represent the divine or apostolic Fishes, or the Fish of the Church's net. The net is more rarely represented than the hook and line, but St. Peter is represented in an ancient ivory (in Mamachi, "Costumi I." Prefaz. p. 1) casting the net. The net of St. Peter, with the Lord fishing with the line, is a device of the Papal Signets. In the Callixtine Catacomb (De Rossi, "Roma Sott.," vol. i. tav. xv. n. 4), the fisherman is drawing forth a fish from the waters which flow from the Rock in Horeb. See also Bottari, vol. i. tav. xlii. At St. Zenone in Verona, the patron Saint is thus represented; and this subject, with those of Abraham's Sacrifice, Noah's Ark, and others on the bronze doors and marble front of that most important church, are specially valuable as connecting the earlier Lombard carvings with the most ancient and scriptural subjects of primitive church-work.

FOSSOR.

The Fossores (fodere, to dig) were a class of men employed in the offices of Christian sepulture, and in opening fresh graves and catacombs. They must have been very numerous, considering the great extent of the subterranean world of Rome, which is calculated at from 350 to 900 miles of passages, at various distances from the surface. These are all hollowed in the soft tufa-rock with the pickaxe or mattock: and an instrument of this kind, or a small lamp, is always placed in the hands of the memorial pictures near the graves of these men. As the extent of the catacombs went on increasing, the number and importance of the Fossores must have increased; their acquaintance with the dark and labyrinthine passages of the various catacombs must have made them guides to places of refuge in time of persecution. A woodcut in Bottari [1] (vol. ii. p. 126) gives us the portrait of one of these men, perhaps of superior rank in his craft. The shoulder and skirts of his long tunic are marked with a peculiar cross, of one of the shapes called *formes dissimulées* by Father Martigny (s.v. Croix, "Dict. des Antiquités Chrét."): he wears long boots, carries a heavy pickaxe, and is surrounded by other tools of his occupation. He is placed under a dark arch, on which are two doves with the epitaph:

Diogenes. Fossor.in. pace. depositus
Octabu. Kalendas. Octobris.

Father Martigny discusses the question of how far the Fossores were considered clerical persons. This seems difficult to decide, as he admits, from the fact that the offices of sepulture in the catacombs were various, and devolved on different classes of men, styled lecticarii, libitinarii, copiatæ, decani, &c. Of their organization under Constantine, he says, "The Emperor Constantine assigned special places of call to the fossores, in different parts of Rome: and we possess the epitaphs of some of these Church-officers, which inform us of the neighbourhood to which they were attached—as, for example, 'Junius, Fossor of the Aventine, made (this grave) for himself.'" [2]

The importance of these men's labour may be judged by the greatness of their work, and on this Dr. Theodore Mommsen makes the following observation,

[1] "Fossores" are represented at plates xciv. and ci. vol. ii., and clxxi. vol. iii.

[2] "L'empereur Constantin assigna aux '*fossores*' des habitations spéciales (*officinas*), dans les différents quartiers de Rome ; et nous avons des épitaphes de quelques-uns de ces fonctionnaires de l'Eglise, qui indiquent la région à laquelle ils étaient attachés ; par exemple, celle-ci : 'Iunius. Fossor. Aventinus. fecit. sibi.'"

after allowing for the existence of non-Christian catacombs. " The enormous space occupied by the burial
vaults of Christian Rome, in their extent not surpassed
even by the system of cloacæ or sewers of Republican
Rome, is certainly the work of that community which
St. Paul addressed in his Epistle to the Romans; a
living witness of its immense development."

FOUNTAIN OR WELL. (See Rock in Horeb; and Evan-
    gelists.)

Our Lord is represented (in Bottari, tav. xvi., Buonarotti,
    " Vetri." tav. vi. et passim) as the Source of the Gospel
    and Fons Pietatis, from under Whose feet flow the Four
    Rivers of Paradise (see Paradise, Four Rivers). In
    the Lateran and other Baptismal Crosses, the Holy
    Dove is the Fount or Source from which the sacred
    rivers flow. The Well, springing in the wilderness, is
    rather a Hebrew, Arab, or universally Eastern image,
    than a specially Christian one. In some early Baptisms
    of Our Lord, as that in the ancient Baptistery of
    Ravenna, the River-God, or presiding deity of the
    Source of the Jordan, is introduced. For the fountain
    or stream flowing from the Rock of Moses and fishes
    therein, see articles Fisherman and Rock in Horeb.

FURNACE. (See Three Children.)

GOAT OR KID.

In Bottari, tav. clxxix. there is an engraving from a picture
    in the Cemetery of St. Priscilla, on the Via Salaria, of
    the Good Shepherd bearing a kid, with goats and sheep
    alike looking to Him. This is perhaps the earliest
    existing allusion to the Last Judgment: but the
    shepherd bearing the kid seems to be a thought
    consonant with the prayer for all men permitted in our

Litany. See Prof. Arnold, "New Poems." See also Bottari, tav. lxxviii.

GOD THE FATHER, Representations of.

(Most representations of the Divine presence have their proper place under the word Trinity). For the first four centuries at least, no attempt was ever made at representing the actual presence of the First Person of the Trinity. It was indicated invariably by the symbolic Hand, proceeding from a cloud. Martigny quotes the words of St. Augustine, Epist. cxlviii. 4 · "When we hear of His Hand, we ought to understand His Working,"[1] from which it would seem that the great Western Father foresaw a tendency to anthropomorphic misapplication of the words, Hand, and Eye, or Ear of God, as they are frequently used in the Old Testament. The distinction between analogy and similitude has been so often neglected, that bodily parts as well as passions (like those of anger, repentance, &c.) are often attributed to the Incorporeal and Infinite Being. This has been repeatedly noticed, and last by Drs. Whately and Mansel. St. Augustine's expressions show that he was thoroughly awake to the misconception, and consequent irreverence, which is involved in the forgetful use of such terms as the Divine Hand, or Eye, for the Divine Power or Knowledge. "When thou thinkest of these things, whatever notion of bodily likeness may have occurred to thee, reject it, deny it, refuse it, shun it, fly from it."[2] The symbolic Hand appears in Christian representations of several subjects from the Old Testament, principally connected with events in the lives of Abraham and Moses. The two are found corresponding

---

[1] "Quum audimus manum, operationem intelligere debemus."
"Quidquid dum ista cogitas, corporeæ similitudinis occurrerit, abige, abnue, nega, respue, fuge."

to each other in Bottari, vol. i. tav. xxvii. also vol. i. tav. lxxxix.   Moses is receiving the Book of the Law, so also in vol. ii. tav cxxviii.   Abraham alone, vol. ii. tavv. lix. and xxxiii. from the Callixtine Catacomb.   In vol. iii. tav. xxxvii. (from Cemetery of St. Agnes) the Deity appears to be represented in human form.   He is de-livering to Adam and Eve respectively the ears of corn and the lamb, as tokens of the labour of their fallen state, and their sentence " to delve and spin."   See also Buonarotti, p. 1.   In Bosio, p. 159, Cain and Abel are apparently making their offerings.   Cardinal Bosio, and M. Perret (vol. i. 57 pl.) give a copy of a painting of Moses striking the Rock, and also in the act of loosening the shoe from his foot.   Ciampini's plates, " Vet. Mon." tav. ii. pp. 81, 82, tav. xxiv. tav. xvii. D. are important illustrations of this symbol, more especially those of the mosaic of the Transfiguration in St. Apollinaris in Classe, and of the Sacrifice of Isaac in St. Vitale.   The Hand proceeding from clouds appears in the Sacra-mentary written for Drogon, Bishop of Metz, and son of Charlemagne, above the Canon of the Mass.   The Creator is represented in the MS. of Alcuin.   See Westwood's " Palæographia Sacra."

GOURD.   (See Jonah.)

HAND.   (See supra.   Representations of God the Father.)

HARE.

The boy who represents Spring among the four seasons frequently carries a hare in his hand.   The idea of speed in the Christian course was associated with it. It is sometimes connected with the horse (Perret, v. lvii.) or with the Palm.   Boldetti, 506.   Its appearance may be connected with the Roman taste for pet animals, which had much to do with their ornament. See p. 120.

HORSE.

Attending on the Orpheus-Shepherd. Bott. tav. lxxi. with the Magi, tav. cxxxiii. Two bearing Crosses, tav. lxiii. The Horse occurs, of course, in the frequent representations of the translation of Elijah found in the Sarcophagi and elsewhere. (See Elias.) The horses of Egypt are commemorated by a rider as well as a chariot, in representations of Pharaoh and the Red Sea. Aringhi, p. 331.

HOUSE.

In Aringhi, i. p. 522, ii. 658, are woodcuts of houses from ancient tombs. This either refers to the grave as the House of the Dead, Boldetti, p. 463; even Domus Æterna (Perret, v. pl. 36, x. 110), or to the deserted House of the Soul, the buried body (2 Cor. v. 1), "For we know that if our earthly house of this tabernacle were dissolved, we have a building of God," &c. &c. There is in Aringhi (sub verbo, ii. 658) a House of the Grave with a small mummy—Lazarus, laid up alone, as it were, to abide the Resurrection. The Houses of Jerusalem and .Bethlehem, representing the Jewish and Gentile Churches, occur frequently in early Mosaics.

INNOCENTS, THE HOLY; Massacre of.

Represented in the mosaics of Sta. Maria Maggiore, and in two ivories, one of which (from a diptych in the Cathedral of Milan) is given by Martigny, sub verbo. Also on a Sarcophagus at St. Maximin, South of France.

ISSUE OF BLOOD.

The cure of the woman thus afflicted is repeated on many Sarcophagi. See Bottari, tavv. xix. xxi. xxxiv. xxxix. xli. lxxxiv. lxxxv. lxxxix. cxxxv. She has been taken to represent the Gentile Church, specially by St. Ambrose (Lib.

ii. in Luc. c. viii.). She is of small stature in the carvings, like the other subjects of our Lord's miraculous cures. In Euseb. "Ec. Hist." vii. 18, mention is made of the bronze statue of our Lord, supposed to have existed at Cæsarea Philippi, Dan (or Baneas at this day), attributed to this woman, who was represented kneeling at its feet.

JERUSALEM.   (See Bethlehem and House.)

JESUS CHRIST, Representations of.   See chapters on Cata-combs, Mosaics, the Monogram, Cross, and Crucifix.

JOB.

Pictures of Job occur in the cemeteries of Domitilla, St. Callixtus, and SS. Marcellinus and Peter "inter duas lauros." They are attributed to the third century, but a certain uncertainty hangs over these paintings. However, their antiquity is confirmed by a carving of Job (on the dunghill or heap of ashes, with his wife and one of his friends), on the sarcophagus of Junius Bassus, A.D. 359. This is of high merit, like the rest of the tomb. It insists on the painful and offensive suffering of the Patriarch; his wife is covering her nose and lips with her garment, while she offers him a panis decussatus, or cross-cake, at the end of a stick. This is Martigny's conjecture, fully borne out by the sculp ture, and far more satisfactory than Père Garrucci's ("Hagioglypt." p. 69, note) that she is preparing to beat her husband with her distaff.

JONAH.

Is represented, passim, in the Catacombs and on the Sarcophagi. He is either cast into the sea, or ejected by the Whale on the shores of Joppa, or reclining under his gourd. Aringhi, i. p. 315, ii. 143, i. 533, ii. 59, &c.

Bottari, tav. xlii. lvi. As a parable or figure concerning Himself, from our Lord's mouth, the greatest
reverence must always have been felt for this subject,
and it is repeated constantly, in consequence, especially in the earliest times, as His solemn promise of the
Resurrection. St. Augustine (Ep. ad Deo gratias quæst.
vi. De Jona) carries the typical resemblance much further, and affords a most ingenious and harmless, though
perhaps not perfectly satisfactory, example of comment,
out-running the words of our Lord, instead of contemplating them. "Christ," he says, " passed from the Wood
of the Cross, as Jonah from the ship, to the whale (or
power of Death) ; the endangered crew are the human
race battered by the tempests of the world—and as
Jonah preached to Nineveh after his return to life, so
the Gentile Church only heard the Lord's word after
His Resurrection." The fresco at Bott. tav. lvi. from
St. Callixtus is perhaps the best typical representation
of this subject.

For the Whale, or Fish, all manner of draconic, hippo-
campic and other forms are assigned it, which are not
very important to our purpose; nor yet is the controversy
as to whether the Hedera of St. Jerome, or the Cucur-
bita of the Vulgate, be the proper term for the plant
which overshadowed him. The early Church painters
seem to have adhered to the later idea of it.

JORDAN.   (See chapter on Sacramental Emblems.)

The Jordan is often personified as a River-God, as in
Bottari, tav. xxvii. with Elias; in the Baptisteries of
Ravenna, on the Borghese sarcophagus at the Louvre,
and in various early MSS., particularly that of St.
Mark's Library at Venice. Its violent windings are
generally dwelt on, and sometimes two of its sources,
named according to the fanciful etymology of its name

(Jor or Ghòr? and Dan) are inserted. The four
Evangelical Rivers sometimes unite in the Baptismal
Jordan, as below the Lateran Cross. (Woodcut, p.
192, and pp. 153 and 207.)

JORDAN, as River God.

Represented, Bottari, tav. xxix. from a sarcophagus from
the Vatican Cemetery, in an Ascension of Elijah. Also
in various Baptisms of Our Lord, as in the Baptisteries
at Ravenna.

JOSEPH, Saint.

Appears in the Nativity, the Adoration of the Shepherds
and of the Magi, and in the discovery of Our Lord in
the Temple, Bottari, tavv. lxxxv. and xxii.

JOSEPH, the Patriarch.

As a typical person standing for the God Man, rejected
and sold by his brethren to the Gentiles for thirty pieces
of silver, we might expect that Joseph would be more
frequently represented in early art than he is. But he
is hardly seen on mural decoration or on the Sarcophagi.
There is a painting given by D'Agincourt (Atlas, pl.
19. Peinture) from a 'MS. in the Imperial Library at
Vienna, which seems to represent the Blessing of
Ephraim and Manasseh. Another dubious fresco
(Bottari, tav. lvii.) from the Callixtine Catacombs is
considered by him and Aringhi to represent the funeral
of Jacob. The ivory chair in the Duomo at Ravenna
contains events of Joseph's history; but it is not till
the Mosaics of the Atrium of St. Mark's at Venice
that it is fully dwelt on.

JUDGMENT, Last.

It may also be said that representations of this tremendous
subject hardly belong to early Christian art, that is to

say, to that period of Christian art which ends with the death of Charlemagne. The great mosaic of the Duomo at Torcello, the mother-city of Venice, still exists ; and if (as is Mr. Ruskin's opinion, agreeing with that of the Marchese Selvatico) the present Duomo is identical with the earliest building in 641, the mosaic cannot be considered of much later date. It was in that year that Altinum was finally destroyed in the Lombard invasion ; the first flight to the Lagoons having been from Attila in the fifth century. (Appendix 4 to vol. ii. of " Stones of Venice.") The original Duomo of Torcello was restored in 1108 ; and certain carvings appear to have been altered, as also the pulpit and chancel screen ; but the mosaics are supposed to form part of the Church as first built. That of the Last Judgment is quite an anticipation of the conceptions of Giotto and Orgagna, the latter of whom certainly gave an inspiration, by his works in the Campo Santo at Pisa, to Michael Angelo for his Sistine frescoes. The Torcellese mosaic is of the rudest, yet most forcible, description. Skulls are in the foreground with worms issuing from the eyes, enforcing the victory of Death over our flesh ; and there is this peculiarity about the conception of the Everlasting Fire, that it is not represented as a conflagration, or monstrous prison-house, as in other works, but as a red stream issuing from beneath the Throne of God. This work is perhaps the earliest known pictorial imagination of the Judgment. If it be of the early twelfth century, it is of course posterior to the celebrated painting of Methodius for Bogoris of Bulgaria, 853-861. This would seem to have been a direction of art untried before; as the King's taste for pictures of battles, and other exciting subjects, is said to have given the painter-apostle of Bohemia the idea of representing the punishment of the

wicked to him.   Whatever we may think of the direction thus given to sacred art, there is no doubt it has
been followed too eagerly, and with deplorable result.
And it is remarkable that the first paintings of this
nature, entirely different in spirit from the peaceful
works of praise, faith, and rejoicing found in the
Catacombs, should be found at the corner of Europe,
where Eastern theology, and asceticism, found their
first and strongest bearing on the animal fierceness
of the Teutonic races.   The monk's indifference to
suffering and the Gothic recklessness of infliction seem
united in many Last Judgments.   (See Orgagna's
Triumph of Death, Inferno, &c. in Kügler, and
Lasinio's Campo Santo of Pisa, and elsewhere; also
Lecky's " History of Rationalism," ch. iii. Æsthetic
Social, and Moral Developments, &c.)   The present
writer remembers no representation of the Last Judgment at Mount Sinai, and the one or two at Mar
Saba seem of late date.   There are many at Mount
Athos, but Mr. Tozer considers them entirely out of our
period.   A heathen painting of Judgment or Presentation
of the Soul after death to the Lower Powers has been
found in the Catacomb of St. Prætextatus.   See Perret,
i. 73.   Diespiter and Mercurius Nuntius are named in
it, as also Alcestis.   See also the " Inductio Vibies " in
the Gnostic Catacomb, which certainly represents the
Presentation of the buried Vivia to some assembled
Divinities.

LAMB.

As the sheep accompanying the Good Shepherd, and
the doves, stand for human members of the Church, so
the Lamb is the emblem of the Lord submitting to
death for man ; the victim Whom every Paschal sacrifice
prefigured.   In this sense it occurs most frequently

in Sarcophagi and mosaics after the time of Constantine. It was not, perhaps, till the triumph of the Cross under Constantine, when the upright or penal Cross had taken the place of the decussated symbol (which really was the Monogram, or name of Christ)—that the Lamb, as the victim of the Cross, came to be an object of constant contemplation; and its image was frequently combined with the Cross. See chapter on the Cross; also Ciampini, de Sacr. Ædif. tab. xiii. where the Lamb is represented "as it were slain" bearing the nimbus, and with the chalice receiving His blood. This begins as early as the first part of the sixth century, and about this time the Lamb is placed in a medallion at the intersection of the limbs of crosses, as the celebrated Vatican Cross. See Borgia, de Cruce Vaticano.

On the sarcophagus of Junius Bassus, or rather on its pillars, there is a most curious sculpture of the symbolic Lamb performing miracles and acts, mystically selected from the Old and New Testament. He is striking water from the Rock, multiplying the Loaves, administering baptism to another Lamb, touching a mummy with a wand, as Lazarus, and receiving the Tables of the Law.

As accompanying representations of the Fall of Man, see Adam and Eve. The Apocalyptic Lamb occurs frequently in the great mosaics of Rome and Ravenna in St. Prassede for example (see chapter on Mosaics), and in the Sarcophagi of the chapel of Galla Placidia.

LAZARUS, Raising of.

This great miracle, amounting to anticipation of Our Lord's final Triumph over Death, is one of those most frequently represented in all kinds of Christian art, alike in sculpture, mosaic and fresco painting. Metallic or ivory images were fastened to the outer doors or lids of tombs

with actual or symbolical representations of it (Bold etti,
"Cimit. di Santi Mort. et antichi Christ. di Roma," p.
:23.) Lazarus is generally represented as a small figure
swathed in linen, exactly like a mummy ; as in the representations of other miracles the human figures present
are often made much smaller than that of Our Lord,
Who sometimes touches Lazarus with a wand, some
times (Bottari, tav. xxviii. 42) holds a volume, or
blesses him with the Latin benediction (two fingers
raised), Aringhi, ii. 121; sometimes the hand is laid on
the head, Aringhi, ii. 183.   In this as in many of the
earliest representations of the Crucifixion, the sepulchre
is represented as a small house ; sometimes it is
hollowed in natural rock, Aringhi, ii. 331.   In several
instances, Aringhi, i. and 335, 323, 423, Bottari, tav.
xlii. Martha with Mary, or one of them alone is present ;
generally kneeling before the Lord, and of small stature.
The idea of a Chrysalis, Aringhi, i. 565, is supposed by
Martigny to be attached to one of these representations
(in a cubiculum of the Callixtine).   The allusion to the
Resurrection is obvious, as the little mummy-figure
recalls that of an infant in swaddling clothes.
Moses and the Rock are frequently opposed to this miracle
on Sarcophagi.

LETTERS ON APOSTOLIC ROBES.

In some of the Roman mosaics of Byzantine type, and
particularly in the Baptisteries of Ravenna, it will be
observed that letters are placed on the skirts of the
figures of Apostles and Saints.   The reason is very
doubtful ; the only probable conjecture is Aringhi's, that
they involve a reference to Ezekiel, ix. 4.   But as the
mark there mentioned is set on the foreheads of the
mourners for iniquity, the passage cannot be thought
an explanation of the symbol.   He refers to Origen,

Serm. 8, De Epiphania; and also to the beginning of
Boëthius de Consolatione, where the heavenly visitant
has the letters P and T on her robe. H, A, N, and Z
occur at Ravenna, and T is spoken of by Aringhi as
most frequent of all, representing the Cross, " Rom.
Sott." ii. 592. The fossor or grave-digger in Bottari, vol.
ii. p. 126, certainly bears a Cross on the skirt of his long
vestment, though of irregular or disguised form.

LION.

The earlier ideas connected with this animal appear to
regard principally the nobler qualities generally attributed to him. He is taken to symbolize watchfulness,
and vigour, or authority in the faith. Until Raffaelle's
St. Margaret, he is rarely coupled with the Dragon in
art, or made symbolic of the Evil One, as in Ps. x. 9.
and xci. 13. See however Gori, " Thes. Diptychorum,"
vol. ii. His head appears, of course, as an ornamental
carving, in all work, Christian and Gentile, Bottari,
ii. lxix; Boldetti, 369. As a supporter to columns
of ambons (see Ciampini, i. tab. xvii. and many later
Lombard carvings) it is to be hoped that he was not
needed or used in early times as a hortatory symbol of
wakefulness. He appears with Daniel very frequently
on the Sarcophagi, and in mosaics as the symbol of St.
Mark (see Evangelists). For his form as compounded
with other animals, see the description of the Lombard
Griffins in " Modern Painters," vol. iii. p. 106.

LITURGICAL BOOKS, Decoration of.

Evangeliaries or MSS. of the Gospels, with the Psalters, are
stated by Dom Guéranger ("Institutions Liturgiques,"
8vo. Le Mans, 1840) to be the earliest examples
of ecclesiastical decorative art now in existence. The
Rabula or Laurentian MS. is one of the very first (see
Miniatures, Crucifix, &c.). This work, invaluable in

every respect, is particularly so in a historical point of view, as a premonitory sign of the divergence of Eastern and Western art.   In Eastern MSS. as Professor Westwood remarks ("Palæographia Sacra," Introd.) the miniatures are of rectangular form let into the text, and unconnected with the writing; whereas in Western work, miniature-art begins as decorative writing; and is, in all the best early examples, associated with it and dependent on it.   (See s. v. Miniature).   The greater number of the richer MSS. are not at very early dates decorated with miniatures, but written altogether on purple or azure vellum in letters of gold.   The Evangeliary of Ulfilas, on purple vellum, and those of Brescia, Verona, and Perugia, are all referred to the sixth century; as also the Psalters of St. Germain des Près and Zurich; these are all in gold or silver writing on purple vellum, though the Psalter last mentioned has faded into a kind of violet tint.   Silver-ink MSS. are much rarer than the chrysographs.   The MSS. of Ulfilas, of Verona, and Brescia are examples, gold being used for the initials.   Other very ancient works still in existence are the Greek Evangeliary of St. John de Carbonara of Naples, now in the Library at Vienna, of the eighth century, the Antiphonary of St. Gregory at Monza, which once belonged to Queen Theodolinda; one belonging to Charlemagne at Aix-la-Chapelle, and another of his, now at Abbeville.

The purple vellum begins to be economized in or before the ninth century, as in Charlemagne's Psalter presented to Adrian VIII. about the end of the eighth (now at Vienna).   This MS. has a limited number of purple pages.   Evangeliaries of this time are still purple throughout.   The use of this colour, however, may be said to go out in the tenth century.   There is in the Bodleian a purple vellum MS. of the eleventh century, which contains whole-page miniatures. Of chrysographs on white vellum, in gold and silver characters, the Evangeliary of St. Martin des Champs,[1] of the time of Charlemagne, and that of St. Médard of Soissons, are mentioned with great admiration by Guéranger, as also that of the monastery of St. Emmeran, near Ratisbon, now at Munich. Gold writing in great measure disappears in the eleventh century, gold backgrounds taking its place. In the Western Church, miniature ornament (see s. v.) begins, and runs parallel with splendour of caligraphy, from the eighth century. In the ninth, design begins to prevail, as in the Missale Francorum. The stories of Alfred's being inclined to learn to read by the beauty of an illuminated book, and of Charlemagne's vigorous but unsuccessful attempts to learn the art of caligraphy himself, are in all probability well founded: for the latter, see Eginhard, "De Vitâ et Gestis Caroli Magni," cap. 25. "Tentabat et scribere, tabulasque et codicillos ad hoc in lectulo sub cervicalibus circumferre solebat, ut cum vacuum tempus esset, manum effingendis literis assuefaceret. Sed parùm prosperè successit labor præposterus et sero inchoatus." "He used to try to write, and was wont to carry about tablets and pocket-books in his bed, under his pillow, that when he had spare time he might accustom his hand to shaping the letters. But it was vexatious labour, and begun too late, and did not turn out successfully."

Design and miniature of course began with the initial letters. The "Sacramentaire de Gellone," ninth century, contains a miniature of the Crucifix in the Canon of the Mass; the Cross forming the T in the words Te igitur. In the same MS. the Mass of the Invention

---

[1] The MSS. of St. Médard and St. Martin are beautifully illustrated in Count Bastard's first volume.

of the Cross has in its initial letter the figure of a
man squaring a tree-trunk, as if to form the upright
stem. The "Leofric" Sacramentary, ninth century, in
the Bodleian, has highly ornamented initials in the
Canon of the Mass, but is without figures. There are
whole-page illuminations of the Four Evangelists in
the Hours of Charlemagne; and in the Evangeliary
of St. Médard, Our Lord sits in the initial of the
word Quoniam, with which the Gospel of St. Luke
commences. Such are the earliest steps of the transition
from caligraphy to painting, and Lange's remark
appears a valuable one, that the labours of the later
miniaturists or illuminators who worked from nature,
gave much originality and confidence to the rising efforts
of the fresco or panel painters; who were very commonly
skilled in MS. decoration, as well as in their special
work. So late an example as Angelico's may prove
how both branches of art went together.

A point of interest on this subject is the frequent use of
ancient consular diptychs as bindings of service-books,
&c. The "Diptychon Leodiense" of the Consul
Flavius Astyrius was made into one of the side covers
of an Evangeliary; so also that of Flavius Taurus
Clementinus, now at Nuremberg. But the most interesting of these adaptations occurs in the well-known
Antiphonary of Monza, where the two consular figures
of the fifth century have been altered into representations of David and Gregory the Great, by means
of cutting the names in the ivory. A tonsure has
also been pratiqué, as Guéranger calls it, on the
head of the consul who represents the Pope. See
Gori, "Thes. Diptych.," t. ii. tav. vi.

A grotesque Eagle of the early ninth century at the end
of this book is traced from Count Bastard's second
volume. See Miniatures.

LYRE.

A symbol of the human body and physical frame, to be kept in harmony with the precepts and duties of the Faith. The Lyre of Orpheus (Aringhi, ii. 562) is likened to the Cross of Christ, as "drawing all men unto Him." See article Calf. The lyre is of course in the hands of Orpheus and, as an ornament adopted from common use, is often, perhaps, without meaning. Bottari gives many different forms of the instrument.

MAGI.

The representation of the Three Sages or Kings of the East, who were led to the presence of the Saviour soon after His birth, is very commonly found in fresco and on the sarcophagi. It was evidently felt to be an assertion alike of the Divinity of Our Lord, and of His Incarnation; and it introduced the Virgin Mother in the most impressive manner, without setting her forth with Divine attributes as a Receiver of Prayer. As an Epiphany also, or manifestation of the object of their Faith to the Gentile Church in particular, it must also have claimed attention from the first. The pictures and carvings greatly resemble each other and are described in the chapter on the Catacombs. See Bottari, passim, especially tav. lxxxii, where the Magi wear boots and spurs, and cxxxiii. &c. where they lead their horses. They almost always wear the Phrygian cap and anaxyrides, or leggings, or Roman caligæ; and are commonly of youthful appearance. Martigny refers to Perret, vol. ii. pl. 48, for their appearance before Herod, from a fresco in St. Agnes: on a Sarcophagus given by Millin ("Midi de la France," pl. 76), and on the gates of St. Zenone they are observing the star. The great procession of Holy Women in St. Apollinare Nuova at Ravenna ends at the altar-end of the church with an adoration of the Magi, evidently intended to introduce the Blessed Virgin, as Mother of the Lord, and blessed among women on the female side of the Church.

MILK OR MILKPAIL.

Often represented in the Callixtine Catacomb in connection with the Eucharist. Bosio, p. 249: third Cubiculum of St. Callixtus; also in De Rossi, "Roma Sotteranea," with apparent allusion to the Good Shepherd, and the pastoral life of the ministry.

MINIATURES.

This term, in its modern sense, signifies only portrait painting on ivory, or on a small scale. It is derived from minium or red lead, the pigment universally made use of, in the earliest days of ornamental writing, in order to decorate the capital letters, titles, and margins of various MSS. This is a parallel etymology to the word Rubric; as the service-books, which employed the attention of the most skilful copyists, were generally most freely ornamented. The use of this term indicates the principle, long sustained in the best illuminations, that the pictures they contained were to be considered only as ornamental adjuncts to the writing, by no means as earnest attempts to represent real scenes or things. The beautiful work of Count Bastard contains every necessary gradation of examples of the progress made in the first eight centuries, from simple writing in red letters, with dotted borders or strokes,—to ornamented letters,—then to letters composed of natural objects, or grotesques of them,—finally to completed pictures of persons or things. The term miniature also serves to distinguish two classes of the most ancient MSS., those in which colour is used for the ground of the page, and those in which the letters and ornaments are in metallic or coloured relief on a white page. For some of the earliest service books on purple or azure vellum, see Art. Liturgical Books, and Dom Guéranger's work on Liturgies.

The Chrysograph of St. Médard of Soissons in the Bibliothèque Nationale, a purple MS. of extreme beauty, is mentioned by Guéranger as containing architectural drawings of great interest, affording much information on Byzantine buildings, and displaying curious feelings after perspective. This Evangeliary contains, as he says, various "gracieux et étonnants édifices." The "Ménologe de Basile" he says, is the store-house of examples of Byzantine architecture, resembling the buildings found in some of the earliest Italian paintings, as in Giunto's of Pisa at Assisi (in the lower Church of St. Francis). The necessity for arrangement in columns, in Liturgical books, gave great occasion for the use of architectural forms in decoration. These will be found in Count Bastard's work, passim, and in the MS. of Rabula ; for a full account of which see Dom Guéranger, "Instit. Liturgiques," vol. iii. Appendix. A beautiful copy in colour of the Miracle of Bethesda in this MS. will be found in Professor Westwood's "Palæographia Sacra." The division of subjects by columns and arches, &c. may be connected with the carvings on ancient Sarcophagi ; see Bottari, passim.

The strict distinction between the terms miniature and illumination seems to be that the latter word applies to the earliest *realist* miniatures, or representations of natural objects. It cannot indeed be denied that the Eastern Church used actual picture miniatures, or representations of events, from a far earlier date than the Western, as the Laurentian MS. abundantly proves. The Illuminators (enlumineurs) and their system of realist decoration date from the ninth century. Their subjects for ornament were not confined to flowers, fruits, leaves, insects, &c., as there are important figure subjects in MSS. of Charlemagne's period. With these began a school of miniature which had advanced into painting of all kinds by the time of Cimabue and Giotto.

These works are beyond the range of our period, but a few remarks and examples, chosen principally from the books of Count Bastard, and Professor Westwood, may be allowed with reference to caligraphy and miniature. The former illustrates the principal French MSS. now in existence; the latter is our chief authority for Saxon and Irish work. Count Bastard virtually gives us access to all the riches of the Bibliothèque Royale, beginning with a splendid purple page in gold and silver from the sixth-century Psalter of St. Germain des Près. Red initials seem to have been used from the first, at all events they appear in a fifth-century MS. of Prudentius (Bast. vol. i.), but the earliest ornament of red and black dots seems to be in an uncial MS. (Bast. i. 5) of the Merovingian type (sixth century). Next is a treatise of St. Ambrose, c. vii. uncial with capitals; the colours used are red. green, and brown, and the interlaced ornament which prevails, for centuries after, over all Northern work has already begun. See also the St. Augustine MS. of the Abbey of Corbie. The first architectural ornament is in a fragment of the Canons of Eusebius, of the early seventh century.

But the earliest ornament which indicates a glance at nature in the caligraphist is in a MS. of extracts from St. Augustine of Hippo, seventh century (second half) the property, in the eighteenth century, of Uhri Obrecht, Préteur Royal de Strasburg. Birds and flowers (daffodils carefully observed and drawn) are used here; and from this point, Frank fancy runs stark distracted in every form of grotesque combination; of birds, fishes, and faces in particular. Flowers and beasts come rather later in Carlovingian work, eighth centuiy. The colours are still red, green, and brown, with purple and yellow, and interlaced work prevails.

But a Merovingian MS. of the second half of the seventh century (Bast. vol. i. ; a Receuil des chroniques de St. Jérôme, d'Idace de Lamégo, Coll. des Jésuites) possesses special interest from the beautiful and spirited work of the true scribe-draughtsman. Its capitals are drawn brilliantly and precisely with the pen, without colour (lettres blanches ou à jour) and point to the real origin and principles of miniature very admirably. So also some of the best Carlovingian MSS., where the pen breaks out vigorously in all manner of grotesques, ornithographic, zoographic, ichthyographic, and even anthropomorphographic (such, inherited from Benedictine comment, are Count Bastard's formidable adjectives). The most amusing triumph of penmanship ever attained we apprehend to be an initial portrait of a monk-physician in a lettres-à-jour MS. of the medical works of Orbaces, Alexander of Tralles, and Dioscorides. (Bast. vol. i. eighth cent.) Gothic humour can hardly go farther. No offensive or outrageous allusion or idea occurs anywhere in these records, as might be expected. In the examples of Visigothic decoration, however, a crucifixion with angels occurs in an early Sacramentary of the eighth or ninth century, Abbaye de Gellone, where much blood is used, and the drawing is very inferior. It soon recovers, however, in the Visigothic MSS. where many human figures and angels are represented, and which may, perhaps, be distinguished from the earlier works by the number of beasts of chase represented in them, boars and hares in particular. These are drawn with the greatest spirit, but the strange northern taste for distortion begins to prevail in the human

figures.   Count Bastard's work only gives one example
of a thoroughly Italian-Lombard MS. It is conspicuous
by the absence of interlaced work, and by a tendency to
geometrical arrangement, which is a marked feature in the
French-Lombard examples.   They are more numerous,
but all dwell much on interlacings.   ·Some of the most
delightful and valuable of the earlier illustrations are
those given from the great MS. of St. Médard of
Soissons, written for Charlemagne. The mystic fountain,
which occupies a whole page of this great work, is
probably a reminiscence of Constantine's fountain of
Baptism.   (See Dove, Stag, Baptist, Jordan, &c.)
The dove, stag, and peacock occur here, and the swan,
stork, and other birds are added. Another picture is the
Church as a building; the Lamb above with circular
nimbus, and light radiating from Him to the four
Evangelists below; then come the walls, windows, and
pillars.   At the base are the words: Qui Erat et Qui
Est et Qui " Enturus " est.

The use of gold and scarlet in the Charlemagne MS. of
St. Martin des Champs is very brilliant, and new
" Initiales fleuronnées," with evidence of fresh study
from nature, occur in Drogon's Sacramentary.

The importance of ancient miniature as representing architecture, ceremonial, and costume cannot be overrated ·
but some MSS. contain actual portraits.   The Emperor
Lothaire is represented in his Evangeliary, and Emma
his wife.   Also Henry III., and the Empress Agnes.
A MS. is said to be now in the Escurial which contains
portraits of Conrad the Salic and Gisela, and the
Countess Matilda is depicted in her Evangeliary in the
Vatican.

The connection between Miniature and Glass painting is
still maintained by some of the best or most promising
of our modern artists.   In the early times it was even

more strict, since the same men used the same colours in both branches of art, whether for transparent or opaque effect. The entirely conventional use of colour, both in illuminated pages and illuminated windows ; absence of effort after any pictorial effect ; and the simple wish to tell a story or represent an event in pleasant colour without regard to correct form, and with endless play of grotesque fancy, are the principal characteristics of the ,best periods of both book and glass-painting. Attempts at absolute realization, correct chiaroscuro, and glass copies of great canvasses, are happily far distant from the period on which we are employed.

Professor Westwood's "Palæographia Sacra," and his larger " Illustrations of Irish and Anglo-Saxon MSS." are standard works which contain, or give references for, the whole subject of early caligraphy and miniature in this country ; and the first of them is universally accessible. The author's able and apparently valid plea for the antiquity of MSS. such as the Gospels of Mœil Brith MacDurnan, and the " Book of Kells," and that of St. Columba, gives us reason for commending the account of them in " Palæographia Sacra " to the student of our period. They seem to date from the earliest out-spreading, under St. Columba, of Irish or Gaelic Christianity ; which may be said to be connected with the Anglo-Saxon Church, after the colonization of Lindisfarne from Iona in 634, forty years after Columba's death. The Gospels of Lindisfarne and St. Chad are probably of the seventh century, and mark this connection. Without entering on the characteristics of the miniature-art of our own islands, however, reference must be made to the Gregorian Gospels of St. Augustine and St. Cuthbert, with others described in " Palæographia Sacra," and now preserved, one in the library of Corpus Christi College, Cambridge, No 286, the other in the Bodleian Library,

Oxford. These Westwood believes to be original Gregorian-Augustinian MSS.[1] Their ornament is purely Romano-Byzantine. Four miniatures are given in " Pal. Sac. "; besides a large one of St. Luke from the Cambridge MS. They are of the highest interest, as probably the oldest known specimens of this kind of Roman pictorial art now in this country or elsewhere; probably a few years anterior to the great Syriac Florentine MS. of Rabula. With the exception of a leaf of a Gospel of St. Luke in Greek, with miniatures of the Evangelists, preserved at Vienna, together with the illuminated Greek Pentateuch of the fourth century; they are held to be the oldest remaining specimens of Roman-Christian iconography written or painted. The Entry into Jerusalem, the Raising of Lazarus, the Capture of our Lord, and the Lord bearing His Cross are four of the twelve subjects of the Cambridge MS. Three of them correspond to those so frequently repeated in the Catacomb-paintings, and on various Sarcophagi. (Bottari, &c. passim.) The initial letters are plain red, and the writing a fine uncial.

Considering the Anglo-Saxon school of miniature orna-ment as derived rather from Irish, than from directly Romano-Byzantine instruction, we may quote from Prof. Westwood a few of the characteristics of Irish work of the sixth and seventh centuries. They pre-vail also in the Anglo-Saxon, and of course in some degree in all northern ornaments.

The first is the constant use of interlaced decoration : traced variously to Gothic hurdles, British wicker-work, Runic knots, Saxon leg-bandages, &c. However, the type of this ornament is found also in Eastern or Byzantine

[1] The Golden Gospels of Stockholm (sixth to ninth century) should be taken in connection with the Augustine Gospels. Westwood, " Fac-similes of Anglo-Saxon and Irish Gospels," 1868.

architecture ("Stones of Venice," vol. ii.) and originated possibly in the chequer-work of the Temple of Solomon.[1] It is universal in northern miniature and writing, Merovingian, Carlovingian, Lombard, and Visigothic, and in the "Book of Kells," &c. reaches a wonderful and distressing intricacy. The use of purple and green colour in that book is very beautiful, as some of the azure and green ornament in Brith MacDurnan. It is paralleled in the Ravenna mosaics only, as far as the present writer has observed. With this intricacy of crossed patterns is combined every variety of ribboned and spotty ornament, and the use of lacertine or ophidian heads everywhere. This seems to have offended the Benedictine authors of the " Nouv. Traité de Diplom." (ii. 122) as they complain rather acrimoniously of the " imaginations atroces et mélancoliques" of Anglo-Saxon MSS. Some echo or reflection of contests with ophidian worship, or Gnostic symbolism, may perhaps have given occasion to work of this kind; but it seems to have more to do with the Gothic tendency to put wrong heads in right places, as manifested from Pavia and Lucca to Iona and Lindisfarne. The initials in Irish works are generally of great size, with intricate spirals within spirals, and circles within circles. Altogether, as the Crucifixion in the St. John's College, Cambridge, MS. proves,[2] art expires in colour-complication.

The principal accessible works on this subject, besides those quoted from, are Astle's volume on the " Origin and Progress of Writing," about seventy years old, with 31 plates the works of Shaw and Strutt; and on the

[1] Interlaced work does not appear in the Syriac (Florentine) MS. of Rabula; though it contains chevrons, lozenges, zigzags, flowers, fruit, and birds. See also Count Bastard's Lombard-Roman illustration.
[2] See chapter on the Crucifix.

Continent, D'Agincourt's " Histoire de l'Art par les
Monuments," Willemin's " Monuments Français inédits,
pour servir à l'Histoire des Arts," and more especially
Silvestre and Champollion, " Palæographie Universelle ;"
and finally Ct. Bastard ; though the enormously high
price of the last two works makes them somewhat
difficult of access, except in the largest public libraries.
In interest, splendour, and accuracy of reproduction,
Professor Westwood's works yield to none.

MONOGRAM. See chapter on Cross, and all records of ancient
Christian sepulchral inscriptions, passim.

MOSES AS A TYPE OF CHRIST.

One of the earliest and most constantly insisted on of all
typical persons in the Old Testament History, various
actions of his life being selected.   He is represented :
1. Removing his shoe from his foot (Exod. iii. 5) at
God's command from the Burning Bush. The presence
of God is signified by a Hand issuing from a cloud
(see Bottari, tav. lxxxiii. and Ciampini from Ravenna
" Vet. Mon." II. tab. xxi. 3).   Martigny refers to
Laborde for a mosaic of this subject in the Convent of
Mount Sinai, which contains a Chapel of the Burning
Bush on the supposed spot of its appearance.[1]
2. The Passage of the Red Sea is, on the whole, less
frequently represented than might have been supposed from its universal acceptation as a figure of
our Baptism, 1 Cor. x. 1 and 2, "All (our fathers)
were baptized unto Moses in the Cloud and in
the Sea." Augustine, Enarratio in Ps. 80. p. 861.
c. ed. Ben. Par. 1590. " Nihil aliud tunc in figura

[1] This the present writer regrets to have failed to observe, but it
is represented in the late Ordnance Survey, vol. i. illustrations
at end.

portendebat transitus populi per mare nisi transitus fidelium per Baptismum." "The passage of the People through the Red Sea meant nothing else than the passage of the faithful through Baptism." This subject is more frequent, however, in the ancient Christian monuments of the South of France.

3, The Manna is represented, Bottari, tav. lvii. Nos. 3 and 5, but Moses striking the Rock is far more frequent (1 Cor. x. 4). This is one of the most frequent subjects in early Christian art, and is generally set opposite to a corresponding picture of Our Lord raising Lazarus from the dead, the drapery of His Form being made to correspond in its lines to that of Moses on the other side, Bottari, tav. cxxix. The Rock has been made to represent St. Peter, instead of Christ, in late Roman art and comment; against which the Abbé Martigny wisely protests.

4. The Book of the Covenant is perhaps given on a sarco- phagus from the Vatican Cemetery (Bottari, tav. xl.) See Exodus, xxiv. 7. Moses is receiving the Tables of the Law, above the great Transfiguration at Mount Sinai, in the Church of the Convent now named after St. Catherine. See Bottari, xxvii. lxvii. clxi. The following events of the Scriptural Life of Moses are given in the great Mosaics of Sta. Maria Maggiore. 1.' The Delivery of Moses to his mother by the daughter of Pharaoh. 2. Marriage of Moses and Zipporah; with her flock (also in St. Vitale at Ravenna). 3. His Return to Egypt with the Wand, and meeting with Aaron. 4. The Quails. 5. The Golden Calf. 6 and 7. The battle with the Amalekites at Rephidim. 8. and 9. The Revolt of Korah and the delivery of the Book of Deuteronomy to the people. These mosaics are represented in Ciampini's "Vet. Monumenta," but his plates have been reproduced in photograph by Mr.

J. H. Parker, who also gives the originals in their present state, to be compared with them ; with profoundly
interesting results.

For Moses' presence at the Transfiguration, the only early
representations of it of which we are aware are : 1.
That at the Convent of St. Catherine at Mount Sinai.
2. That of St. Apollinaris in Classe at Ravenna.

NATIVITY.   Bottari, tavv. lxxxv. and lxxxvi.

In the first, Joseph stands behind the Madonna ; on the
left the Magi are presenting their offering, the Holy
Child alone as a new-born in swaddling clothes is on the
right, with the shepherds, an Angel, and the heads of
the ox and ass. The Magi lead their horses. In lxxxvi.
the three Magi approach, on the spectator's left ; St.
Joseph and the Blessed Virgin are on the right ; the
Cradle and Infant, with the animals at full length, in the
centre.   In a fragment in the Lateran a camel accompanies the Magi.   (See Camel.)

NIMBUS.

Originally a heathen symbol of divinity or glory ; though
appendages resembling nimbi, and called μηνίσκοι, are
supposed to have been attached to the heads of statues
to protect them from birds.   Schol. Aristoph. " Aves,"
1114.   Trajan bears it in the bas-relief of the Arch of
Constantine, and Antoninus Pius on the reverse of one
of his coins.   Constantine also bears it on a coin, and
Justinian, and Theodora at Ravenna in St. Vitale. The
Emperors of Constantinople adopted it on their statues,
and it even passed to some figures of the Merovingian
kings, said to have existed in time past at St. Germain
des Prés. Mabillon, "Annal." Benedict, ann. 577. On
cups, &c. Our Lord and the Blessed Virgin are frequently
adorned with the nimbus. Its constant use seems to begin

with the mosaics, those of St. Constantia in particular. The Phœnix has it on a cup in the Vatican (Northcote).

OLIVE.

This tree is represented (to all appearance) among the trees which surround the mystic Orpheus, or Orpheus-Shepherd. Bottari, lxi. In tavv. cxviii. cxxv. and others, it seems to accompany the Good Shepherd, at least the trees represented are very like young olives, or willows; and in cxxv. the olive is distinctly drawn. Less attention however seems to have been paid to St. Paul's allegory on the tree than might have been expected. The olive-branch is borne by Noah's Dove (see Noah), and olive crowns occur in some of the mixed or Gentile ornament of the sarcophagi. I can find no representation of Zechariah's vision of the Two Olives and Candlestick.

ORANTI.

The figures which bear this name, and are so frequently found in the Catacomb-frescoes, are generally to be described as male or female forms in the Eastern attitude of prayer. The former of course more frequently represent or symbolize some special personage or character. They are for the most part in a standing position, with the arms extended. In some instances they may be taken as symbolizing the Church of believers; but most frequently they appear to be portraits, or rather memorial pictures, of the dead. The celebrated one in SS. Saturninus and Thrason, somewhat grand in form and conception, though grotesquely ill-drawn, is seen in its present state in Parker's Photographs, 469 and 1470, also in Bottari, tav. clxxx. Others are on tavv. clxxii. clxxxiii. and elsewhere. Female Oranti are often represented in rich garments, and profusely adorned with necklaces and other jewellery. See Parker's Photographs, 467, 475-6, 1751-2, 1775, 1777, and the mosaics of SS. Prassede and Pudentiana, 1481-2, Parker. This Martigny rightly explains, " Ces vête-ments somptueux sembleraient au premier abord consti-tuer une contradiction ou une contraste avec la modestie bien connue des femmes Chrétiennes de la primitive Église. Mais en décorant ainsi leur image, on avait bien moins pour but de retracer aux yeux ce qu'elles avaient été dans la vie, que d'expliquer allégoriquement la gloire dont elles jouissaient dans le ciel. Dans les sépultures de tout genre, l'Orante, placée ordinairement entre deux arbres, était le symbole de l'âme devenue l'épouse de Jésus Christ, et admise à ce titre au festin céleste." " These rich dresses would seem at first sight to indicate contrast or contradiction to the well-known modesty of the Christian women of the Primitive Church. But in thus decorating their pictures, the object was much less to represent to the sight what they had been in life, than to give an allegorical idea of the glory they enjoyed in heaven. In graves of every kind, the Orante (commonly placed between two trees) was the emblem of the soul become the spouse of Jesus Christ, and admitted by that title to the Heavenly Feast." (Compare Ruskin, " Modern Painters," vol. iii. p. 49, for similar treatment of the Blessed Virgin by Francia and Perugino, with comments.)

ORPHEUS.

There are two or more fresco-paintings in St. Callixtus, Bottari, VII. tav. lxiii. and vol. ii. lxxi., which represent Orpheus surrounded by the listening animals. It is apparently a heathen subject, favoured and adopted by Christians. The camel, horse, lion, and peacock, are prominent among the creatures ; and the composition of one or both of the pictures reminds us of the celebrated mosaic of the Good Shepherd in the Chapel of Galla

Placidia. Orpheus is clad in a sort of Phrygian tunic and anaxyrides, not unlike the dress in which the Three Kings are frequently represented at Rome and Ravenna. See chapter on Catacombs. The connection in the Christian imagination between the mythical Orpheus and the historic Saviour is not difficult to understand, and is very ancient. See De Rossi, vol. ii. chap. 14, p. 357. The association may have arisen from the Lord's promise to draw all men to Himself. It is highly interesting, to say the least ; because it shows how well the Christian mind was prepared to look back on the myths of the Greek fathers, as well as on Hebrew history, in the light of the Gospel. It does not seem to have been done only to exercise Neo-Platonic ingenuity in mythical interpre tation ; far more likely, it was a natural and right yielding to feelings of common charity and hope for Gentile forefathers, who might be believed to have looked for the coming Redeemer of mankind in their comparative darkness. The earlier habit of christianizing the myths seems to be, in part, the habit of indulging a Christian hope of the salvation of the fathers.

PALM.

The palm-branch occurs everywhere in Christian sepulchral inscriptions, often accompanied by the Dove or other birds. The tree is common on sarcophagi, and in the mosaics, particularly at Ravenna, as in St. Apollinaris in Classe, and the sarcophagi of Galla Placidia's Chapel. See descriptions of the mosaics, in Chap. V., and Bottari, tavv. xix. xxii. lxxviii. &c. In xxii. it is beautifully used as a pillar to divide compartments. For the Army of Martyrs with Palms in St. Prassede, see chapter on Mosaics. See also the Peter and Paul Cup of the Vatican Museum, given in woodcut by Northcote, where the Phœnix sits, bearing the nimbus.   Also woodcut of the Lateran Cross, facing Chap. VIII.

PARALYTIC MAN, Healing of.

Universally represented, in fresco and mosaic, by sculpture, and on diptychs, and glass.   The healed man is always in the act of carrying away his bed.   Our Lord raises His hand in the act of blessing, and the cure is effected.   Whenever He is present, difference of stature is insisted on, but in some instances the miracle is simply represented by the patient carrying that whereon he lay. In Bottari, tav. xxxi. a Scribe is present (John v. 10).

PEACOCK.

A favourite ornament in Gentile work, for the sake of its colours and graceful form ; for which reason ducks and other birds are represented in mosaic and illumination. It is found in the Jewish Catacombs, and in nearly all the others.   In St. Callixtus peacocks are very beauti fully arranged as an ornament of a round vault.   It was willingly adopted by Christian decorators, and treated as a symbol of the Resurrection, from the bird's annual loss and renewal of his beautiful feathers.   See Aringhi, II. book vi. c. 36, p. 612.   It is found in SS. Marcellinus and Peter, Bottari, II. tav. xcvii., and in St. Agnes, Bottari, III. tav. clxxxiv.   In tav. lxiii. it is one of the animals grouped around the symbolic Orpheus.

PHARAOH AND PASSAGE OF RED SEA.   Aringhi, p. 331. See Moses.

PHŒNIX.

As the Phœnix is certainly represented on coins and medals of Constantine, it may be supposed that a strange bird occasionally found in mosaics, placed on the palm-tree or branch, and sometimes wearing the nimbus (as in the mosaics of St. Cecilia at Rome), is intended for it. It is connected with Baptism, as a type of Death, and Resurrection. Clement, Epp. 1 Cor. xxv. It is found in the mosaics of SS. Cosmas and Damianus at Rome, and also in St. Prassede ; Ciampini, "Vet. Monumenta," II. tav. xlvii. li. and tav. xvi. A Phœnix with the nimbus is placed in one of the palm-trees by the side of the curious Peter and Paul Cup in the Vatican, given in woodcut by Dr. Northcote ; p. 316. See Lateran Cross, p. 192 in text.

PILATE.

Our Lord's appearance before Pilate is almost the only scene of His Passion to be found on the Sarcophagi, or indeed anywhere in very early Christian art. See Bottari, xxiv. Pilate is seated on a curule chair, John xix. 13. Bottari, tavv. xv. xxii. xxxiii. xxxv. An expression of anxiety and reluctance is generally given to Pilate, and in some instances water is being brought for his hands.

PORTRAIT OF OUR LORD. See chapter on Catacombs, in text, and woodcut from the Callixtine Catacomb, p. 98 ; also p. 305.

PORTRAITS.

The majority, perhaps, of the Oranti or praying figures in the Catacombs (male or female) may be supposed to be portraits or memorial figures of the dead. Two medallion portraits, one of them apparently of considerable merit, occur in the Cemetery of St. Priscilla. Bottari, tavv. clx. and clxi. Both apparently commemorate military men, and Bottari mentions a conjecture, without giving any opinion of his own, that seventy-two soldiers, martyred in the reign of Numerianus, with Claudius their tribune, may have been buried here. The first and most striking example certainly contains a medallion of a young man of apparently Gothic countenance, and mould of neck, and shoulders, with short hair and beard; and has a chariot on each side of the half dome of the apse or arcosolium on which the paintings are. No specially Christian imagery is introduced. The other has a medallion of an older man armed with a spear, with Abraham in a girded and striped tunic, on his left, and Moses, probably, on his right. Many figures in the mosaics are undoubtedly portraits, as those of Justinian and Theodora, in St. Vitale; and possibly at Mount Sinai; and the marked countenances of many saints of the Byzantine and Eastern works can hardly be ideal.

ROCK.

See Moses, Bóttari, tav. xlix. &c. also Lazarus, Bott. cxxix. The ancient artists seem rather to have dwelt on Moses, as a type of Christ in the office of Leader and Lawgiver, than on St. Paul's words, " That Rock was Christ." At least, I do not know where the Rock appears alone in early art, unless, which is probable, the Lord's standing on a Rock from whence flow the Four Rivers of the Gospel is meant to call attention to that text. Rocks are often represented in Baptismal pictures.

SAMARIA, Woman of.

Bottari, tav. xxiii. and tav. cxxxvii. from Sarcophagi, and tav. lxvi. from a fresco in St. Callixtus. Also Perret, i. pl. 81. The well, and the figures of Our Lord and the woman, seem to leave little or no doubt of the intended subject of these works.

SEASONS, FOUR.

Pictures of the Seasons are among the adopted subjects of Christian art. They had long been a favourite subject of Roman decoration, and one of the most pleasing kind ; so that the Church speedily invested them with a meaning of her own. To the heathen they were a subject of contemplation on natural growth, and change ; in Christian thought the hope of the Resurrection was added.[1] "All this rolling order of things bears witness to the Resurrection." Accordingly, as Martigny remarks, the Good Shepherd accompanies the pictures of the Seasons almost invariably. The Seasons of the Domitilla Catacomb are photographed in their present condition in Mr. Parker's collection. They appear to have been retouched or repainted, as they must be of considerable antiquity. The recently discovered frescoes of the Catacomb of St. Prætextatus are more beautiful, and almost to a certainty in their primitive condition (see text, chapter on Catacombs). Agricultural work corresponding to the four seasons is combined with decoration in four vegetable forms, vines, laurels, corn, and roses. See Parker's Photographs, Bottari, tav. lv. and where the seasons are represented on the small ends of the sarcophagus of Junius Bassus (Bott. vol. i. p. 1). Youths or boys are the usual personifications.

SERPENT, BRAZEN.

Aringhi in his "Roma Subt." vol. ii. p. 453 (book iv. 4) says that the Brazen Serpent (the original, as broken by Hezekiah) was given to Arnulf, Bishop of Milan, by Nicephorus of Constantinople (probably Nicephorus III. about 973, scarcely Phocas). It is preserved to

[1] See Tertullian, De Resurrect. xii. "Totus hic ordo revolubilis rerum testatio est resurrectionis mortuorum."

this day in St. Ambrogio, he continues, with apparent
gravity and conviction. It may be an Alexandrian
talisman. For that at Constantinople, see De Quincey.
"Miscellanies," *Modern Superstitions*, p. 345, vol. 1854,
Hogg, Edinburgh.

SERPENT.   (See s. v. Dragon.)

There is this distinction between representations of the
Serpent and the Dragon in Christian symbolism, that
the former represents the evil power in its tempting
office as inviting to sin,[1] and the latter generally points
to Evil, or the Evil One in the destructive function, as
the permitted agent of punishment. A gem given by
Gori, Thes. Diptych. vol. iii. p. 160, represents the
Serpent twined about the Cross, and apparently tempting
two doves. Whether the serpent on the Cross may
not in this instance have reference to the Brazen
Serpent (Numbers xxi. 9, St. John iii. 14) seems
doubtful. In Bottari, Vol. I. tav. xix. Daniel is
offering the destructive cakes to a serpent, which has
here taken the place of the Dragon of the Apocrypha.
The serpent is of course a part of most representations
of the Fall of Man, Boldetti, p. 200, book i. also
Bottari, tav. xv. 9 (tomb of Junius Bassus, A.D. 358),
and tavv. clvi. lxxx. Continual use is made of the
serpentine or lacertine form in Irish and Anglo-Saxon
ornament from the earliest date ; see "Palæographia
Sacra" on the "Book of Kells," and other ancient MSS.
This is of course in great part a result of the northern
taste for plaited and interlaced ornament, and the forms
to which snake-heads are attached are generally mere
ribbons. The MS. of Alcuin contains one of the
latest in our period, Westwood "Pal. Sac." Prof.
Westwood appears inclined to connect their continual

---

[1] See the various representations of the Fall of Man in Bottari.

recurrence with symbolism of Temptation, the Fall of Man, and his spiritual enemies; and perhaps also to traditions of ancient ophidian worship. A very curious illustration in this direction will be found in the " Alpine Journal," vol. iv. p. 173 (by the Rev. T. G. Bonney, M.A., F.G.S., &c. Fellow of St. John's College, Cambridge). A strange woodcut is given of the Abyssinian Saint Tekla Haimanout, who founded the Monastery of Debra Damo on a mountain near Axum. It is so situated that those who go to it are obliged to be drawn up by a rope: but the saint was originally raised to the summit by hanging on to the tail of a mighty serpent. There is a singular analogy between these dragon and serpent stories, and there is little doubt of their ancient symbolical meaning and Eastern origin. "Profane sceptics," says our author, "may perhaps say that this story is only to the mountaineer symbolical of the use of the rope." Those who are acquainted with the illustrations of Hindoo mythology may remember the forms of Vishnu suffering, and Vishnu triumphant; in the one case folded in the coils of a serpent who bites his foot, in the other stamping upon the head of the defeated monster.

SHEEP. (See Lamb.)

Two sheep very frequently accompany the Good Shepherd besides the one generally laid on His shoulders. They are often represented looking to Him with an expression of awe and affection. His Hand is sometimes raised to bless them. In Bott. tav. xxi. a Lamb stands beside Him bearing the Cross-monogram on its head. In tav. xxii. there are six, and the seventh has the simple Cross. For the twelve sheep around the greater Lamb, see Bott. tav. xxviii. (See in particular Martigny's " Étude archéologique sur l'Agneau, et le Bon-Pasteur.")

SHIP.   (See Church.)

The Navicella of Giotto is one of the chief modern examples of the symbolism of the Church by a vessel at sea.   The emblematic architecture of some of the early Greek churches, as that at Torcello, is mentioned under

known sign of the accomplished voyage of Life (see Death).   The Ship occurs of course in all the representations of Jonah, and in some mosaics, as in the ancient seaport from the Callixtine Catacomb (Parker, Photographs, Antique Mosaics).   Theophylact (on Jonah, ii.) says the ship is a type of our Flesh, which the Antitype of Jonah " went down into," and took upon Himself, and again, that it stands for the Jewish synagogue in the same relation.   Aringhi, tav. ii. p. 507.

STAG.   See chapter on Sacramental Representation.

ST. PAUL.

Generally associated with St. Peter; he appears with St. Lawrence in the Neapolitan Catacombs.

ST. PETER AND ST. PAUL.

An early sarcophagus at Avignon, perhaps of the fourth century, as Dr. Appell informs us, contains the Delivery of the Keys to St. Peter.   Some principal examples of portraits or commemorative pictures of the two Apostles are on glass cups or drinking vessels, Boldetti, p. 202, tav. vii. 22, Northcote, p. 316.   The statue in St. Peter's at Rome, and the lost statuette of St. Peter, are mentioned in the chapter on Sculpture, p. 178.   St. Peter appears in some of the Roman mosaics of early date, e.g. that of St. Pudentiana.   Ciampini, " Vet. Mon." I. tab. xviii. ; and several of the sarcophagi given in Bottari represent the two Apostles.   Their appearance is, generally speaking, distinguished by the greater age and stature of St. Peter, who bears originally one, and afterwards two keys. St. Paul often holds a roll (volumen) or book (liber). In Greek portraits, says Martigny, both Saints are represented bald, which distinguishes such pictures from the ideals of the Western Church.

The Good Shepherd.

See chapter on the Catacombs, and all illustrations of Christian paintings. The antiquity of this symbol of Our Lord, dictated as it is by His own mouth, is quite undisputed; and it is the most frequent of Christian images in painting, or mosaic, and perhaps in bas-relief. One marble statue from the Lateran Museum is given by Martigny, and still exists (see wood-cut in this volume, p. 174); a work of really great beauty, and probably of very early date. For the connection of this symbolic figure with that of Orpheus, see that name. It occurs in the South of France (Millin, "Midi," p. 65), and in Africa and Cyrene. "Annal. Archéologiques," vi. ann. p. 376. As an allegory of Divine, or Kingly care, the symbol dates probably from the earliest patriarchal life. Compare Müller ("Chips from a German Workshop," vol. i.). The 22nd Psalm, Isaiah xliv. 28, Ezek. xxxiv., points to its Hebrew use; and its Homeric application to Kings, as Shepherds of the people, will be remembered. D'Agincourt considers ("Hist. de la Peinture," t. v. p. 20) that one of Bosio's prints of this subject is taken from an original of the end of the second century. As an image not infrequent in Gentile decoration, it would be more likely to be used in the early days of persecution.

THREE CHILDREN.

Bottari, tav. clxix. (with attendant bearing logs and perishing in the flames), tav. clxxxi. in a kind of Phrygian dress with braccæ ; clxxxvi. 6, standing in a regularly built smelting furnace, with striped pallia. Also cxcv. cxliii. cxlix. and passim. The original state of one of these, from the Catacomb of SS. Marcellinus, &c., is given in Parker's Photographs. Also Bottari, xli. and xliii. from St. Pontianus. The Furnace is always literally insisted on. In one instance there are only two youths ; and in another, Bottari, tav. clxxxi. Noah's Dove, with the Olive-branch, is hovering above them.

TRIANGLE.

A not frequent symbol, more commonly used after the fourth century, like the A ω ; with which it is frequently combined, as in Aringhi, R.S. 1, p. 605. M. de Rossi has collected six or seven examples, two or which are from Lyons, and one from Africa. See Martigny, and Boldetti, " Cimiteri," &c. p. 402. Three fishes disposed in the form of a triangle are represented, Münter's " Symbolica," p. 49, tab. i. 26. (See next article.)

TRINITY, the Holy.

It is impossible to separate the Doctrine of the Holy Trinity from that of the Divinity and Incarnation of Our Lord. Accordingly we find that the symbolic Triangle is almost invariably combined with the Monogram, and seems to have special relation to the Second Person of the Trinity. The central mystery of the Faith was hardly a subject for graphic art ; but the various representations from Genesis xviii. of the appearance of the Three to Abraham have always been considered as adumbrations of it. See Ciampini, "Vet. M." tab. li. 1, from the mosaics of Sta. Maria Maggiore at Rome, and Parker's photographs of the actual state of that picture, and of the more beautiful one of St. Vitale at Ravenna. In all Baptismal pictures, as in the Form of Baptism, the Trinity is represented by the Hand, the Cross, or Present Person of the Saviour, and the Dove. St. Paulinus of Nola thus describes the type of all these paintings:—"The Trinity appears in full mystery of brightness; Christ stands in the river; the voice of the Father thunders from heaven, and the Holy Spirit glides down in the dove."

> " Pleno coruscat Trinitas mysterio,
> Stat Christus amni ; vox Patris celo tonat
> Et per columbam Spiritus Sanctus fluit."

ULYSSES AND THE SIRENS.

See chapter on Catacombs (De Rossi, " Roma Sott." vol. i. tav. xxx. p. 5) for a fragment of bas-relief evidently representing the hero's escape with his crew, symbolic of temptation.

VIRGIN MARY, the Blessed.

See in text, chapters on Catacombs and Mosaics ; and Mr. Hemans's article, "Contemporary Review," vol. iii. 1866, p. 155. Also Rev. Wharton Marriott, " Testimony of the Catacombs."

VINE.

Perhaps the most ancient of all symbols of the Lord, or of His Church ; see examples and illustrations in the chapter on the Catacombs. The vintages, &c. in St. Constantia at Rome are some of the most ancient Christian examples in mosaic; and the vines in St. Prætextatus, Bottari, vol. ii. tav. lxxiv. in fresco. The beautiful stuccoes in the Cemetery on the Latin

Way, Bottari, II. tav. xcviii., must also be of great antiquity. The Vine which covers the roof of the Chapel of Galla Placidia is another grand example; and so on to St. Mark's at Venice, and the constant modern use of the symbol. On Sarcophagi, see Bottari, tav. iii. p. 19. The massive porphyry Sarcophagus of St. Constantia (daughter of Constantine, died 354) has bas-reliefs of boys treading out grapes.

R. St. J. T.

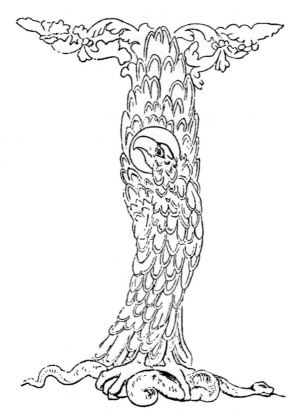

EAGLE SYMBOL.

EVANGELIARY OF LOUIS LE DEBONNAIRE, FIRST HALF OF NINTH CENTURY.

PUBLICATIONS OF THE
Society for Promoting Christian Knowledge.

CPSIA information can be obtained
at www.ICGtesting.com
Printed in the USA
LVOW07s0129071017
551546LV00002B/324/P

9 781331 720621